Adirondac

P9-APZ-648

Faith and Reason

Faith and Reason

RICHARD SWINBURNE

OXFORD
AT THE CLARENDON PRESS
1981

Oxford University Press, Walton Street, Oxford OX2 6DP

London Glasgow New York Toronto
Delhi Bombay Calcutta Madras Karachi
Kuala Lumpur Singapore Hong Kong Tokyo
Nairobi Dar es Salaam Cape Town
Melbourne Auckland

and associate companies in
Beirut Berlin Ibadan Mexico City

Published in the United States by
Oxford University Press, New York

© Richard Swinburne 1981

All rights reserved. No part of this publication may be reproduced,
stored in a retrieval system, or transmitted, in any form or by any means,
electronic, mechanical, photocopying, recording, or otherwise, without
the prior permission of Oxford University Press

British Library Cataloguing in Publication Data

Swinburne, Richard
  Faith and reason.
  1. Faith and reason
  200'.1   BT50

ISBN 0-19-824663-3

Printed in Great Britain
at the University Press, Oxford
by Eric Buckley
Printer to the University

Preface

THIS book is based on the third of my three series of Wilde Lectures, given in the University of Oxford in Hilary Term 1978. (The first two series came to form my book *The Existence of God*.) I am most grateful to those who elected me to the Wilde Lectureship; and to the President and Fellows of St. John's College, Oxford, for the very generous hospitality which they showed me during the terms in which I delivered the lectures. I am also most grateful to Mrs Yvonne Quirke for her patient typing of various versions of the book.

Contents

Introduction   1

1. The Nature of Belief   3

2. Rational Belief   33

3. The Value of Rational Religious Belief   72

4. The Nature of Faith   104

5. The Purpose of Religion   125

6. The Role of Creeds   143

7. The Comparison of Creeds   173

   Epilogue: Faith is Voluntary   198

   Index   203

Introduction

Faith and Reason is the final volume of a trilogy on philosophical theology. The first volume, *The Coherence of Theism*, was concerned with what it means to say that there is a God, and whether the claim that there is a God is internally coherent. It argued that the claim was not demonstrably incoherent, that it was proper to look for evidence of its truth, and that evidence that it was true would be evidence that it was coherent. The second volume, *The Existence of God*, was concerned with evidence that the claim was true. It was concerned to assess the force of arguments from experience for and against the existence of God. It argued that, although it could not be proved conclusively that there was a God, on balance the various arguments taken together showed that it was more probable than not there was a God. *Faith and Reason* is concerned with the relevance of such judgements of probability (either the particular judgement which I reached, or a different one—e.g. that it is very improbable that there is a God) to religious faith.

The practice of religion is usually said to involve 'faith' of some kind. But what sort of faith is needed for the practice of religion, and what sort of faith ought churches to demand of their members? Faith certainly seems to involve trust in God and commitment to him, but what does such trust amount to? Does it involve believing that there is a God and believing certain truths about him; and, if so, how strong do these beliefs have to be? If the trust can exist without the belief, is it rational to put your trust in God without the belief that he exists? And, anyway, what is it to believe that there is God, and when would it be rational for a man to believe that there is a God? Finally, when is faith in God obligatory and when is it rational? These are the topics of this book. Although I shall seek general results about when faith in any kind of God is rational or obligatory, I shall fill them out mainly by considering faith in the God of Christian theology, and so the kind of faith which a Christian Church ought to demand of its members. This work is thus centred more on Christianity than its predecessors. It is in no way necessary for a reader to have read the earlier works in order to understand this one; this work does not in any way presuppose the results of earlier ones. But the conclusion of the *Existence of God*, that it is more probable than not that there is a God, can be slotted in to the results of this work, to obtain a particular conclusion about the rationality of faith in the Christian God.

As in both the earlier works, my primary aim has been to justify my conclusions by rigorous and careful arguments. This has meant, inevitably, that there are long sections on general philosophical topics, such as belief and rationality, in which philosophical views are developed, which are applied only subsequently to religious issues. I can only ask for patience from those whose main interest lies in my conclusions about religious faith rather than in my discussions about the nature of belief. Well-justified conclusions about religious faith can only be reached through a thorough understanding of the nature of belief. The road may be dry and secular, but we shall reach our destination in the end.

1

The Nature of Belief

MANY religious traditions extol the virtue of faith, and in the Christian tradition, faith in God who has revealed himself in Christ is seen as a major virtue.[1] You need it in order to travel the Christian road to Heaven. But what is it to have faith in God? In the Christian tradition there have been various views on this, and in a later chapter I shall need to distinguish between these views. A major constituent of faith, on most such views, is belief-that or propositional belief. The man who has faith in God, on these views, believes that there is a God and believes certain propositions about him. However one view claims that belief-that is not important; what matters is action. The man of faith is the man who acts on or lives by the assumption that there is a God and certain other assumptions. There are thus two important concepts which come into definitions of faith, and which require analysis before we can investigate head-on the concept of faith itself; these are the concept of believing that so-and-so, e.g. that there is a God, and the concept of acting on the assumption that (or acting as if) so-and-so, e.g. that there is a God. This chapter will be devoted to analysing these concepts and to exhibiting the relation between them. We shall find that the concept of belief is not a completely clear one, and that to make it useful we shall need to tidy it a bit at the edges.

Belief as Relative to Alternatives

So, then, what is it to believe that so-and-so, that today is Monday or that there is a God? I suggest that the primary concept of belief picked

[1] Or an essential component of a major virtue. In his sense of 'faith', Aquinas claimed that faith by itself was not a virtue; but he went on to claim that what he called 'formed faith' was the virtue. On this see Chapter 4.

out by public criteria is the concept of believing so-and-so more probable (or more likely) than such-and-such. I shall be arguing for this suggestion shortly. If it is correct, then belief is relative to alternatives, and this is something that a number of writers[1] have urged in recent years. You believe of one proposition as against another proposition, or propositions, that the former is more probable than any of the latter; and what your belief in the former amounts to depends on what are the latter. The normal alternative with which a belief is contrasted is its negation. The negation of a proposition p is the proposition not-p, or 'it is not the case that p'. The negation of 'today is Monday' is 'it is not the case that today is Monday' or 'today is not Monday'. The negation of 'there is a God' is 'there is no God'. Normally to believe that p is to believe that p is more probable than not-p. To believe that Labour will win the next general election is to believe that it is more probable that Labour will win than that anything else will happen (e.g. the Conservatives win, or the Liberals win, or no party win). To believe that today is Monday is to believe that it is more probable that today is Monday than that it is any other day of the week.

If p is more probable than not-p, then p is probable *simpliciter* (and conversely). So my claim is that normally to believe that p is to believe that p is probable. (I understand p being certain as an extreme case of p being probable; it is p having a probability of 1 or close thereto.) What can be said in favour of this claim? To start with, if I do not believe that p is probable, I cannot believe that p is true. If I believe that it is more probable that not-p than that p, I cannot believe that p. Examples bear this out. If I believe that it is not probable that Liverpool will win their next game, then (barring considerations to be discussed below arising from the existence of a number of alternatives) I cannot believe that they will win. But what about the other way round? Suppose that I do believe that p is probable. Must I believe that p? Clearly if either I am to believe that p or I am to believe that not-p, I must believe the former. But might I not believe that p is probable without believing that p or believing that not-p? If I believe that p is very very probable, surely I believe that p. Cases where we would say the former are always cases where we would say the latter. If I believe that it is very very probable that Liverpool will win the F.A. Cup, then I believe that Liverpool will win. The only difficulty arises when I believe that p is marginally more probable than not. Here we might be hesitant about whether to say that I believe that p.

[1] See especially Isaac Levi, *Gambling with Truth* (New York and London, 1967).

The hesitation arises not from ignorance about any unobserved matters, but because the rules for the application of the concept of belief are not sufficiently precise. Maybe some men do use 'believe' so that S has to believe that p is significantly more probable than not if S is to believe that p. But certainly others are prepared to allow that S believes that p if S believes merely that p is marginally more probable than not. It seems tidier to follow this latter usage. For, if we do not follow this usage, there would have to be some value of probability θ between $\frac{1}{2}$ and 1, such that only if a man believed that p had a probability greater then θ would he believe that p. But any value chosen for θ would be extremely arbitrary. I conclude that although our ordinary rules for the use of words *may* not be sufficiently precise for my suggestion to be clearly analytic, there is a case if we are to have a clear concept of 'believe' for tightening up usage so that the words of my suggestion do now express an analytic (i.e. logically necessary) truth.

Although normally the sole alternative to a belief that p is its negation, sometimes there will be other alternatives. This will be the case where p is one of a number of alternatives being considered in a certain context. In that case to believe that p will be to believe that p is more probable than any one of these alternatives (but not necessarily more probable than the disjunction of the alternatives).[1] Suppose that we are discussing who will win the F.A. Cup and a number of teams are being considered. Let p = 'Liverpool will win the Cup', q = 'Leeds will win the Cup', r = 'Manchester United will win the Cup', and so on. Suppose that S believes that p is more probable than q, or than r, or than any similar proposition, but not more probable than not-p, 'Liverpool will not win the Cup' (the disjunction of q, r, and similar propositions). Does he then believe that p? Again, I do not think that ordinary usage is very clear, but I am inclined to think that it favours the view that it is correct to say that S does believe that p. If we asked S 'Who do you believe will win the Cup?', he would surely not be lying if he said 'Liverpool' rather than 'I do not believe of any particular team that it will win'.[2] For this reason our earlier suggestion must be expressed as follows: S believes that p if and only

[1] The disjunction of a number of propositions is the proposition which says that at least one of them is true. The disjunction of q, r, and s is the proposition 'either q or r or s'. The conjunction of a number of propositions is the proposition which says that they are all true. The conjunction of q, r, and s is the proposition 'q and r and s'.

[2] I argue this point at greater length in my *An Introduction to Confirmation Theory* (London, 1973), pp. 185 ff. I claim that it provides a ready solution to a paradox known as the lottery paradox .

if he believes that p is more probable than any alternative. The normal alternative is not-p, but p may on occasion be contrasted with several alternatives. So the meaning of 'S believes that Liverpool will win the Cup' will vary with the contrast being made. If the talk is about whether Liverpool will win or not, then to believe that Liverpool will win, I have to believe that it is more probable than not that Liverpool will win; whereas if the talk is about which of a number of clubs will win, to believe that Liverpool will win I have to believe that it is more probable that Liverpool will win than that any other named club will win.

It may be objected to my account that it leads to an infinite regress. For on that account normally to believe that p is to believe that p is more probable than not-p, i.e. to believe that p is probable. If S believes that p, then S believes that p is probable. So, by substitution, it follows that S believes that it is probable that p is probable. And so on. But this is no good objection to the claimed logical equivalence. Many undoubted logical equivalences lead to similar infinite regresses. $1 = 1 \times 1$. So $1 = 1 \times 1 = 1 \times 1 \times 1 = 1 \times 1 \times 1 \times 1$, and so *ad infinitum*. An infinite regress of this character would be objectionable, would be vicious, only if it occurred in a definition. If the equivalence in question was supposed to be a definition of 'believes', intended to convey its meaning to someone who had no idea of the meaning of that word in any context, then indeed the infinite regress would be objectionable. It would be objectionable because the word 'believes' occurs both in the definiendum and in the definiens, and so the definition would be of no help to anyone in ignorance of the meaning of 'believes'. But the suggestion was not intended as a definition of 'believes' in all contexts any more than '$1 = 1 \times 1$' is intended as a definition of '1'. Rather I am attempting to draw out some of the logical relations of a word 'believe', the meaning of which, I shall suggest, gets introduced by public situations which give us ground for saying of a man that he believes one proposition p to be more probable than some other proposition q.

We can now apply our claim that belief is relative to alternatives, to religious beliefs. The normal alternative today to 'there is a God' is its negation 'there is no God'. But to many religious beliefs in the past there were surely more alternatives than one. The alternatives, for example, to the orthodox faith of the Council of Chalcedon, that Christ had two natures in one person, might naturally be thought of as the various heresies that were its rivals—Nestorianism and monophysitism. In that case a man who said that he believed that

Christ had two natures in one person, might thereby be committed only to believing that this view was more probable than that Christ had only one nature in his one person, and more probable than that Christ was really two persons. A man today who expresses his belief in such propositions may have various alternatives in mind or he may simply have the negations in mind. Belief-that is relative to alternatives; and where this is not realized or where the alternatives are not clearly specified, a man who expresses belief may not be saying anything very clear.

I believe that this simple point, generally unrecognized, is of very considerable importance for the Christian religion. What it is to be a Christian believer is unclear until we have made clear what are the alternatives with which the propositions of Christianity are being contrasted. I suspect that in the course of twenty centuries implicitly a more restrictive understanding of what it is to be a Christian believer has developed than existed earlier. In early centuries you had merely to believe that the whole Christian system was more probable than various rivals. In later centuries you have had to believe that various items of the system are each more probable than their negation. I shall argue at a little greater length for this historical conjecture when I come in Chapter 4 to distinguish between the different understandings in the Christian tradition of the nature of faith. When I come in Chapter 6 to consider the kind of faith, and so the kind of belief, that a church ought to demand of its adherents, I shall argue that in the course of the centuries the Christian Church has become rather too demanding in the beliefs which it requires of its adherents.

The point that belief is relative to alternatives is connected closely with the issue of the conjunctivity of belief. If S believes that p, and S believes that q (where p is being contrasted with not-p, and q with not-q), it does *not* follow that he believes (p and q) (where the alternative to this is its negation, (not-both-p-and-q)). It follows only that he believes (p and q), where this is being contrasted with (p and not-q), (q and not-p), and (not p and not-q). For S may believe that it is more probable that in a match between them A will beat B rather than B beat A, and more probable that in a match between them C will beat D rather than D beat C, without believing that it is more probable that both A and C will win than that there will be any other outcome of the two matches. Hence it is that many a wise man believes that he has some false beliefs. He believes p, and believes q, and believes r, etc., because he believes that each is more probable than any alternative (and we may suppose that the only alternative is the negation), but he believes that (*p* and *q* and *r* . . .) is less probable than its negation, viz. that he has at least one false belief. The application to Christian creeds, understood as expressions of belief-that, should be apparent. One who believes the Nicene Creed may believe each item of the Creed, because he believes that each item is more probable than any alternative (and we may even suppose that the only alternative is the negation); but he need not believe that the Creed as a whole is more probable than its negation (i.e. the negation of the conjunction of all the items in the Creed, that is the proposition that says that there is a false item in the Creed). He may still believe that somewhere in the Creed he has made a mistake.

Belief and Action

So much for the connection between believing that *p* and believing *p* to be more probable than not-*p*, or than *q*. But what of the latter, believing something to be more probable than something else, which I called earlier the primary concept of belief? What is it to have such a belief? Belief has consequences for action, for it is in part a matter of the way in which one seeks to achieve one's purposes.

Suppose that I seek to get to London, and I come to a junction in the road. Then clearly if I believe that it is more probable that the road on my right leads to London than that the road on the left does, I shall take the road on the right. More generally, if *S* seeks to achieve *X* and believes *p* to be more probable than *q*, where *p* entails that doing A_1 will bring about *X* and doing A_2 will not bring about *X*, and *q* entails that doing A_2 will and doing A_1 will not bring about *X*, where A_1 and A_2 are actions which cannot both be done, then if *S* can do A_1, he will do A_1 and not A_2. At least, this holds so long as *S*'s beliefs have no other relevant consequences, and *S* has no other purposes in life except to bring about *X*. The relation of belief to action becomes more complicated if *S*'s beliefs have further consequences and *S* has other purposes. But clearly, given all these restrictions, the consequence does follow. I *could not* believe that it is more probable that the right-hand road leads to London, have the sole purpose in life of going to London, and take the left-hand road.

S may have various beliefs relevant to the attainment of any given purposes. Although he may believe that the right-hand road leads to London and the left does not, he may also believe that if he waits at the junction there is some possibility that he can get a bus which goes to London, or if that he reverses his steps, he will probably find a railway station from which he can get a train to London. The connection between belief and action now becomes more tenuous. But what we can still say is the following. If S has various beliefs about the probability of different actions, A_1, A_2, A_3, etc., attaining his one goal X, that it is more probable that A_1 will attain it than that A_2 will or that A_3 will or that any other action will, and if he can only do one of these actions, he will do that action which, he believes, will most probably attain his goal. S's beliefs about the probability of different actions attaining his goal are what I shall call means–ends beliefs. They will normally follow from more theoretical beliefs—e.g. his belief that if he waits at the junction, there is a certain probability that he can get a bus which goes to London, will follow from beliefs such as that probably buses stop at the junction, probably they are not always full up, and probably those buses go to London.

Men have many beliefs which in fact never affect their actions, but what the theory which I am advocating claims is that if circumstances arise in which I seek to achieve some purpose, where my beliefs entail that it is more probable that it can be realized by one means rather than some other incompatible means, if there are no other means, I shall if I can bring about the former means. I may believe it more probable that the Pharaoh of the Exile referred to in the Book of Genesis was Ramses II, than that it was any other Pharaoh. This belief may in fact have no effect on my conduct. I may not have any other beliefs with which it can join for it to entail a relevant means–end belief, a belief about the means by which some purpose of mine can be achieved. All that the theory claims is that if circumstances were to arise such that this belief together with other beliefs entail a belief about the means by which a purpose of mine is to be achieved, I will use that means. My belief about Ramses II could well have a significant effect on my conduct. It follows from it that if I am seeking to provide you with true information about the Book of Genesis, I shall do so by saying that Ramses II was the Pharaoh of the Exile rather than by saying that Merneptah was. Further, together with other beliefs my original belief may entail that it is more probable that some document K discovered by an archaeologist is a forgery than that document J is. In that case it will follow that if I am seeking to acquire a genuine historical document for a museum, I will acquire J rather than K.

My account of the consequences for his actions of a man's beliefs, complex though it may sound, is over-simple in neglecting the fact that a man may and normally does have more than one purpose which he is seeking to achieve. He does not normally just seek to get to London but to get there without travelling a long time, not seek merely to acquire documents for museums but to acquire them without spending much money, and so on. (Some of his purposes may even be ones which he is not prepared to admit, even to himself—e.g. the purpose of not expressing an opinion different from one accepted by his fellows.) What dictates what he will do is then not merely his belief as to whether his action is more likely than some other action to achieve a given purpose, but his belief as to how much more likely it is to achieve the purposes on which he is most keen than is some other action. Which action a man will perform depends on just how keen he is on the fulfilment of the various purposes X_1, X_2, X_3, and so on; and just how probable he believes that it is that the various actions A_1, A_2, A_3, etc. will lead to the fulfilment or non-fulfilment of each of them. Suppose that it follows from my belief about Ramses II that it is more probable that K is a forgery than that J is. Then if my sole aim is to acquire a genuine document for the museum, I will acquire J rather than K. But suppose that I have the further goal of spending as little money as possible, and J is expensive while K is very cheap. What I will do will then depend on my belief about how much more probable it is that K is a forgery than that J is (if there is not much difference in this respect between them, I am more likely to acquire K); and on how keen I am on getting a genuine document as opposed to spending little money. If J is very expensive and K is very cheap, and I do not mind too much about the risk of K being a forgery, I am much more likely to acquire K.

For the case where a man has more than one purpose, I suggest that the following more general account holds. If S has the purposes to achieve goals X_1, X_2, X_3, etc., he will do an action A_1 (rather than actions incompatible with A_1—A_2, A_3 etc.) in so far as his beliefs have the consequences that the probability that

(1) A_1 will lead to the attainment of X_1

is greater than the probability of any other statement of the form

(1a) A_n ($n \neq 1$) will lead to the attainment of X_1;[1]

and that

(2) A_1 will lead to the attainment of X_2

is greater than the probability of any other statement of the form

---

[1] '$A_n(n \neq 1)$' is a symbol which allows us to substitute for it any of A_2, A_3, A_4 . . . etc. other than A_1.

(2a) $A_n (n \neq 1)$ will lead to the attainment of X_2;

and that

(3) A_1 will lead to the attainment of X_3

is greater than the probability of any other statement of the form

(3a) $A_n (n \neq 1)$ will lead to the attainment of X_3,

and so on.

If S's beliefs entail that some of these conditions are satisfied, and that in no case the converse is satisfied (e.g. the probability a statement of the form of (2a) is greater than that of (2)), S will do A_1. In other cases, S may or may not do A_1. S is more likely to do A_1, the more the purposes which he wants most to achieve are ones which will, he believes, most probably be achieved by doing A_1—e.g. if he is most keen on achieving X_1, and his beliefs entail that the probability of (1) greatly exceeds that of any statement of the form of (1a), whereas although his beliefs entail that the probability of some statement of the form of (2a) exceeds that of (2), he does not mind very much about achieving X_2.

Having now drawn attention to the complexity of the relation between belief and action, I shall henceforward, unless I state otherwise, assume that the agent has only one purpose, to achieve X, that the only possible actions are doing A and doing not-A, that p has the consequence that A will attain X and not-A will not, and not-p has the reverse consequence. In such a case if S believes p to be more probable than not-p, and has no other relevant beliefs, S will do A. I do not think that the vast over-simplification involved in this formula will vitiate my subsequent analysis. However my discussion of the past few pages should have illustrated the point that the belief which has consequences for action is a belief about one means being more likely to achieve a result than some other means. A student may seek to gain admission to a University. If that is his sole purpose in life, what dictates whether he will take the entrance exam is not whether he believes that he will pass the exam and so gain admission, but whether he believes that he is more likely to gain admission by taking the exam than by doing something else. This confirms my earlier suggestion that the primary concept of belief is the belief that some proposition is more probable than any alternative.

Before advancing the argument, I must mention at this point one further complication. This is that the theory so far advanced holds only if S believes that his beliefs have the entailments in question. He will probably believe this if the entailments are fairly immediate, for necessarily a man believes many of the immediate entailments of any proposition which he believes. If I believe that if someone points a loaded gun at a man's heart and pulls the trigger, the bullet will enter the man's heart and make a bullet-sized hole in it, and if a man has a bullet-sized hole in his heart, he will die immediately, then I can hardly fail to believe that if I fire a loaded gun at a man's heart, he will die immediately. But I may believe a complicated scientific theory which has a remote consequence that doing r will bring about not-q, and yet I may not realize that the theory does entail this. In that case I may believe the theory and still do r in order to bring about q. So we need to add that S believes that the relevant consequence is a consequence of p before the general claim holds.

The main claim which I have made so far is that a man's beliefs carry consequences about how he will seek to bring about his purposes. That this is so is certainly part of the claim of what is called the Dispositional Theory of belief. That theory, however, normally makes the stronger claim that this is all there is to belief—your beliefs just are a matter of the way you seek to bring about your purposes.[1] That however I deny. For even if we know what a man's purpose is and what public action he is performing, the most that that can show us is that the man has a certain means–end belief. If, seeking baked beans, I open a certain can, that perhaps shows that I believe that opening the can will get me baked beans. But people normally hold means–end beliefs because they hold more theoretical beliefs from which those means–end beliefs follow; and a particular course of conduct does not show which more theoretical beliefs a man has. Thus I may hold the means–end belief, that opening the can will secure baked beans for me, because I hold the more theoretical belief that there are baked beans in the can. But there are other more theoretical beliefs from which the means–end belief also follows. It follows from the belief that the tin contains peas, and that if I open it, my wife will find and open for me a tin of baked beans. It also follows from the belief that there is a genie whom I can force to give me baked beans by opening this magic can. The same public action may, for men of the same purpose, be a case of acting on different theoretical beliefs.

[1] There is a well-known exposition of a qualified version of the Dispositional Theory by R. B. Braithwaite in 'The Nature of Believing', *Proceedings of the Aristotelian Society*, 1932–3, **33**, 129–46. (Reprinted in *Knowledge and Belief*, ed. A. Phillips Griffiths, London, 1967.)

The consequences for action of a man's beliefs will also depend on what are his purposes, what he is seeking to achieve, and that too is not something visible on the surface of what he does. I may believe that the cliff path is dangerous, but what I will do to act on this belief will depend on what I am seeking to achieve. If I want to preserve my life I will not use the path but travel by another route. But if I want to commit suicide without it being known that I have done so, I may well use the path.

It will be clear by now that a given stretch of a man's public behaviour is compatible with his having various beliefs and purposes. If you are prepared to attribute any strange purpose you like to him, you can attribute any belief you like to him. I fire a gun at someone. This is compatible with any belief you like to take about guns or anything else—e.g. the belief that firing a gun at someone gives him long blond hair—so long as you are prepared also to attribute to a man strange purposes in his actions—e.g. to make someone have long blond hair. However, although compatible with any given belief or purpose, a man's conduct rules out very many combinations of beliefs and purposes. If *S* fires a gun at *T*, it cannot be both that *S* has the purpose of keeping *T* alive and that *S* believes that firing guns at them kills people.

The Grounds for Attributing Beliefs

Although a man's public behaviour may be formally compatible with his having all sorts of extraordinary beliefs and purposes, we infer from their public behaviour to the beliefs and purposes of others, and we do so using certain inductive principles (in the wide sense of principles which yield merely probable results).[1] First, we use the principle of simplicity. We attribute to men relatively stable purposes and beliefs. We assume that in general the beliefs and purposes manifested in a man's actions today and yesterday are similar; that different men have similar beliefs and purposes; and that people's beliefs change when presented with stimuli in regular and similar ways. Secondly, we use what has been called the principle of charity. Other things being equal, we assume that other people have purposes of a kind which we also have ourselves, and come to acquire beliefs in ways similar to that in which we do. Application of the principles of

---

[1] I repeat here the kind of description of the inductive principles at work, given (e.g.) in David Lewis, 'Radical Interpretation', *Synthese*, 1974, **27**, 331–44.

simplicity and charity allow us to reach reasonably justified conclusions about what a man believes. If we show to a man S other men being killed by being shot in the heart, we reasonably suppose that S will come to believe that shooting kills (since we ourselves would come to hold that belief when shown what S was shown), and so if we then see S intentionally shooting someone else T, we infer that he believes that he will kill T, and so has the purpose of killing T. We assume that purposes do not come and go completely randomly, and so if failing to hit T with his shot, S then tries to strangle him, we infer that S believes that strangling kills (because S's purpose of killing T has remained). And so on. One way in which we apply the principle of charity is in assuming that others are like ourselves in seeking to convey true information by what they say. Hence, in the absence of grounds for supposing otherwise, we believe what others say about their beliefs and purposes.

Although we infer to a man's beliefs from his behaviour by means of the principles of simplicity and charity, we assume that the conclusion yielded by such principles is only probable, not necessarily true. S may ask R for an aspirin, R may take a pill out of his aspirin bottle and give it to S, R may in general have behaved benevolently towards S so far; yet the pill turns out to be a cyanide pill which kills S. We infer from his generally benevolent behaviour that R did not have the purpose of killing S, and hence that he did not believe that the pill would kill S. But we could be wrong, and R could know that we were wrong. A man's beliefs are not necessarily what an inference from his observable behaviour would by the principles of simplicity and charity lead us to infer that they are. And the same goes for his purposes.

This account of how we infer the beliefs and purposes of others presupposes that we have non-inferential knowledge of our own beliefs and purposes. That is surely so. A man's purposes are, paradigmatically, what he consciously sets himself to bring about (and although he may repress some purposes from consciousness, they remain purposes of which he is half-aware, but which he will not admit to himself). Just as a man must know (in some degree) what are his purposes, so he must know what actions he is performing—a movement of your limb would not constitute an action unless you knew that it was occurring and that you were bringing about its occurrence. If a man knows what action he is performing and what purpose he is seeking to realize by it, he must know what are the means–ends beliefs on which he is acting, because a means–end belief is a belief about how an action will attain a purpose—although if he is only *half*-aware of his purpose, he may be only *half*-aware of his belief. If he can put his knowledge into words, and is not attempting to deceive anyone by what he says, he will give a true account of these beliefs. Since a man knows what he would do to achieve many other purposes which he is not currently seeking to achieve, he has non-inferential knowledge of other means–ends beliefs (the ones on which he is not currently acting); and in so far as he does not know how he would set about achieving some purpose, he does not have any relevant means–end belief. He may be consciously aware of the beliefs or, never having given any thought to them, be able to become aware of them by self-examination (i.e. asking himself how he would seek to achieve certain purposes). But if honest self-examination yields no answer as to which way or ways he would use to achieve some purpose, then he cannot have a means–end belief on this matter. If the man can put his means–ends beliefs into words, and is not attempting to deceive anyone, he will give a true account of these beliefs. And it seems too part of the logic of belief that unless a man is in some way deceiving himself, what he naturally admits to himself about his more theoretical beliefs—that he believes this proposition of astronomy or that proposition of history—rather than what others infer about his beliefs from a study of his behaviour, is what he believes.[1] Similarly, with regard to purposes—there may be states of affairs which a man's behaviour tends to bring about, but if he is totally unconcerned about them, then bringing such states about is wrongly called a purpose of his. And if a man is totally unaware that his actions do have such consequences, that they do is no belief of his. A man's beliefs and purposes are mental states of which a subject is aware or can be made aware by self-examination.

What, then, in summary is the connection between the public criteria of a man's beliefs and the man's own awareness of those beliefs? First, nothing will count as a belief unless it is compatible with the way in which the believer seeks to realize his purposes. This

[1] In saying this I go against the article of Lewis referred to in n. 1, p. 13 above. Lewis claims that if we knew all the actual and hypothetical behaviour of a person (i.e. not merely what he does, but what he would do in unrealized circumstances), all described in physical terms, and draw conclusions therefrom about his beliefs and purposes, we would know everything about his beliefs and purposes. If the data gave equal support to more than one theory about the man's beliefs and purposes, there would be no factual difference between such theories. My argument above suggests that this is false. If, for example, there was more than one such theory, what a man admitted to himself, although not publicly, about his beliefs and purposes would seem to select one such theory as true and another as false.

we have already seen. Very roughly—if *S* believes that doing *A* is the way to achieve *X*, and he seeks to achieve *X*, he will do *A*. Secondly, within this limit by and large men must be judged to have the purposes and beliefs which the public criteria of simplicity and charity would indicate that they have. 'Belief', 'purpose', and similar words are public words and when it is reasonable to apply them is constrained by the public criteria. Hence a man can only reasonably claim, when talking about his 'beliefs' and 'purposes', to be talking about beliefs and purposes in the public sense, if he claims, on the whole, to have those beliefs and purposes which the public criteria indicate that he does have. The public criteria show which of his attitudes towards propositions he is justified in calling 'belief' (as opposed, e.g., to 'doubt' or 'disbelief' or 'knowledge'). Thirdly, however, once he has in this way got hold of the concept, he can rightly call cases of that same attitude towards some other proposition an attitude of 'belief', even if the public criteria do not indicate that he believes the proposition in question, and even if they indicate that he does not. Belief is thus an inner attitude towards propositions which is manifested in action and often evidenced by public criteria, but which may exist independently of its manifestations and of evidence shown in public behaviour.

The account which I have given of the nature of belief brings out, I believe, what is right in the main philosophical theories about the nature of belief. We saw earlier how my account takes over from the Dispositional Theory the doctrine that a man's beliefs carry consequences about how he will seek to bring about his purposes. It also takes over Hume's doctrine[1] that belief is an inner attitude towards a proposition, and the connected doctrine of others[2] that in general a man will have the beliefs which he naturally admits to himself and to others to having. But it affirms the obvious point that a man may still have a belief even when he is not currently thinking about it. Most writers who affirm the connection of belief with what a man would admit, assert that a man has a belief if he would affirm it, were he to think or be asked about the matter. But some who espouse the above

---

[1] For Hume an idea is believed if it presents itself to the subject in a certain way, that is by being more 'lively', having more 'force' and 'vivacity', than ideas which are merely entertained. See David Hume, *A Treatise of Human Nature* (first published 1739), ed. L. A. Selby Bigge, 2nd edn. revised by P. H. Nidditch, Oxford, 1978), I. 3. 7.

[2] For example, Dummett. 'Roughly speaking, a person believes something to be the case if an expression of that belief can fairly easily be elicited from him by prompting him appropriately'—Michael Dummett, *Frege, Philosophy of Language* (London, 1973), p. 285.

doctrines deny that a man may have beliefs of which he has never thought.[1] But this seems wrong—a man may believe that the distance from his office to his home is less than two-thirds of a mile; and yet the thought that this is so may never have crossed his mind. Yet the man has the belief, because if some occasion arose where the way to fulfil his purposes would be crucially affected by whether or not that distance was less than two-thirds of a mile, he would do the action which would be the way to fulfil his purposes, if that distance were less than two-thirds of a mile. For example, if offered a bet as to whether the distance was less than two-thirds of a mile, he would bet that it was. Finally, my account affirms that a man may deceive himself about his beliefs and not admit some of his beliefs even to himself.

So then with complications and qualifications, I have defended the view that a man's belief is a mental attitude towards a proposition which, perhaps together with other beliefs, entails how he will seek to realize his purposes. But there is more to a belief than just a disposition to realize purposes in certain ways. For the same disposition to realize purposes in a certain way may result from different beliefs.

What applies to beliefs generally applies to the belief that there is a God. Those who have that belief have a certain attitude towards the proposition or claim that there is a God, an attitude of setting it epistemologically above the alternative that there is no God, an attitude which has consequences for the believer's behaviour. In the sense which I have been careful to distinguish, a man must act on his beliefs; he cannot have beliefs which could not in any circumstances make any conceivable difference to his conduct. One who really believes that there is a God will in some circumstances act differently from one who does not. If he seeks to tell the truth, he will say that there is a God. If he believes as well as that there is a God, that any God punishes the wicked, and if he seeks to avoid punishment, he will not be wicked. And so on. A man with the same purposes and the same other beliefs, would not do the same actions without the belief that there is a God. What are the consequences for action of a man's belief that there is a God will depend crucially on which other beliefs he holds and what his purposes are. Thus suppose that he also believes that if there is a God, it is man's duty to worship him; and he has the purpose of doing his duty, then he will worship. But he may

---

[1] Thus Dummett, ibid., p. 286—'We should argue that I can hardly be said to believe some proposition which has never occurred to me.'

believe that there is a God and yet not worship if he does not hold the other belief or does not have the purpose of doing his duty.

Whether a man believes that there is a God is something of which he is aware or of which he can become aware by asking himself whether or not he believes. However, a belief of this kind is of course one about which we may be rather more inclined to self-deception than about more mundane beliefs. We may want to believe, although really we do not, and so persuade ourselves that we do—or conversely, we may want not to believe, although really we do, and yet persuade ourselves that we do not. Clearly some vigilance is necessary here. Because of the possibility of a man deceiving himself about his religious beliefs, public criteria may sometimes show what are a man's religious beliefs rather better than will his apparently honest avowal.

Belief and Evidence

I claimed earlier that belief is relative to alternatives. To believe that p is to believe that p is more probable than any alternative. The normal alternative is the negation, not-p. To believe that Labour will win the next general election is to believe that it is more probable that Labour will win than they will not win. But sometimes there may be more than one alternative. Then to believe that p is to believe that p is more probable than any alternative q, r, s, etc.; more probable than q, and more probable than r, and so on. There might be listed in the betting shop a number of alternative results of the election—'Labour will win', 'Conservatives will win', 'no party will win', etc. To affirm a belief that Labour will win in this context is to affirm a belief that that result of the election is more probable than any other of the listed results you like to name but not necessarily more probable than that Labour will not win. (In subsequent discussion I shall normally assume, unless I state otherwise, that the only alternative to a belief is its negation, and so that S believes that p if and only if he believes that p is more probable than not-p, i.e. probable *simpliciter*. My treatment can easily be generalized to deal with other cases.)

But what is it for one proposition to be more probable than another proposition? Philosophers have distinguished different kinds of probability. The kind of probability at stake here is evidently epistemic probability. The epistemic probability of a proposition is a measure of the extent to which evidence renders it likely to be true. Epistemic probability is relative to evidence. Whether a proposition is epistemically probable or not depends on the evidence-class relative to which the probability is assessed. On the evidence that a certain pack is an ordinary pack of playing cards, the probability that the top card is the ace of hearts is $1/52$; but on the evidence that it is a normal pack of playing cards and the top card is a heart, the probability that the top card is the ace of hearts is $1/13$. The epistemic probability of most ordinary claims cannot of course be given an exact numerical value; the most that one can say about the probability of most ordinary claims is that one claim is more probable than some other claim. (If one claim is more probable than its negation, it has a probability of more than $1/2$. If on the evidence a claim is certainly true it has a probability of 1; if it is certainly false, it has a probability of 0.) If it is not stated explicitly what is the evidence in question, the assumption is that the evidence is the total evidence available to the person assessing the probability; or, sometimes it may be, the total evidence available to the community to which he belongs—to say today that it is probable that Einstein's General Theory of Relativity is true is to say that the total evidence available to us today makes it likely that Einstein's General Theory is true. In statements about an individual's beliefs it is presumably the evidence available to the man himself rather than the evidence available to any community which is involved. So my claim that S believes that p if and only if S believes that p is more probable than any alternative, amounts to the claim that S believes that p if and only if S believes that the total evidence available to him makes p more probable than any alternative; that, on the total evidence available to him, p is more probable than any alternative.

But presumably the only thing which can make a proposition probable is another proposition, or something formulable as a proposition; and so a man's evidence must consist of propositions which he believes. And how are these propositions to be distinguished from other propositions which the man believes?

Some of the propositions which a man believes, he believes solely on the grounds of other propositions which he believes, and which, he believes, make the former probable; but some of the propositions which a man believes, he does not believe only for this reason. I believe that a train will leave Oxford for Birmingham tomorrow at 10.11 a.m. solely because it says that it will on the timetable and railway timetables are on the whole reliable (which latter propositions I believe). Yet my belief that the clock says that it is 5.10 is not something which I believe for the sole reason that it is made probable by others of my beliefs (e.g. my beliefs that it is now 5.10 and that clocks in this house are usually reliable). On the contrary, I believe that the clock says that it is now 5.10 because it looks[1] to me as if it does say 5.10. My system of beliefs has here an anchorage in what I believe to be my experience of the world.

I shall call those propositions which seem to a man to be true and which he is inclined to believe, but not solely on the ground that they are made probable by other propositions which he believes, his basic propositions. Among a man's basic propositions are those propositions which report his perceptions ('I see a clock') or what he perceives ('the clock reads 5.10'), his memories ('I remember going to London yesterday') or what he remembers ('it rained in London yesterday'). He is inclined to believe these, not solely because he believes something else, but because he is inclined to believe that they are forced upon him by his experience of the world.[2]

In terming all such propositions basic I do not mean to imply either that they are known infallibly (i.e. without the possibility of error) or that they are known incorrigibly (i.e. without the possibility of the subject subsequently rationally believing that he has been in error about them) or that they are known at all. On the contrary the subject will have different degrees of confidence in them (i.e. he ascribes to them different degrees of prior probability). I am much more confident that the clock reads 5.10 than that it rained in London yesterday. (Maybe it was not yesterday, but the day before yesterday that I was in London.) When a man is asked why he is initially inclined to believe some basic proposition, with the degree of confidence in question, the only answer which he can give is that his experiences have been such that it seems to him to be probable to that degree. The subject's evidence is then this set of propositions, reporting what he is initially inclined to believe, together with the degree of prior probability which he ascribes to each, the degree of his initial confidence in them. A claim that a belief is probable is then a claim that it is made probable by this set.[3] The greater the prior

---

[1] I here use 'looks' in what Chisholm calls its 'epistemic' sense, i.e. in saying that it looks to me as if the clock says 5.10, I am saying that on the basis of my visual experience I am inclined to believe that it is 5.10. See R. M. Chisholm, *Perception* (Ithaca, N.Y., 1957), Ch. 4.

[2] All these examples of the basic propositions are of propositions grounded in the subject's experiences. I shall argue in Chapter 2 that there are basic propositions in the sense defined above, which are not grounded in a subject's experience but rather report 'truths of reason' of which he seems to be aware.

[3] The view that a man's system of beliefs must ultimately be justified by their being

probability of basic propositions p, and the greater the conditional probability of a further proposition q on the basic propositions p (i.e. the probability that if p then q), the greater the resultant probability of the further proposition. In so far as the subject believes that the prior and conditional probabilities are great, the more probable he will believe the further proposition to be.[1]

A basic proposition will acquire the status of a belief (and we may then call it a basic belief) unless other of a man's basic beliefs render it improbable. Most of a man's basic propositions acquire the status of beliefs, but some do not.

It may seem strongly to me that I saw a ghost in my room last night. 'There was a ghost in my room last night' is then a basic proposition of mine. But my evidence of what I have read and been told about what kinds of thing there are in the world may in my view make it very unlikely; and so I do not in fact come to believe what seemed to me, on the evidence of my senses at the time, to be the case. Whether the basic proposition wins through in such circumstances depends on the believer's judgement of its prior probability (his initial degree of confidence in it) as opposed to his assessment of the probability on his other evidence of some claim which conflicts with it, and how improbable the latter makes the basic proposition.

In saying that men believe things if and only if they believe that their evidence makes them probable, I do not mean to imply that men make very explicit calculations. Normally for example men do not

made probable by some basic set of beliefs which just seem (on grounds of experience or reason) to the man to be so, is usually called Foundationalism. The alternative is the view that each of a man's beliefs might be justified solely by being made probable by some other belief, and so there could be an infinite regress of justification, or justification in a circle (e.g. belief A by belief B, belief B by belief C, and belief C by belief A). I do not find it coherent to suppose that each of a man's beliefs could be justified only by some other belief. But I do not assume this in the text. I assume only that in practice for humans things are not like this. Human beliefs find their foundation in beliefs whose justification is not solely in terms of other beliefs. Those called foundationalists often hold that basic propositions are incorrigible; as I say, I am not claiming that.

My account of the structure of actual belief is similar to that given as an account of the structure of all possible belief by Chisholm. See Roderick Chisholm, *Theory of Knowledge* (2nd edn., Englewood Cliffs, N.J., 1977). Thus he claims (p. 85): 'every proposition we are justified in believing is justified, in part, because of some relation that it bears to the directly evident.'

[1] Most confirmation theories do not allow for the fallibility of evidence. They take for granted that evidential propositions are unchallengeable. The confirmation theory which seems to me to take this point into account most adequately is that of Richard Jeffrey. See his *The Logic of Decision* (New York and London, 1965), especially Chs. 11 and 12.

consider directly whether their evidence makes some proposition probable (or rules out some would-be basic belief), but only whether their other beliefs do this, but this is on the assumption (which can be questioned), that those other beliefs are rendered probable by evidence. Once a proposition (e.g. 'there are no such things as ghosts') is admitted into the belief-corpus, it plays its part in promoting further beliefs, without the extent of its own evidential support very often being brought explicitly into question.

Nor do I imply that a man who on some evidence believes a proposition, can say why his evidence makes the proposition probable, can state explicitly the inductive standards (i.e. standards for one proposition making another probable) which he uses. I may believe that a man to whom I was introduced was hostile to me because of the way he smiled at me, without being able to say *why* the latter is evidence for the former. A professional reasoner may be able to set out his reasons; but if a man cannot do that he may be guided by reasons all the same.

Also, I do not imply any restriction on the kind of propositions which can function as basic propositions. A man's basic propositions may include not merely ordinary reports of things perceived and remembered, but his 'hunches' and 'intuitions' which he thinks are justified by the experiences to which he has been subjected but cannot justify in terms of propositions. A man lost in a wood may have a strong hunch that a particular path is the way home—without this hunch having grounds which he can state.

A man may continue to believe a proposition while his evidence for it changes. I may a few years ago have assembled a lot of historical evidence which, I believed, made it probable that Jesus was raised physically from the dead. I therefore believed the latter proposition. I may now have forgotten the historical evidence, and yet continue to believe that Jesus was raised. My evidence now may be only that I once did, honestly and conscientiously, examine historical evidence and reach the conclusion that Jesus was raised. This evidence about my past investigation may be my present grounds for belief.

With all of these qualifications needed to save the claim, my original claim that a man believes *p* if and only if he believes that his total evidence makes *p* more probable than any alternative, viz. (normally) probable, may seem to be becoming trivial. For originally it might have seemed to rule out a man having beliefs for which he could not cite public evidence. But now it turns out that it is compatible with a man having almost any beliefs, supported or not supported by any public evidence or indeed anything puttable into words. Where a man's belief has no evidence expressible in words, we just say that the proposition believed is one of the man's basic propositions which acquired the status of a belief because he had such confidence in it that it was not overruled by any other evidence. Yet although this is so, the claim is far from useless, for it provides a framework in which we can describe kinds of belief in terms of the different kinds of evidence by which they are supported and the different standards of probability involved in the judgement that certain evidence supports a certain belief. Further, it still does rule out certain apparent possibilities. It means, for example, that a man can only claim to believe a proposition *p* which he admits that the public evidence renders improbable if he claims to have the kind of access which men have to their perceptual experiences, to something which justifies him in asserting a proposition *q* which counts in favour of *p*. Consider the mother who admits that the public evidence seems to indicate that her son is dead and yet says that she continues to believe that he is alive. If she really continues to believe, she must believe either that the public evidence does not show what others think that it shows (e.g. because there are hidden discrepancies in it) or that she has private evidence which counts the other way. If she claims to believe that the son is alive, not on the basis of anything else, and so treats it as one of her basic propositions, she is in effect claiming clairvoyance; for she is claiming the sort of justification for it that others claim for ordinary perceptual statements. My formula brings this out.

The same goes for the man who claims to believe that there is a God, while admitting that public evidence seems to count against his belief. He must claim either that the public evidence has been wrongly assessed or that he has private evidence. He may claim that while at first sight it looks as if the various arguments do not render probable the existence of God, in fact their force has not been appreciated by the public or that there is public evidence which others have not noticed, which does render probable the existence of God. If the man's appeal is to private evidence, it will often be to something other than the claim that there is a God, which makes the latter probable— e.g. it might be strange prophetic visions. Otherwise 'there is a God' will be functioning as the man's basic proposition. But in that case the believer is claiming an awareness of God similar to the awareness men have of material objects. The formula brings this out.

My formula rules out the suggestion that a man could believe a proposition while admitting that the public evidence rendered it

improbable and denying that he had any other evidence. That surely
is so. For what sense can we make of the suggestion that Holmes can
believe that Smith is innocent of the crime of which he is charged,
although admitting that on balance all the evidence points to his guilt
(including evidence about Smith's character, etc.)? 'There's no
doubt', Holmes says, 'that the public evidence shows strongly that
Smith is guilty. I have no hunch or feeling that it shows anything else.
What I know of his character and the clues which the police found
point to his guilt and I have nothing else to go on, except this public
evidence.' A man who heard Holmes say this and believed him to be
truthful would naturally report Holmes as believing that Smith was
guilty.

Finally, what of Tertullian who claimed that 'the Son of God died'
was 'worthy of belief, because it [was] absurd'; that 'He was buried
and rose again' was 'certain because it [was] impossible'?[1] There are
ways in which we can interpret Tertullian as making an intelligible
claim. For example, we could suppose that 'absurd' and 'impossible'
are being used in 'inverted comma senses'. 'Absurd' could be taken to
mean 'apparently absurd', and 'impossible' to mean 'impossible by
normal standards'. Tertullian might be saying that one would not
expect a true claim about a matter of very deep significance to look
plausible or likely at a first glance by the average man. True
propositions of very deep significance must be very different from
normal propositions about the world of sense, and true claims of very
deep significance will in consequence seem absurd at first glance.
Hence, Tertullian might be saying, the fact that a claim purporting to
be a very deep truth seems absurd at first glance is evidence that it is
such a truth. Similarly, he might be saying that because the most
significant and fundamental happenings must be very different from
normal ones, they will be impossible by normal criteria—so a claim
about such a happening would be more likely to be true if it
concerned the apparently impossible.

But if Tertullian is saying that the fact that some proposition really
is 'absurd' or 'impossible' is grounds for believing it to be true, then
we must respond that not merely are these not good grounds for
believing a proposition, but that no one *can* believe any proposition
on the ground that it is absurd or impossible. For to claim the latter
involves claiming that all the evidence counts against the proposition.
And if Tertullian believes that all the evidence is against a proposi-

---

[1] 'credibile est quia ineptum. . . . certum est quia impossibile.' *De Carne Christi* 5.

tion, he must believe that that proposition is improbable, and in that case he cannot believe that it is true. He may die rather than deny the proposition in public; he may in some sense plan his life on the assumption that the proposition is true, but he does not *believe* it. There are logical limits to the possibilities for human irrationality, and even Tertullian cannot step outside them.

Belief is Involuntary

All of this has consequences for the question of the voluntariness of belief. In general a man cannot choose what to believe there and then. Believing is something that happens to a man, not something that he does. I believe that today is Monday, that I am now in Keele, that Aquinas died in AD 1274, etc., etc. I cannot suddenly decide to believe that today is Tuesday, that I am now in Italy, or that Aquinas lived in the eighteenth century. That belief is passive was a claim of Hume's. 'Belief consists', he wrote, 'merely in a certain feeling or sentiment; in something, that depends not on the will, but must arise from certain determinate causes and principles, of which we are not masters.'[1] But what Hume does not bring out is that this is a logical matter, not a contingent feature of our psychology. For if my arguments so far are correct, then a man believes that p if and only if he believes that the total evidence available to him makes p more probable than any alternative. His beliefs are a function of his basic propositions (and the degree of confidence which he has in them) and his inductive standards. If his beliefs were to be under his voluntary control, then either his basic propositions and the degree of his confidence in them, or his inductive standards, would have to be under his voluntary control. Yet our reason for trusting our basic propositions is our conviction that they are formed by outside factors independently of our will. If I were to control at will my basic propositions and the degree of my confidence in them, I would know that I would; and hence I would know that whether a proposition was among my basic propositions was not determined or even influenced by whether what it reported was the case. If I chose at will to believe that I now see a table, then I would realize that this belief originated from my will and so had no connection with whether or not there was a table there, and so I would know that I had no reason for trusting my belief, and so I would not really believe. A similar point goes for

[1] Hume, *A Treatise of Human Nature*, Appendix, p. 624.

our inductive standards. If I were to decide there and then what to count as evidence for what, I would realize that I was doing this, and so that my resultant beliefs were the result of my choice and so not in any way connected with whether or not things were as they claimed. It is because one set of inductive standards seem to me intuitively right and my use of them is not under the control of my will, that I trust that the resultant beliefs indicate how things are. If I decided there and then whether to adopt historical standards which ensured that no evidence counted as evidence for the physical resurrection of Christ, or to adopt standards which ensured that just one piece of testimony for that event would by itself make the occurrence of that event very probable, then I would know that I had no reason for trusting the resultant belief, and so I would not really believe it.

While I cannot change my beliefs at will, what I can do is to set myself to change them over a period. I can set myself to look for more evidence, knowing that that *may* lead to a change in my beliefs. Or I can deliberately set about cultivating a belief—e.g. by looking selectively for favourable evidence, and then trying to forget the selective character of my investigation. I can bring before my mind the evidential force of certain evidence, and try to forget about the evidential force of other evidence. And I can try to persuade myself that my old inductive standards were wrong standards. All this can and does happen, and in a later chapter I shall inquire if it is ever a good thing that it should happen. But the point here is that at any instant our beliefs are dependent on the view we then have of the evidence, and only if the process of changing our beliefs is a long and hard one can we persuade ourselves that our current view of what the evidence supports does not depend on our will, but rather on the evidence itself. For if we knew that some attitude of ours depended on our will we could not call it a belief.[1]

Acting on One's Beliefs

The account of belief which I have been expounding in this chapter involves the view that to believe a proposition is to have a mental attitude towards that proposition which logically constrains the way in which the believer can seek to achieve his purposes. As we saw, if I believe that p is more probable than q, and p entails that doing A_1 will bring about X, and q (unlike p) entails that doing an incompatible

---

[1] See my *An Introduction to Confirmation Theory*, pp. 182 f., for a somewhat lengthier defence of this view.

action A_2 will bring about X, and my sole purpose is to bring about X, then (if I have no other relevant beliefs) I will do A_1 rather than A_2. If I believe that it is more probable that this road leads to London than that one does, and if my sole purpose is to go to London, necessarily I shall take this road rather than that road. In this way a man cannot but act on his beliefs. Yet men are often criticized for not 'acting on' or 'living by' their beliefs. This seems to suggest that it is one thing to have a belief, another to act on it. What is being said when it is said that a man does not act on his beliefs? I suggest that when it is said that a man is not 'acting on' his beliefs, one of three things may be meant. My account of belief allows that although in the sense which I delineated a man must act on his beliefs, in these senses he may not. In considering each sense I shall consider in particular how a man may fail to 'act on' his belief that there is a God.

First, and least commonly, a man may fail to 'act on' his beliefs because he fails to draw those consequences for action which in fact follow from his beliefs. I did explicitly make the assumption when analysing the connection between belief and action, that the believer was aware of the means–ends beliefs entailed by his more theoretical beliefs; but, as we saw, he might not be. Thus, to take the religious example, a man may believe that there is a God, and also believe a whole series of religious propositions about God of a traditional Roman Catholic kind. The man may be a teacher of religion in school and have the purpose of teaching in school nothing but true religious doctrines. He may nevertheless teach out of a book which teaches things inconsistent with the religious propositions which he believes; he may teach these things because he fails to realize that they are inconsistent with his beliefs. In this way he fails to act on his beliefs. His failure is a failure of logic.

Secondly, a man may fail to 'act on' his beliefs because he lacks other beliefs with which the former can mesh to give rise to consequences for action. If a belief is of a theoretical kind logically remote from a man's other beliefs, it may carry little in the way of consequences for action in the circumstances of a man's life. A man's failure to act on that belief will then arise from his having few other beliefs which make the former applicable to the circumstances of his life. It is in this way that many men fail to 'act on' the belief that there is a God. If a man believes that there is a God, and has the purpose of telling the truth as he sees it, when asked, on religious matters, then when asked if there is a God, he will say that there is a God. But a man's belief that there is a God carries little else in the way of consequences for action unless the man has other religious beliefs with which it can mesh. For unless the believer has in addition beliefs about what a God wants men to do for him or about what a God has a right to demand of men, then, whatever his purposes—e.g. whether he wants to please God or to hurt him, to do his duty or not—the mere belief that there is a God dictates nothing in the way of action. The beliefs of a mere theist, a man who believes that there is a God but has little in the way of more detailed beliefs about him, carry so little in the way of consequences for action compared with the beliefs of, say, a fairly conservative Christian. Both act on their beliefs in the original sense which I analysed and yet there is so little for the former to act on.

A man whose religious beliefs are to give rise to much in the way of action may need, not only a number of religious beliefs, but also some simple factual beliefs. I may believe that there is a God, and that he has commanded me to help the poor and underprivileged, have the purpose to do what he commands, and yet fail to help the people on my doorstep through a failure to realize that those people are poor and underprivileged.

The other beliefs which a man lacks in order that certain beliefs may carry consequences for action may not be simply beliefs that some proposition is more probable than some alternative, but beliefs that some proposition is very much more probable than some alternative. A man may believe certain propositions, but only believe them mildly probable; whereas the consequences for action would only follow if he believed them very probable.

Thirdly, a comment that a man does not 'act on' his beliefs may really amount to a comment that he fails to have certain purposes (or to have them in sufficient strength). Although he does 'act on' his beliefs in the way which I originally delineated, he does not do those actions which we might expect him to do, given those beliefs, because he lacks certain purposes. Thus a man may believe that there is a God, and yet fail to worship God or render thanks to him—through a failure to have the purpose to worship whatever God there may be, or through a failure to have any purpose to express gratitude to any one who has benefited him. Or a man may believe that there is a God, who gives to (and only to) the virtuous a life of happiness after death, and yet fail to be virtuous through a failure to have the purpose of securing his long-term well-being. In these cases we describe a man as not 'acting on' his beliefs, because we naturally expect him to have, or think that he ought to have, the purposes in question.

In all cases where a man would do an action A_1 rather than A_2 if his beliefs relevant to it were stronger, he would also do A_1 rather than A_2, if his purpose to achieve the believed consequence of A_1 was stronger, relative to his purpose to achieve the believed consequence of A_2; and conversely. The failure may be either one of belief or one of purpose; how we classify it will depend on whether we think that the man has wrong beliefs or wrong purposes. An example will illustrate this. Suppose S believes that, on balance, just probably, there is a God, and that, on balance, just probably, God wants to be worshipped in church on Sunday morning, and that, on balance, just probably, if you do not do what God wants, you will suffer quite a bit for it in the next life. S has the purpose of avoiding such suffering, but also the purpose of staying in bed on Sunday morning. In the end he stays in bed. We accuse him of not 'acting on' his beliefs. The beliefs have failed to influence conduct because they were not strong enough for purposes of given strength. If S had believed the religious propositions with much greater confidence, he would have got up and gone to church; but, as it was, he stayed in bed—the religious propositions seemed somewhat speculative, and so it seemed worth taking a gamble on their falsity. But if S had had a stronger purpose to avoid suffering in the after-life, then given the beliefs of the strength which he had, he would still have gone to church.

In all these various cases which I have been discussing, if we criticize a man for not 'acting on' his beliefs, we may be saying either that, objectively speaking, he ought to have done so-and-so; or that he is culpable for not doing so-and-so. Objectively speaking a man ought to do those actions which he would do if he had all true beliefs and the purposes which objectively he ought to have. If a man has a belief that there is a God, and if in fact he ought to worship any God there may be, then, objectively speaking, he ought to act on his belief, by worshipping. If, in addition, in fact he ought to secure his long-term well-being and if in fact God gives to (and only to) the virtuous a life of happiness after death, then the man ought to seek virtue. He ought to 'act on' his belief by doing the actions which would follow by adding to his belief other relevant true beliefs and also right purposes. However, a man is only culpable for failure to do those actions which are dictated by the beliefs which he actually has and their consequences of which he is aware, given the purposes on which he recognizes an obligation to act. As I argued earlier, a man cannot there and then choose his beliefs; and so any culpability there may be for failure to have beliefs can only be culpability for failure to acquire them over a long period. A man may have obligations to pursue inquiries leading to possible changes of belief, or to cultivate specific beliefs over a period; and how far there are such obligations I shall investigate in Chapters 2 and 3. Likewise a man may have obligations over a period to check the consequences of his beliefs. But a culpable failure to act on some belief at a time can only be a failure of purpose. It is a failure to have (i.e. to seek to fulfil) those purposes which the man recognizes that he ought to have (i.e. ought to govern his behaviour). It is a failure to have certain purposes or to have them in sufficient strength. Clearly we can and do recognize purposes which ought to govern our actions, and yet fail to pursue those purposes. We may recognize an obligation to seek our long-term well-being or to worship any God there may be, and yet, while holding beliefs that God exists and wants us to do so-and-so, and will provide long-term well-being for those who do what he wants, fail to act on those beliefs through a failure to have the purposes which we recognize that we ought to have. Such failure is culpable failure to 'act on' beliefs in the third sense—i.e. the failure is basically one of purpose rather than of belief.

We have seen that one of three things may be meant when it is said that a man fails to act on his beliefs. It follows that one of three things can be meant when we say of a man that he *does* 'act on' or 'live by' his beliefs. We may be saying that he does not fail to act on his beliefs in any of the ways which we have spelled out: that he draws the right consequences from his beliefs, that he combines those beliefs with other beliefs which objectively he ought to hold, or that he has the right purposes (either objectively or as he sees it himself) in the actions to which his beliefs have application. Note however that, although a man may or may not act on his beliefs in one of these ways, nevertheless in the primary sense which I delineated earlier a man cannot fail to act on his beliefs—for a man's beliefs necessarily dictate the ways in which the man seeks to achieve his purposes.[1]

[1] It always appears strange when men have beliefs and yet do not 'act on' them. This fact led Newman to distinguish between two kinds of assent to propositions, 'notional' and 'real'. (J. H. Newman, *An Essay in Aid of a Grammar of Assent*, first published in 1870, Notre Dame, Indiana, 1979.) Notional assent involves unthinking, nominal, or half-hearted or unconvinced belief; real assent involves living conviction. He contrasts them by saying (p. 87) that 'we shall not . . . be very wrong in pronouncing that acts of notional assent . . . do not affect our conduct, and acts of belief, that is, of real assent, do (not necessarily, but do) affect it'. But what Newman calls 'notional assent' clearly has some effect on conduct—e.g. it may make a difference to what we say in casual conversation, even if it does not make a difference to what we are prepared to die for. Beliefs differ in strength and, as we have seen, for that reason differently affect

Acting on Assumptions

As well as talking of men acting on their beliefs (which in our primary sense they must do) we may also talk of men acting on assumptions. The only point of talking of this arises where the assumptions are propositions which the agents do not believe. For example, an Englishman in Turkey who speaks no Turkish and seeks directions from a native, will, if he believes that the native speaks English, address him in English. He will do just the same if he does not believe that the native speaks English. This will be because only if the native does speak English will the Englishman be able to achieve his purpose (obtaining comprehensible directions), and so realizing this, as he does not speak Turkish, he does the only action which has any chance of achieving his purpose. We may then describe him as acting on the assumption that the native speaks English. Or again, a man in an underground cave may believe that none of the several exits lead to the surface. He may nevertheless take a certain exit, because only by taking some exit has he any chance of achieving his purpose of getting to the surface. We may say of him that although he does not believe that this exit leads to the surface he is acting on the assumption that it does. These examples suggest the following relation between having a belief and acting on an assumption. To act on an assumption that p (or to act as if p) is to do those actions which you would do if you believed that p. It is to use p in your practical inferences, to take it for granted when working out what to do. If you do A on the assumption that p, you believe that there is a small probability that p, and that given the existence of at least that probability, the action most likely to realize your purpose is A. Hence you would still do A if you believed that the probability that p was greater, and so you would do it if you believed that p. In short, when a man acts on an assumption that p his action can also be described as acting on the belief that there is some (albeit small) probability that p.

Pascal recognized the difference between believing that there is a God and acting on the assumption that there is a God. He replies to a man who says 'But I can't believe' with the following recipe of how to acquire belief in God: 'You want to be cured of unbelief and you ask for the remedy; learn from those who were once bound like you and who now wager all they have. They behaved just as

conduct. There seems no justification for making a sharp division between two kinds of belief or 'assent'.

if they did believe, taking holy water, having masses said, and so on. That will make you believe quite naturally.'[1] Acting 'as if', i.e. on the assumption that p, is thus distinguished as a stage causally efficacious in producing belief that p.

[1] B. Pascal, *Pensées*, translated by A. J. Krailsheimer (Harmondsworth, Middlesex, 1966), No. 418.

2

Rational Belief

I N Chapter 1, I considered the nature of actual belief. We saw how in a sense all beliefs give rise to action and must be based on evidence. But not all beliefs are rational beliefs. A belief will fail to be rational if it is based on evidence in the wrong way or if it is based on the wrong sort of evidence. In this chapter I begin by considering the kinds of evidence which different people have for different beliefs, and the different ways in which they treat such evidence, and I then go on to examine what kinds of relation of evidence to belief make the belief rational. I do this because it is often suggested that people ought to hold only rational beliefs. I shall however find that the concept of rationality is ambiguous, and that we need to distinguish five different kinds of rationality which may be possessed by beliefs. Once we have distinguished these, we can consider how far it is incumbent on men to hold only rational beliefs.

Different Kinds of Evidence

A man's evidence, as I am using the term, is the set of his basic propositions, each together with his initial degree of confidence in it (the prior probability which he ascribes to it). A man's basic propositions are those propositions which seem to him to be true and which he is inclined to believe, but not solely on the ground that they are made probable by other propositions which he believes; propositions which he would believe unless they were overruled by other propositions which he believes. Men's basic propositions cover a vast range, but it is important to distinguish two kinds. To start with there are those which the subject believes because he thinks that they report his experiences or things experienced by him. Such propositions are the only ones which I have considered so far, and I will call them

initial propositions. Among all men's initial propositions are those
which report their apparent sense experiences or mental states or
events—'it looks to me as if there is a table in front of me' or 'I feel
giddy'. So too are propositions which report apparent perceivings—
'I see a table' or 'I see a rough surface'—and apparent perceptions—
'there is a table in front of me' or 'the clock says 5.10'. So too are
propositions which report apparent memories of past events, and the
past events which men think that they remember—'I remember going
to France when I was a boy' or 'yesterday I was in London'. Among
propositions which report things remembered are ones which report
the results of past investigations—'I examined the accounts and
checked that they balanced', or 'I looked on the shelf and in every
cupboard and my book was not there'. Some men may even include
among their initial propositions, propositions reporting experiences
of telepathy or propositions reporting future experiences or even universal propositions covering both past and future. (For whether or
not men can see into the future, some men may believe that they can.)

Men have different degrees of initial conviction with respect to
such propositions. I am a great deal more confident that there is a
table in front of me than that I was in London yesterday. (Just
possibly it may have been the day before yesterday). The greater the
confidence which the subject has in an initial proposition, the more
likely it is to acquire the status of an initial belief and to continue to be
believed despite counter-evidence.

As I noted in the last chapter, most of a man's initial propositions
acquire the status of beliefs, but some do not. Once initial propositions have acquired the status of beliefs, they help to promote further
beliefs (in virtue of being rendered probable, in the subject's view, by
his evidence), which in their turn may interact back with initial
propositions. Long observations by S of the behaviour of swallows
makes it probable, S believes, that p, virtually all swallows fly south
from England in autumn. Believing this, S then thinks that he has
seen a swallow one December day. This latter proposition q is an
initial proposition in which S has high initial confidence. But S's
confidence is diminished because S believes that his past observations
make p probable and so make it probable that he has misobserved on
this occasion. His final judgement may then be that q is rendered
improbable by his total evidence, that is, propositions reporting his
past observations together with q and his initial degree of confidence
in each.

Now two men, both concerned to judge the probability of a

proposition *p* may have different evidence, and/or different criteria, for when one proposition makes another probable (that is, different inductive standards), and for either of these reasons make different judgements of the probability. The simplest case of this is where one man perceives something which the other was in no position to perceive, but would have perceived if he had been in the right place at the right time. Two detectives investigating a crime may have seen different clues and for that reason come to different beliefs about who committed the crime. The difference of evidence may however have a deeper source. One case, on which I commented briefly, is that a man may claim to have evidence of a kind that the other never has—e.g. information provided by a sixth sense, by telepathy or clairvoyance. But more common is the case where one man is inclined to describe his experiences in a certain way as a result of having certain sensations, whereas another man who had the same sensations is inclined to give an entirely different description of his experiences. One man may have certain visual or olfactory sensations as a result of which he has great confidence in an initial belief—'I smelt an evil demon' or 'I saw a UFO land on Port Meadow'. Most of us, had we had those sensations, would have described our experiences differently—'I smelt a nasty cold smell' or 'I saw a white light moving over Port Meadow'. In each case there may be background beliefs which lead the subject to modify or reject his initial propositions, but our concern for the moment is merely with the initial propositions, the description of apparent experience. My point here is simply that men differ in the descriptions they consider themselves justified in giving of their experiences.

Men differ too in the degrees of confidence with which they hold initial propositions. The same sensations may lead two men each to have an initial proposition that he saw a UFO. Both may admit that the same background evidence counts against their proposition—that no one else saw the UFO, that there was a fire-engine with flashing lights in the vicinity which could easily have been mistaken for a UFO, that there have been no well-substantiated cases of UFOs or any other grounds for believing that beings from other planets have ever visited this planet, etc., etc. Both men may admit all this, and admit that in itself it all tends to count against the initial proposition. Yet the same background evidence which leads one man not to promote his initial proposition to the status of belief, will be insufficient for the other man. He may have much more confidence in the initial proposition. He may say: 'I saw the UFO. I cannot deny the testimony of my senses.' On the other hand there are men with such little confidence in the deliveries of their senses, that any proposition put forward on the basis of experience is immediately rejected if it comes into conflict with antecedent beliefs. No doubt Galileo's opponents, after looking through his telescope, were initially inclined to believe that the Moon has an earthlike surface, but immediately rejected that belief because of its conflict with other propositions (e.g. about the quintessential nature of the Moon) which they believed to be better established.

A man's basic propositions, as I defined this term, are those which seem to him to be true and which he is inclined to believe, but not solely on the ground that they are made probable by other propositions. Among such basic propositions I distinguished initial propositions as those which he is inclined to believe because he thinks that they report his experiences or things experienced by him. But men have basic propositions which they are inclined to believe, not on the basis of *experience* but because *reason* seems to show them true. Intuitively it seems to men that those propositions must hold. Basic propositions which are not initial propositions I will call prior propositions. Prior propositions which acquire the status of beliefs I will call prior beliefs. Men's beliefs in the truth of many of the propositions which philosophers call analytic[1] are often prior beliefs. My belief that if A is taller than B and B is taller than C, then A is taller than C, is not based on experience, but on reason. It is part of the armoury of reason with which I come to experience. The same applies to my belief that $2 + 2 = 4$ and my beliefs that various other propositions of mathematics are true. The beliefs of those who believe that every event has a cause is also normally a prior, rather than an initial, belief—an assumption with which they approach experience rather than a belief derived from experience. And, as we shall shortly see, many of men's beliefs about the correctness of inductive principles are also prior beliefs.

Men have different prior beliefs from each other; a mathematical assertion which seems self-evident to one man, for another man needs

[1] A proposition p is analytic (roughly) if and only if its negation (the proposition 'it is not the case that p') contains a contradiction. Thus 'all squares have four sides' is analytic because 'not all squares have four sides' contains a contradiction; it involves a claim that there is a figure with four equal sides and four equal angles which does not have four sides. A proposition which does not itself contain a contradiction and whose negation does not contain a contradiction is called synthetic. For a more detailed account of when propositions are analytic and when they are synthetic see my *The Coherence of Theism* (Oxford, 1977), Ch. 2.

to be justified by being shown deducible from some other proposition. Men *may* also have very different *kinds* of prior belief from each other. Some men may well have beliefs of very different kinds from those which I have mentioned, which are in no way based on experience but which intuitively seem to them correct and form starting-points for their belief structures—e.g. propositions about which states of affairs there are. Alvin Plantinga has recently in effect suggested that 'there is a God' may be a prior proposition for some people, and indeed one in which the believer may have enormous initial confidence.[1] Any of a man's prior beliefs which amount to knowledge (i.e. are beliefs which are true and justified, and satisfy whatever other conditions for knowledge there may be), are, in Kant's terminology, truths known *a priori*.

Some prior propositions seem self-evident to all who understand them and reflect on them—for example 'anything red is coloured' and '$2 + 2 = 4$'. The truth of these propositions seems to stare the thinker in the face; he judges that it is impossible that they could be false. Other prior propositions, such as 'every event has a cause', may seem to many thinkers to be true on grounds of reason; and yet they might judge them to be only highly probable, not certain.

Different Inductive Standards

Two men, both concerned to judge the probability of a proposition, may differ not in their evidence, but in their inductive standards, that is, in what conclusions they judge to be probable on the basis of what evidence.[2] Among their inductive standards all men have some kind of generalization principle; some principle to the effect that if all (or most) objects of some kind which have been observed have had a certain property, then it is (very) probable that some other object of that kind to be observed will have that property. A man who has observed that all observed heavy-feeling bodies (stones, chunks of

---

[1] See his 'Is Belief in God Rational?' in C. F. Delaney (ed.), *Rationality and Religious Belief* (South Bend, Indiana, 1979). He claims that it has not been shown that there is anything irrational in a man treating 'there is a God' as a basic belief. As he seems not to be suggesting that it would be a belief derived from anything analogous to sensory experience, his suggestion, in my terms, amounts to the claim that it might be a prior belief (along with such self-evident truths as '$2 + 2 = 4$').

[2] I am counting deduction as a special case of induction, since I count 'making certain' as a special case of 'making probable'. A deductive argument is one in which the premisses, if true, guarantee (i.e. make certain) the truth of the conclusion. As well as differing generally over what makes what probable men may differ in their beliefs about what entails what; that is, they may differ in their deductive standards.

wood, animals, etc.) when liberated from the hand fall to the ground, will judge that it is probable that the next such body, liberated from the hand, will fall to the ground. As Hume reminded us, some such principle is the foundation of all our beliefs about things beyond our immediate experience.[1] But men differ in the way in which they interpret the principle. One man may claim that it applies to predictions of the results of gambling games and another may deny that it has application here. Thus a man may claim that the fact that red has won much more frequently than green at a certain game of roulette is grounds for supposing that red will win next time (and so for betting on red next time), while another claims that the same evidence is grounds for supposing that green will win next time. Men may differ as to how far they may extrapolate from evidence obtained in a narrow spatio-temporal region. Can I reach a conclusion about how bodies will behave on Sirius in 10,000 million years time from a study of how they have behaved on Earth over a couple of millenia? And men will differ as to how many observations are needed before a judgement of high probability can be made. On the whole those who practice what we call science share fairly similar standards by which they make judgements of probability. They believe that a scientific theory is probable in so far as (1) it predicts accurately many and varied data, and (2) it fits in well with other scientific theories and is simple and intelligible.[2] But even scientists will differ in the way they interpret these standards. Scientists with different mathematical training may well differ in their claims about when a scientific theory is simple. To Kepler his theory that each planet moved on an elliptical path with the Sun at one focus no doubt seemed a fairly simple theory.

---

[1] Nelson Goodman claimed that there could be tribes which extrapolated properties totally different from the ones which we extrapolate. He invented the predicate 'grue' which (developing his idea in a way in which many philosophers have developed it) we may understand as follows. An object x is grue at a time t if and only if *either* the object is green and t is before AD 2000 *or* the object is green and t is AD 2000 or after. Then the grass is now both green and grue, but if it stays green in AD 2000, it will be no longer grue (since neither condition applies). So a tribe which used 'grue' instead of 'green' to describe objects would describe leaves in spring as now grue, and would use the generalization principle to conclude that leaves in spring in AD 2000 will also be grue. Whereas we, describing objects in terms of 'green', will conclude by the generalization principle that leaves in spring in AD 2000 will be green. But while what is grue in 1981 is also green in 1981, what is grue in 2000 will not be green. We get different predictions according to whether we extrapolate the property of being green or the property of being grue. See N. Goodman, *Fact, Fiction and Forecast* (2nd edn., Indianapolis, 1965), Chs. 3 and 4.

[2] For a somewhat fuller account of these criteria see my *The Existence of God* (Oxford, 1979), pp. 51–7 and 64–9.

But then he was one of the very few men of his time to understand the mathematics of the ellipse. To most of his contemporaries theories which claimed that the path of a planet was the product of many different circular motions may well have seemed simpler. To take a more up-to-date example—ten years ago there was the well-known dispute between 'big bang' and 'steady state' theories in cosmology. Both parties to the dispute accepted each other's reports about the amount of red-shift shown by different galaxies and quasars etc.; the disagreement concerned what this showed, and hence turned on the standards for what makes what probable.

Some men may have inductive standards very different from the rest of us. In a well-known article, 'Understanding a Primitive Society',[1] Peter Winch described the standards by which the Azande assess a claim to have put a spell on someone, and pointed out that although they are not our standards, they are ones which intuitively seem right to the Azande. Even within our own culture there are men with very different standards from our own—for example gambling addicts. Thus a gambler who has just become a father of a baby boy may go to the races and find that a horse called 'Sonny Boy' is running. He immediately judges this an omen; and on this basis being convinced that the horse will win, bets a large sum on it. His belief arises from the fact that his inductive standards include a principle roughly to the effect that apparently coincidental resemblances of name between recent or important past events in someone's life and future events which can be 'backed' or invested in, make it probable that such backing or investment will bring great reward. Most of us do not have such principles among our inductive standards.

As I noted in Chapter 1, many men just use inductive standards without ever putting into words what the standards are which they use. The point that a man may be altogether rational in his acquisition of beliefs, acquire them only on good grounds, and yet be unable to set out those grounds, was made very forcibly by Newman both in his *University Sermons* and in the *Grammar of Assent*.[2] Others of us are more sophisticated, and have explicit beliefs about what makes what probable, e.g. a belief that a scientific theory which satisfies certain statable criteria is probably true. Some of these beliefs are based on experience; some of their experiences provide men's grounds for holding these beliefs. Thus a man may believe that if n per cent of a

[1] *American Philosophical Quarterly*, 1964, **1**, 307-24.
[2] J. H. Newman, *University Sermons* (first published 1871; London 1970), see especially Sermons 11 and 13; *Grammar of Assent*, Ch. 8, §3, *'Natural Inference'*.

sample of a population picked by a process of choosing every
hundredth person in the telephone directory has a property P, then it
is highly probable that n per cent of the whole population have the
property P. A man's experiences which are his grounds for this belief
may be what he has found and what others have told him about the
differences and similarities in other respects between different groups
picked by such a telephone directory sampling procedure and
between such groups and whole populations. But although some
beliefs about what are correct inductive standards have their grounds
in experience, not all inductive standards can have their grounds in
experience. For although experience E may make probable a belief B
about what are correct inductive standards, it will only do so in virtue
of some inductive standard G—e.g. the generalization priniciple
which I cited earlier. A man may infer by the generalization principle
from the fact that in almost all cases studies where n per cent of a
sample picked by the method described have a property P, n per cent
of the population have that property, that very probably such a cor-
relation (between sample and population) will hold in a future case.
And if G were rendered probable by experience it could only do so in
virtue of another inductive principle. Men have, and must have in
order to infer from things experienced to things not experienced,
inductive principles which are independent of experience. Such
principles I shall call a man's primary inductive principles—to be
contrasted with his secondary inductive principles, which are principles which, using his primary inductive principles, he believes on the
basis of experience.

One inductive principle which all men accept is what I may call the
testimony principle, that, other things being equal, if someone tells
you that p, then probably p. What other people tell us is the main
source of our knowledge about the world beyond our immediate
experience. Our complex beliefs about the history of the human race
long before our birth, the geography of the Earth beyond our narrow
experience, the structure of the heavens and of the atom, come from
what others have told us. The principle only says that *other things
being equal*, if someone tells you that p, probably p. But other things
may not be equal. You may have other evidence which promotes the
contrary belief—you may have seen for yourself or some third person
may have told you that not-p. In that case, despite being told that p,
you may still come to hold the belief that not-p, or may ascribe equal
probabilities to p and to not-p.

It is sometimes suggested that the testimony principle is a

secondary inductive principle because it is justified, via the generalization principle, from our experience that in the past when people
have told us things we have usually found those things to be true. I do
not think that is correct, for we could not even understand what
people say to us (which we need to do in order to test whether they are
telling the truth) unless we had already made an assumption that they
normally tell the truth. As children we came to understand what our
parents were saying by correlating the words which they uttered with
the states of things which we observed (e.g. the words 'this is a brick'
with the object in front of us), and then assuming that they were
uttering true sentences. The latter could not be a claim which we
proved from experience. The testimony principle is a primary
inductive principle.

What is the case however is that subsequently we come to put
qualifications on the testimony principle, about which informers are
to be believed on which occasions about which matters. Some of
these qualifications come from experience and the application to it of
the generalization principle. Thus we may find that when Bloggs and
Snoggs inform us about things which we subsequently observe for
ourselves, what Bloggs tells us always coincides with what we
observe, whereas what Snoggs tells us often does not. We are inclined
to ascribe high prior probabilities to our own observations. Thus we
conclude that what Snoggs had told us in the past is not always true,
and so (by the generalization principle) that what he tells us in future
will contain a mixture of truth and falsity and so that what he tells us
on a particular occasion is not all that likely to be true; whereas what
Bloggs tells us is very likely to be true. More generally we come to find
in this way that certain sorts of people are more reliable than others;
that people are more reliable in certain circumstances (e.g. on oath,
not under the influence of drink, where what they tell us is not to their
credit or is to their disadvantage, etc.). Further, we may come to
develop theories about the grounds which people need to make
knowledge-claims of various kinds, and hold that they are to be
believed only if they have grounds of those kinds. For example, if
someone makes a claim that a certain scientific theory is true, we may
hold that he has the right to do so only if he has got his information
directly or indirectly from a scientist who has tested his theory to
ensure that it satisfies the criteria sketched on p. 38 above. So we have
reason to believe him if and only if we have reason to believe that his
information does derive from such a source. Or again if someone
makes a claim about an event of past history, we may hold that he has

the right to do so if and only if he has got his information through a chain (of writers or speakers) which derives ultimately from an eyewitness. Our grounds for holding such theories may be *a priori*— i.e. they come to form prior beliefs. Or we may derive them on authority—many teachers, etc., tell us that all knowledge comes from experience in this sort of way. And authority remains perhaps the primary source of our beliefs that these conditions are fulfilled in any given case. How do we know that someone tested Einstein's theories, or that Caesar's *Gallic War* was not written by a nineteenth-century schoolmaster? Our teachers, and books, tell us so. Likewise authorities are often the source of our beliefs about who are the authorities in a field. How does the child know that physics professors in universities rather than scientologists are the ones who are in a position to tell him about physics? Because he is told it by many people.

Most of what we believe, we believe on authority. If there are conflicting claims among purported authorities—one says one thing and the other says the opposite—then, unless we have a doctrine that one authority is more to be believed than another—the issue becomes disputed. Any given issue disputed or not, can be investigated, although, as I shall stress shortly, issues are more worthy of investigation, the more uncertain they are—i.e. the further away from 0 or 1 is the probability of a claim in the area. However, when an issue concerns matters well beyond our immediate experience, any investigation depends on taking for granted other things which we also learn on authority. We can indeed investigate when Caesar's *Gallic War* was written, and can find a number of books which we are told were written by men in various centuries AD between the first and the nineteenth which show knowledge of the *Gallic War*. If we accept on authority when these books were written, we can conclude that the *Gallic War* was written no later than the first century AD. We can in turn investigate when these books were written, but we can only settle the issue if we are prepared to take other things on authority.

It is impossible to discuss anything remote in history or physics or astronomy, unless you take a lot of things for granted. What you take for granted is determined by the climate of opinion, that is by authority. This is not to deny that there is a difference between Britain in the eleventh century and Britain in 1981 in respect of subservience to doctrinal authority. But the difference is not that now there is no stock of propositions believed on authority, taught in primary schools as 'gospel truth'. There always has been and, I have suggested, always will be such a stock of propositions. The main difference is what those propositions are. Then the roundness of the Earth was open to dispute, but the physical resurrection of Christ was not; now the converse is true. (There is of course a further difference in the method of treatment for dissidents; but I pass that over, as unimportant for our purposes.)[1]

The main theme of this section, from which I digressed to discuss the testimony principle in more detail, is the different inductive standards which men have. Sophisticated men, such as philosophers, may hold explicit beliefs about the correctness of the primary inductive principles which they use. These beliefs are prior beliefs. The inductive principles would not be primary if they could be justified by reference to anything else. I have a prior belief in the generalization principle. I am inclined to believe it because it seems to me to be true, but it is reason, not experience, which makes me inclined to believe it.

A man's inductive principles are his beliefs (whether explicit or not) about what makes what probable. As with any other of his beliefs, his beliefs about what makes what probable carry consequences for action, only in this case rather indirect ones. A man's beliefs about what makes what probable carry consequences of the form that if he believes p, then he will believe q. If he believes that if most observed As have been B, the next one will be (for all observable qualities A and B), then if he finds that most balls drawn from a bag have been black, he will believe that the next ball will be black; and this latter belief will have more immediate consequences for action, e.g. he may make a bet that the next ball will be black. Our claims about what are a man's inductive standards must be such that we attribute to him standards which license most of the inferences which he actually makes. We study the evolution of his beliefs. We see that when his evidence is e_1 he comes to believe h_1, and when his evidence is e_2 he comes to believe h_2, and so on. Our account of his inductive standards must be such as to make most of these steps legitimate; must be such that in general

---

[1] In *On Certainty* (translated by Dennis Paul and G. E. M. Anscombe, Oxford, 1969), Wittgenstein stresses the importance in forming the framework of our conceptual system of very general propositions which we are taught as children, and into which we slot anything which we learn from particular experiences. He discusses such examples as that the Earth has existed long before our birth, that the Earth is round, that men's heads are not full of sawdust, that cars do not grow out of the ground. Wittgenstein claims (401) that 'propositions of the form of empirical propositions, and not only propositions of logic, form the foundation of all operating with thoughts', and (318) that 'there is no sharp boundary between methodological propositions and propositions within a method'.

by them e_1 makes h_1 probable, e_2 makes h_2 probable and so on. I say make '*most* of these steps legitimate' rather than 'all' of them, because as we saw in Chapter 1, a man may have beliefs which have no effect on his actions for the reason that he does not realize the consequences of his beliefs for action. A man may have certain general beliefs about what makes what probable, and fail to draw a consequence which follows from them—e.g. that e_5 makes h_5 probable. So given a set of information about which hypotheses a man judges probable on the basis of what evidence, we may set up a theory about his inductive standards which legitimizes most of these inferences. However, as we saw in Chapter 1, compatible with any set of evidential data, there will be many different hypotheses about his beliefs. And this will be the case also where the data are data of what a man believes on the basis of what. Among such theories we must choose, as we saw earlier, by the principles of simplicity and charity. We must attribute to men a few simple general and lasting beliefs about what sorts of thing make other sorts of thing probable. And in so far as we can, we must by the principle of charity attribute to others the same standards for the formation of belief as we have ourselves. As I argued in Chapter 1, it follows from general application of these principles of simplicity and charity that we believe what a man says about his beliefs; and so if he says that he has certain standards for what makes what probable, *ceteris paribus*, we must believe him.

So in this way we may set up on some limited amount of evidence about how his beliefs are influenced by new evidence, an account of the inductive standards which a man uses. Our account could be wrong in being dissonant with the subject's own knowledge of his inductive standards. The subject himself could know that we had misinterpreted his standards—if he had in fact explicitly formulated in words his standards for himself, as of course most people have not. Or the account could be wrong by failing to license other inferences which the subject makes or would make under different circumstances, and of which the investigator is ignorant.

Such then is the structure of men's systems of belief. They start with evidence, basic propositions which seem to them to report experiences or merely to be intuitively right (propositions in which they have varying degrees of confidence), and these interact to give rise to other beliefs which men believe to be rendered probable by the evidence. Men may or may not ever have put into words propositions which set out their inductive principles which are operative in generating those other beliefs.

Among the most influential of men's initial propositions are propositions to the effect that they have been told so-and-so, that the Earth is spherical, that it is many millions of years old, that it revolves round the Sun on an annual orbit, etc., etc. By the testimony principle these propositions then give rise to corresponding beliefs.

Five Kinds of Rationality

Some of men's beliefs are true and some are false, and we may assess beliefs on that dimension. But we also assess beliefs on the dimension of rationality. Roughly, a man's belief is a rational belief if he is justified in holding it—for epistemological reasons. There may be various reasons why it is a good thing that a man hold some belief— e.g. that it gives him peace of mind, or prevents him beating up his wife; but the only reasons which concern us here are reasons which concern the likelihood of it being true—these I will call epistemological reasons. We all want to say that men often hold beliefs which are in fact false but which they have no grounds for believing false and are in fact justified in believing. We might say, for example, that the average man of the first century AD held a rational but false belief in holding that the Earth was stationary. However there are various possible kinds of epistemological justification which a man may have for holding beliefs, and I shall need to distinguish five kinds of rationality which beliefs may possess.

A subject S who believes that p will have what I shall call a rational$_1$ belief if and only if his belief that p is probable, given his inductive standards and given his evidence. A subject must believe that a belief of his is rational$_1$ if he is to have that belief (see Chapter 1); but it may not in fact always be rational$_1$. A failure in respect of rationality$_1$ is a failure of internal coherence in a subject's system of beliefs, a failure of which the subject is unaware. Thus, on the basis of what he has heard in court and outside it, a juryman may hold strong beliefs well-supported by evidence, that (1) the evidence against the prisoner is weak, (2) the police who charged him are intelligent men, (3) the police know far more about the detailed facts than he, the jury-man, does, but (4) often police frame suspects. The juryman's inductive standards may be such that (1), (2), and (3) make probable (5), the prisoner is guilty; but (1), (2), (3), and (4) do not make (5) probable. The juryman then comes to believe that (5) is probable, because he forgets the relevance of his belief that (4), in reaching his conclusion. The juryman's belief that (5) is irrational in the first sense of 'rational'.

A subject's beliefs may be rational in that they are internally coherent, and yet we may feel (loosely) that in holding them the subject is not responding to the world in a justifiable way. To attempt to capture what extra we are looking for I define rationality$_2$. A subject S who believes that p has what I shall call a rational$_2$ belief if and only if p is in fact rendered probable by his evidence, and his evidence consists of basic propositions which he is in fact justified in holding with the degree of confidence with which he does hold them. For his belief to be rational$_2$ his belief has to be grounded in those initial propositions which his present experiences (and memories of his past experiences) in fact justify him in holding or prior propositions which considerations of reason justify him in holding, and to be supported by them in virtue of correct inductive standards. Rationality$_2$ is a matter of conformity to objective standards, which the believer may not recognize and may indeed explicitly deny.

A belief can fail to be rational$_2$ by being grounded in initial propositions which the subject is not justified in holding—e.g. it may be based on a claim to have had a telepathic experience when no conscious experience justified this, or on a claim to have seen a UFO, where the sensations which the subject has had, justify him only in claiming that he has seen a light. Or it may be based on initial propositions about which the subject is excessively over-confident. Or it may fail to be based on initial propositions which the subject, given his experiences, ought to hold.

There are arguments which we can use to show that some man is not justified in holding some initial proposition, with the degree of confidence with which he does hold it, or in failing to hold some initial proposition. To the man who claims telepathic communication, we may attempt to show that what he claims to know telepathically is seldom the case, and hence that he is not justified on a given occasion in having much confidence in initial propositions claiming telepathy. To the man who has excessive confidence in his senses, we can point out how often, when his perceptual judgements can be subjected to objective tests, they fail to be right. Likewise to the man who has too little confidence in his senses, we can point out how often subsequent inquiry showed that what he was hesitant to admit perceiving was in fact there. And so on. But if these arguments are to convince the subject that he has a tendency to hold initial propositions unjustifiably (or not to hold initial propositions which he would have been justified in holding), they must appeal to things which he already accepts, viz. inductive standards and other beliefs which we share with him (e.g. that when many other people in a position to observe report that things are not as he holds, they are right and he is wrong).

Similarly there are arguments which we can use to show that some man is not justified in holding some prior proposition with the degree of confidence with which he does hold it. These arguments would show that he had jumped to the conclusion that the proposition was true without giving enough consideration to whether there was any way in which it could turn out to be false. Thus some man may hold as a prior proposition 'there is no greatest prime number' without ever having thought of the mathematical argument which shows this proposition to be true. We feel that the man should not just believe the proposition without having considered the argument. We can point out to the believer that men who jump too quickly to mathematical conclusions of that complexity often turn out to be wrong.

Arguments to show that a man is not justified in holding basic propositions with the degree of confidence with which he does hold them are arguments to show that he has given to them a wrong prior probability. Note that such arguments are not arguments to show that those propositions are false. A man may include some false proposition among his evidence with perfect rationality—until some good argument is produced to show that it is a false proposition. But the point is that a man may be too hasty in assenting to some proposition on the basis of experience or reason—and we can show him that he is too hasty, and teach him to be more careful in future.

Finally, a belief can fail to be rational$_2$ by not in fact being rendered probable by the subject's evidence, i.e. by his using incorrect inductive standards, like those of the gambler and the Azande discussed earlier. Arguments can be used to show that certain inductive standards are the true ones (the true inductive standards being those which license all and only correct inductive judgements). Clearly the starting-point of such investigation is a large set of judgements which seem to the investigator to be indisputably correct; that e_1 makes h_1 probable, but does not make h_2 probable; that e_2 makes h_2 probable, and more probable than h_1; and so on and so forth. As with all investigation we start from what seems to stare us in the face, although allowing for the possibility of later correction. We then seek, using the principle of simplicity, for the most natural extrapolation from those judgements, an extrapolation which would allow that we had made occasional mistakes but no more. Having reached an account of the true principles of induction we then see whether any necessary corrections to our initial particular judgements are ones which seem plausible. In so far as the general account which we reach fails to license judgements which seem, intuitively, to be obviously correct, we must look for another and perhaps more complicated account of the true principles of induction. But it may be that having formulated general principles, these seem so obviously correct to us that we change some particular judgements in the light of them.[1]

There are arguments which can be used to show that some other man is not justified in using the inductive standards which he uses, but it will be apparent that such arguments will only cut ice if they appeal to particular judgements or general standards which, implicitly or explicitly, the other man already holds. If the gambler accepts that the generalization principle has universal applicability, then we can use it to show him that as some peculiar principle of his has seldom yielded correct results in the past, it is unlikely that it will in the future. But if the gambler does not accept that the generalization principle is of universal application and asserts that it cannot be used to pass judgement on other principles, we may not be able to convince him that his beliefs are not $rational_2$.

However, a subject's beliefs are not $rational_2$ if they are not based on evidence which he is justified in holding or if they are not inferred by correct principles, whether or not we are right in our judgements using our own standards about the matter, and whether or not we can convince the subject about this.

A man must believe that his own beliefs are not merely $rational_1$ but $rational_2$. For a man must believe his basic propositions to have (as a result of his experience of the world) the prior probabilities which he ascribes to them, i.e. believes them to have; and unless a man held that his inductive standards were correct, he could not believe that his beliefs were in fact rendered probable by his evidence. But, for all that, a man's beliefs may not in fact be $rational_2$ and we as outsiders may judge that they are not.

Quite obviously, men of past centuries have often had scientific beliefs which were both $rational_2$ and false. A man of the eighteenth century who studied Newton's *Principia* would have been using the inductive standards which we believe to be correct if he judged that on the observational evidence of astronomy and mechanics which Newton lists, Newton's theory of mechanics was probably true (i.e. that Newton's theory described correctly the behaviour of all

---

[1] My own account of what are the correct inductive standards in assessing when evidence shows that some explanatory theory is correct, are given in *The Existence of God*, Chs. 3 and 4.

material bodies at all points of space and time). He had every reason for believing that the behaviour of planets and moons which Newton cited as evidence was as Newton claimed, and indeed he could have checked it for himself. No other relevant evidence was known. It was only when later evidence turned up in the nineteenth century that men began to doubt the universal applicability of Newton's theory.

The rationality of both rational₁ and rational₂ beliefs is a matter of the believer's response to present sensations and memories of the past and to apparently self-justifying truths of reason at the time in question. The belief is rational₁ if the response satisfies the believer's own standards. The belief is rational₂ if the response satisfies correct standards. However, we often feel that although a man is justified in holding a certain belief at some time, he ought to have looked for more evidence or checked his standards more thoroughly at earlier times. Had he done so, he might have beliefs which were better justified, more probable. And so, according to whether the failure at an earlier stage was a failure by the subject's own standards of which he was aware, a failure by the subject's own standards of which he was not aware, or a failure by correct standards, we have three further kinds of irrationality of belief. In so far as these possible failures have been avoided, we have three further kinds of rationality. The subdivision of 'failure by the subject's own standards' into failure of which he was aware and failure of which he was unaware arises when we are concerned with failure in pursuing investigations, because pursuing investigations is something which a man can choose to do or choose not to do. Whereas the only failure by the subject's own standards with which I was concerned before was failure to respond to evidence in the right way at a time; and here there is no category of failure of which the subject is aware, since, as I argued in Chapter 1, a man cannot but respond in the way in which the evidence seems to him to point; necessarily a man believes what he believes to be probable on the evidence. Hence the only failure of the type with which I was concerned previously was failure of which the subject was unaware. Here we have both types.

A subject S who believes that p has, I shall say, a rational₃ belief if and only if S's evidence results from past investigation which was in S's view adequate, his inductive standards have been subjected to criticism by S which was in S's view adequate, and S has checked in his view adequately that p is made probable by his evidence. Investigation is adequate if it is adequate for the goal of securing true beliefs.

Examples will illustrate the different ways in which beliefs can fail to be rational$_3$. First, there may be a culpable failure, of which the subject is aware, to collect enough true, representative, relevant evidence of good quality. Thus, a detective may have a good case against a suspect, whom, on the evidence available at the time of the trial, he justifiably believes to be guilty of murder. But murder is a serious matter and the detective may not, through culpable idleness, have followed up all leads in the past, checked alibis thoroughly, etc. So although it is rational that the detective should hold the belief at the time of the trial, his belief is in a way irrational because it is not backed by enough relevant evidence. Alternatively, the detective may have acquired plenty of evidence but may have looked only for evidence to support his own point of view. Now, in so far as he remains aware that he has done this, necessarily the detective will take into account the bias of the evidence sample. (For if you know that you have not looked for where damaging evidence is most likely to be found, if there is such evidence, you will know that your failure to find it does not give strong support to your theory.) But the detective may now have forgotten how biased his investigation was, and then on the basis of the evidence which he has recorded, justifiably judge that it points to the subject's guilt. There remains however an element of irrationality in his belief resulting from past failure to investigate—an irrationality which would be compounded if the forgetting of the bias of the investigation was in any way deliberate. The belief may also be irrational$_3$ in being based on initial propositions, on the reliability of which the subject recognizes that he ought to have checked, e.g. claims to have held telepathic communication. In such a case the subject may recognize, as a result of hearing criticism from others, that he ought to have checked whether what he claims to know telepathically is often, by other criteria, as he claims. The second reason why a belief can fail to be rational$_3$ is that the subject has formed it by using inductive standards which he recognizes that he has not subjected to proper criticism. Thus, the gambler referred to earlier may realize that other people think him suspicious, and suspect that his method of reaching conclusions about winners of races is unsatisfactory, and yet not have submitted it to a test which he recognizes to be relevant, e.g. not have tested whether it normally works. Or, although he does not recognize such tests to be relevant (i.e. he treats his principle as a primary inductive principle), he may have refused to take account of philosophical criticisms of it (e.g. that it does not cohere with his other inductive principles, and that it ought to do so). The third reason why a belief can fail to be rational$_3$ is that the subject has culpably failed to check that, given his standards, the belief is made probable by his evidence; he has failed to consider adequately exactly what the evidence does show. A historian may have come to believe some theory on the basis of certain evidence, without having checked whether there were other theories which fitted the evidence equally well and were in fact better supported by it.

For many of our beliefs, however, it surely does not matter whether we look for relevant evidence, or to check their correctness in the other ways. My belief that the distance from London to Edinburgh is 400 miles may not be one which enters into my plans or plans with which I am concerned in any way. In that case any past investigation would have been sufficient, for there was no need for me to do any. It appears that in so far as the rationality of a belief is a matter of whether it results from adequate investigation, it depends on how important it is that the subject should have a correct belief on the matter; or rather, in the case of rationality$_3$, how important the subject believes it to be that he should have a correct belief on the matter. There are some beliefs which matter because they concern issues about which it is important that I have true beliefs—e.g. whether my house is falling down, whether my daughter has had an accident, whether I owe you an apology or a lot of money, whether the old man next door is ill, whether my chemical experiment will blow up the village, and so on. Yet although my judgement about the importance of the belief is one factor which determines whether it matters that I should investigate the relevant evidence, it is not the only factor. Another factor is my belief, to start with, about probabilities in the field. Granted that it is important that I should have a correct belief about whether my house is falling down, there is only point in my investigating the matter if there is, in my view, some significant non-zero probability that it is falling down and some significant non-zero probability that it is not. If it is virtually certain that it is not falling down (none of the available evidence counts in favour of this supposition, and all counts against it), there is no point in investigating the matter; and the same holds if it is certain that it is falling down. I do not have to ring up the police to inquire if my daughter has been involved in a road accident if I have no reason to suspect that she has; and so on. I conclude that the importance of investigating is a function of both (a) the subject's beliefs about the importance of true belief in the field, and (b) the subject's beliefs before possible investigation that the issue is far from certain, that the probabilities to start with are not too close to 0 or 1. (a) and (b) of course interact. How close to 0 or 1 is relevant depends on how important is true belief.

Failure to investigate the truth of a proposition is however excusable in so far as (c) the subject believes strongly that no amount of investigation will make any difference to its probability on evidence, will have any effect on showing how likely it is to be true. An issue may be important and the subject have no belief about it, about which he is in any way confident, and yet it would not be irrational$_3$ of him not to investigate its truth, if he believed it highly probable that no amount of investigation would turn up any new relevant evidence (or show that any mistake had been made in inference). For example, it matters greatly that I shall have a true belief about whether or not a ship on which I am embarking voluntarily in time of war will be blown up by an enemy submarine. Statistics of past enemy successes suggest that there is a probability of 1 in 3 that the ship will be blown up. If, by making a few inquiries, I could discover more relevant evidence, then I should do so; and it would be irrational$_3$ for me not to. But if I have apparently no possible way of finding out anything further about enemy plans or intentions, there is no point in my trying to do so—I must just take my chance. Adequate investigation of a belief in the subject's view is a matter of his having investigated for such time as the importance of the belief and his initial view of its probability, in his view, requires—given that he does not believe it very probable that investigation will achieve nothing. Just how probable the latter belief has to be to excuse failure to investigate, will of course depend on the exact values, in the subject's view, of the other factors. For a belief about a matter which the subject holds to be of supreme importance, perhaps investigation ought always to be undertaken.

The value of investigation may however be outweighed by the value of doing alternative actions; a man may have a duty to act in some way on the belief in question or to do something unrelated. In that case a man is not culpable for not investigating. Important though it is to check whether my house is falling down, it is even more important to get my family out of it if my present belief is that a collapse is imminent. And important though it may be for the detective to check further on a murder accusation, he ought to postpone such checking if he alone is in a position to save a man from drowning. The value of investigation depends finally on (d)—the subject's beliefs about whether he has other important actions to do, e.g. overriding obligations to fulfil. So, in summary, the value of a subject investigating an issue depends on four beliefs of his: (a) about the importance of the issue, (b) about the closeness to 0 or 1 of the probability of his belief about the issue, (c) about the probability that investigation will achieve something, and (d) about whether he has other more important actions to do. A subject's beliefs are rational$_3$ if he has investigated them to the extent determined by these factors.

So, my belief that the distance from London to Edinburgh is 400 miles is rational$_3$ because I believe it to be of little importance whether I have a true belief about the matter. Whereas if I had to bet a considerable sum on the issue, the belief could not in general be rational$_3$ unless I had gone so far as to look up in an encyclopaedia how far it was. Yet if I believed that there were no encyclopaedias or other sources of information available or that I had no time to investigate because of really pressing rival obligation, then the belief would be rational$_3$ after all.

Rationality$_3$ is a matter of the subject's beliefs being backed by investigation which he believed to have been adequate. However, a man can have standards of what is the proper amount of investigation, standards evident in what he says and does on other occasions, judged by which the amount of investigation relevant to a given belief might be inadequate; and yet he might have failed to recognize this. The detective might not have noticed that his investigation of evidence relevant to a particular case was perfunctory, although by his normal standards it was so. Hence we get our fourth kind of rationality. A subject S who believes that p has a rational$_4$ belief if and only if S's evidence results from past investigation which was by S's own standards adequate, and his inductive standards have been subjected to criticism by S which is by S's own standards adequate, and S has checked adequately by his own standards that p is made probable by his evidence.

Rationality$_3$ and rationality$_4$ are both a matter of whether the belief is backed by investigation adequate in some way by the subject's own outlook. Yet of course subjects may be totally blind to the need for investigation and criticism, and beliefs may be irrational because based on inadequate investigation, although the subject may have considered the investigation sufficient, and it may have been sufficient by his own standards. So we come to a fifth kind of rationality. *S*'s belief that *p* is a rational$_5$ belief if an only if *S*'s evidence results from past investigation which was adequate and inductive standards which have been submitted to adequate criticism, and *S* has investigated adequately whether his evidence makes his belief probable. The detective may have thought that his investigations were adequate, but they may not have been so. He may not have collected enough true representative relevant evidence of good quality. In that case his belief that the prisoner was guilty may be irrational in sense (5), even though it be rational in the other four senses. Again, the superstitious gambler may not have recognized the need to investigate his methods, but the need may exist all the same. In that case his beliefs are irrational in sense (5). It follows from earlier considerations that how much investigation is adequate depends on the importance of the belief at stake; whether it is virtually certain that it is true or virtually certain that it is false; whether or not there is some probability that investigation will achieve results;[1] and whether the subject has other important actions to perform. It depends objectively on these facts—not on the subject's beliefs about them. The point of investigation is that it may give the subject beliefs which are not just fairly probable, but very probable.

It is only irrationality in sense (3) which is culpable irrationality, for it results from the subject neglecting investigative procedures which he recognizes that he ought to pursue. Irrationality in senses (4) and (5) are a matter of objective discrepancy between the subject's actual investigative procedures and either those which he normally recognizes or really adequate investigative procedures; but in so far as the subject does not recognize these discrepancies, no blame attaches to his conduct. Irrationality in senses (1) and (2) arises from a failure to recognize certain things at the time in question—discrepancies within the class of the subject's beliefs in the case of irrationality (1), and unjustified evidence and incorrect standards in the case of irrationality (2). But either you recognize the things in question at the time or you do not; either it strikes you or it does not. Recognizing is coming to believe; and if, as I have argued, belief is a passive matter, so too is recognition. No blame is attachable to you for things that happen to you, only for things that you do.

---

[1] Of course the probability of investigation obtaining results and the virtual certainty of the belief being true or false (i.e. its probability being close to 1 or 0) will, like all epistemic probabilities, be relative to the subject's evidence; but the rationality$_5$ of the belief will not depend on the subject's assessment of that evidence.

Men's Evidence for Their Religious Beliefs

Having drawn attention to the different kinds of evidence which men have and the different inductive standards which they use to get their beliefs, and the kinds of rationality which are involved therein, I can now apply these general considerations to men's religious beliefs, inquiring what are the structures of men's religious beliefs and when are those beliefs rational. By a man's religious beliefs I understand, very roughly, his beliefs about transcendent reality, including his belief about whether or not there is a God, and his beliefs about what properties God has (what God is like), and what actions he has performed. However, for the sake of simplicity of exposition, I shall in this chapter consider only men's beliefs about whether or not there is a God.

Quite clearly, different men base their religious beliefs on very different kinds of evidence; pieces of evidence which one man treats as quite irrelevant, another man treats as quite crucial for his belief. Some of the evidence which men have, whether or not regarded as of importance, they share with all other men; other of the evidence which men have is available only to some men. To start with, there are apparently necessary truths of reason, in my terminology, prior beliefs, such as the premisses of some ontological argument,—e.g. 'God is a most perfect being'.[1] The religious belief of the occasional philosopher who believes that an ontological argument works is based on such propositions; but the religious beliefs of few other men are grounded here.

Next, there are certain evident general features of the Universe, which all men can recognize but about the evidential force of which they dispute. These constitute initial beliefs in which all men have great confidence. For example, 'there exists a Universe', the starting-point of most versions of the cosmological argument. Or the propositions of experience which occur at the beginning of Aquinas's first three ways—e.g. 'some things in the world are certainly in

---

[1] The traditional version of the ontological argument was put forward by Descartes, and (probably) originally by St. Anselm. It runs roughly as follows: '(By definition) God is a most perfect being. A being which exists is more perfect than one which does not. Therefore, God, being most perfect, exists.' For ancient and modern versions of the argument and criticisms of it, see (e.g.) the collection edited by A. Plantinga, *The Ontological Argument* (London, 1968). For a very careful analysis leading to a rejection of the argument, see Jonathan Barnes, *The Ontological Argument* (London, 1972). For a new version of the argument, see A. Plantinga, *God, Freedom, and Evil* (London, 1975), pp. 108–12.

process of change.'[1] The starting-points of teleological arguments too can be phrased as propositions which all men believe on grounds of experience—e.g. '(almost) all observed natural phenomena conform to scientific laws'. One evident phenomenon which in the past had, and perhaps still has, some importance for men's religious beliefs is the existence of life on earth; others are the existence of conscious beings, and the existence of beings capable of moral choice. All these propositions form grounds for many men's belief that there is a God, for they believe that the phenomena which the propositions report would not occur unless there were a God. Some men may believe that the phenomena in question make certain the existence of God (because the propositions reporting them, possibly together with certain prior propositions, entail the existence of God). Others believe that one or more of the phenomena render the belief that there is a God probable, because they need explaining, and the creative action of God provides such an explanation. Others believe that each of the phenomena adds to the probability that there is a God (confirms this proposition), and that, together with other phenomena yet to be mentioned, they make it probable overall.

The next influence on men's religion is what they are told about history. Many men's religious beliefs are to a lesser or greater extent rooted in beliefs about history, and these latter beliefs depend on initial beliefs as to what they have been told about history. Some of the things which we are told about history, we are told by more than one person (e.g. we read them in books apparently written by different people), and we are told that they are not the subject of serious dispute (or we are told them in such a tone that we infer this)—e.g. that the Christian Church grew in three hundred years from being a small group in Palestine to being the dominant religious group of the Roman Empire, or that all the books of the New Testament came into existence during this period. But many of the things which we are told are the subject of serious dispute and sometimes we may hear rival views about them from different sources; but perhaps more normally we may simply be told that there are views other than those of our source. In this category might come such claims as that St. Mark's Gospel was written before AD 70, that St. Paul's Epistle to the Galatians was written by St. Paul about AD 49, that Jesus lived on earth in the first thirty years AD and was then crucified, that there are diverse accounts of the Resurrection in the New Testament but all agree in the central facts of a physical

---

[1] St. Thomas Aquinas, *Summa Theologiae*, 1a, 2. 3.

resurrection. According to the society in which we are brought up, so we are given different pieces of information as indisputable-by-reasonable-men. In one society children may be told as beyond dispute that Jesus was raised physically from the dead, that Jesus was born of a Virgin, or that archaeology has discovered the site of the Garden of Eden. In a second society children may be told that these things are probably so (since serious experts have thus pronounced), although there are cultures where men doubt them. In a third society children may be told that these things are questionable.

On the basis of what they are told, using the testimony principle, men come to have different historical beliefs. These historical beliefs they then use as part of their evidence for belief in God. For example, they argue explicitly, or merely come to believe, that the Gospel records would not be as they are or the Church have had the success it did, unless Jesus had been raised physically. But only God could thus have violated nature; and hence there must be a God. Or they argue that Jesus could not have had his honest character and made the claims he did unless he were a special messenger of God. The pattern of argument here is again that certain things need explaining (certain particular historical facts, this time) and that only the existence and action of God can explain them. Hence they make probable his action.

But the source of the historical beliefs which form the jumping-off ground for these arguments to the best explanation is authority. Among historical beliefs which men come to hold as a result of what they are told, we should include not merely beliefs about matters central to a religious tradition, but beliefs about more local matters— e.g. a local miracle—which also form grounds for some men's beliefs that there is a God. Authority is also of course often a more direct source of religious beliefs. Children are told that there is a God, that He became incarnate in Christ, etc.; and, at any rate in certain societies and to start with, they believe what they are told, just because they are told it, even if they are also told that there are men who do not believe that there is a God. So either directly or indirectly (via historical claims) authority is a very powerful source of religious belief.

We saw earlier that all men have as a primary inductive principle the testimony principle that what you are told is probably so. Men learn to put various qualifications on the principle in the course of time: that certain men seek to deceive on certain matters; that only certain men are in a position to inform you on certain matters; that certain areas are the subject of such dispute among experts, that nothing can be taken on authority there, etc. But the principle must come first. Basically, men believe what they are told; and it is by assuming that what they are being told is true, that they have come to understand what they are being told. The qualifications are sometimes the result of personal experience: we find that certain particular acquaintances tell us things which by personal investigation we find to be false. Or we may develop for ourselves or at any rate find that our own experience bears out some theory about who is in a position to give us information about different kinds of matter. But more frequently authority itself provides our grounds for believing the qualifications.

All of this is evident with respect to any religious claims which we are given on authority, or any historical claims which we are given as a basis for religious belief. We may indeed develop partly for ourselves a theory that scientists (not the Bible) are to be trusted on scientific matters. But our grounds for this belief will probably be that scientists have often been proved right about science, where the Bible has been proved wrong. And our grounds for the latter belief will be authority. People tell us that the Bible makes scientific claims which Galileo and Darwin showed to be false.[1]

Again, how do most men know what is and what is not beyond dispute by experts in matters of biblical history? That St. Paul lived in the first century AD is beyond dispute, and that the apostle St. John wrote the fourth gospel is not? By what they have been told. A deep student of the New Testament in Oxford today may have read many books and articles, and as a result come to know by personal experience what is and what is not disputed in that class of literature. But even he has probably not read what Tibetan Communists or Jehovah's Witnesses think about St. Paul—they may well deny what he regards as indisputable. But even if he learns that they deny St. Paul's existence, he will still regard the matter as beyond dispute by *experts*. And how does he know that the Tibetans are not experts on this matter? Because of a general climate of cultivated British opinion which regards them as in no position to comment intelligently on such detailed European historical matters; in other words, on authority.

True, on any given matter (e.g. whether St. Paul lived) a determined investigator could over a period of years set out evidence for what other people take for granted; but he could only do so by taking for granted yet other things (e.g. the general reliability of

---

[1] On this see Chapter 7.

Suetonius as a historian, that Origen lived in the third century, etc., etc. Given such assumptions, we can use the statements which these writers make as evidence.) We take it from our parents and teachers or, as we grow up, from a wider society, what is and what is not the subject of serious dispute among experts. And if we did not, we could not make many claims to knowledge beyond immediate experience. Nevertheless, it remains the case that what we regard as indisputable because it passes our tests in these ways may pass into the category of the disputable. New conflicting evidence may turn up. Or we may, through experience or being exposed to new possibilities, come to develop a new theory about when authorities are to be believed.

So much for the evidence of history, mediated by authority, and of authority direct, on religious matters. I pass now to three further classes of evidence which help to produce men's religious beliefs. First, perceptions of particular public phenomena and private religious experiences. These too provide for many men grounds which (perhaps together with other evidence), they believe, render probable their religious beliefs. A man may see another healed of some affliction subsequent to prayer for the healing, and argue that the healing would not have happened but for supernatural intervention. Or a man may have an experience, which seems to him to be hearing God speak to him, and on that basis conclude that there is a God. Secondly, there may be a man's perceptions of the course of his life or that of others whom he has observed. He may have found that his prayers have always been answered, in that subsequent to his prayers the needs which provoked them have always been satisfied; and also that the events of his life have always provided him with opportunities to do or enjoy worthwhile things. He argues that all this would be unlikely to have happened, had there not been a God who ensured that it did happen. Or he may have seen the lives of some other religious people and watched how deeply satisfying and worthwhile those lives seemed to be; and have reasoned that those lives provided reason for supposing that there is a God. The reasoning here (no doubt normally implicit rather than explicit), it seems, may be of one of several kinds. The observer may be reasoning that the fact that a man acts on an assumption successfully is evidence for the truth of the assumption, and so the fact that the religious people act successfully on the assumption that there is a God is evidence that there is a God. Secondly, the observer may be reasoning that, left to themselves, people would not act in this religious way; so, we need a supernatural explanation of why they do so act, and the

most plausible such explanation is that God helps them. Or, finally,
the observer may be reasoning—the fact that these people have
obviously 'got the measure of life' (in the sense that they have reacted
to the evidence of experience by discovering a satisfying way of life) is
good reason to trust their beliefs generally (whereas the fact that
'clever' scientists, historians, etc. have made such messes of their
personal lives is good reason for supposing that, outside their
academic specialism, there is a lot which they do not know.) The
examples of the lives of others have been a powerful factor in
inducing religious belief, a fact summed up in the slogan 'religion is
caught, and not taught'.

Among a man's initial beliefs may be beliefs about general
phenomena which he has perceived, formulated in ways which others
might regard as question-begging, e.g. 'the world exhibits design' or
'all men are subject to the commands of morality'.

The evidence which I have listed so far is all evidence which tends
to promote the belief that there is a God. Among evidence tending to
promote the belief that there is no God there is again evidence
varying from the public and certain to the private and not so certain
(not so certain in the sense that the believer has less initial confidence
in the basic propositions involved). There are prior beliefs that the
concept of God contains various incoherences. There are initial
beliefs, supported by testimony, of the existence of various kinds and
degrees of evil; which men see as rendering improbable the existence
of a good creator. There are prior beliefs that the concept of free will
is incoherent; and initial beliefs of perceptions which are seen as
evidence against human free will (e.g. a man sees the great influence
of their environment on the actions of other men); and sometimes
men are told on authority that man has no free will. The non-
existence of free will is seen as counting against the existence of God
for more than one reason, but especially because it would make the
existence of evil even more of a difficulty for religion.[1] Then again
there is the enormous influence of authority—'Science has proved
that everything that happens has a cause other than God', 'Science

[1] This is because much of the evil in the world is due to human action. If men do not
have free will, and if there is a God, God would be directly responsible for men's evil
actions; but God, being perfectly good, would not have brought about such evil
actions. So, if men do not have free will, their evil actions are evidence against the
existence of God. If however men do have free will, while a God might have given to
men free will (because of the great goodness of men having free choice), he would not
be responsible for their choosing evil rather than good. For developed argument on the
problem of evil, see my *The Existence of God*, Chs. 9, 10, and 11.

has proved that miracles do not happen', 'We know now that the early Church invented a lot of what was written in the Gospels', or even 'Science has proved that there is no God.'

So much for the diversity of evidence about religion, which different men take into account. Each man is aware of some collection of such evidence, and this he assesses, and judges that it makes probable or improbable the existence of God. In so doing he uses certain inductive standards; for it is in virtue of the evidence having certain characteristics that he judges that it makes probable what it does.

Inductive Standards generating Religious Beliefs

We discover what are a man's inductive standards by discovering the dynamics of his beliefs. We see which beliefs lead him to hold which other beliefs and ask what are the standards involved in this movement. Having reached a reasonable conclusion about what are a man's inductive standards we can, as we saw earlier, then pick out some of his beliefs as not licensed by them, and so as not conforming to them. Studying a man's inferences in all areas including that of religion, we may reach a conclusion about what are his inductive standards, and thereby assess some of his religious beliefs for their rationality. It is however always possible that a man uses different inductive standards in different areas of inquiry. In particular a man's judgements about religion may be formed in accord with different inductive standards from those which he uses elsewhere. We are all familiar with men about whom others find it natural to pass such a judgement. It is natural to pass such a judgement, for example, on the man who claims to have carefully considered the detailed historical evidence of Gospel miracles and thinks that that by itself shows that many of them occurred; while at the same time he pours scorn on claims that modern saints levitate or that Uri Geller bends spoons, on the grounds that science shows that these things do not happen.

There is however a difficulty here, and one must be careful about jumping too quickly to the judgement that a man is using different inductive standards in his judgements about religion from those he uses elsewhere. The difficulty is this. We derive our account of a man's inductive standards by studying the inductive judgements which he makes in different areas. Any attempt to codify standards in any one area is going to involve mention of concepts prevalent in that area—any attempt to codify the standards which a man uses in his

judgements about the purposes and beliefs of other men is obviously
going to involve reference to purposes and beliefs. Yet there will be no
mention of purposes and beliefs in any attempt to codify the
standards which a man uses in physics. Nevertheless in a crucial sense
the same standards may be being used in both areas, because there
are more general standards from which the particular standards
in each area, with particular application to the relevant subject-
matter, can be derived. The more general standards which might
have application to both areas are standards such as Bayes' Theorem,
or 'if from a theory you deduce a prediction, and the prediction
is observed to fail, the theory is certainly false'; or, '*ad hoc* hypotheses
are probably false'.[1] Now clearly the subject-matter of religion—
the possible existence of an extra-mundane being (or beings) with
strange properties—is very different in various ways from the subject-
matter of more mundane sciences. So there will be a danger when
we attempt to codify a man's inductive standards, of giving an
account of them which fits his mundane judgements but which
so incorporates their mundane features that it does not have any
natural application to an extra-mundane subject-matter. To take
a very crude example: we might note that all the factual conclusions
which a man reaches in history, physics, etc., concern the existence
and properties of physical objects, and so judge that his inductive
standards are such that the conclusions of inferences from factual
premises must concern the existence and properties of physical
objects. We then note that in religion he argues from the world to
God, who is no physical object; and so conclude that he is using
different inductive standards here from his normal standards. That
would be a foolish conclusion. What has gone wrong is that we failed
to extrapolate from study of the man's inductive judgements in
other fields a sufficiently general account of his inductive standards to
allow it to apply to very different fields. We built into our account
of the man's inductive standards features peculiar to the areas in
which we studied his inductive behaviour, which did not allow it
to have application to wider fields. It is only reasonable to say that
a man's inductive judgements about religion do not conform to
the standards of inductive inference which he uses elsewhere, if
we have given a sufficiently general account of those standards
to allow them to have application to issues beyond those studies,
to pass judgements one way or the other in new fields dependent
on the evidence.

[1] See *The Existence of God*, Ch. 3, for exposition of such standards.

Rationality₁ and Rationality₂ of Religious Beliefs

A man's beliefs are rational$_1$ if and only if, given his evidence, they are rendered probable on his own inductive standards. A man's belief that p is irrational$_1$ when he has failed to draw the conclusion, using his general inductive beliefs, that his evidence does not make p probable. So when we see what a man's evidence and inductive standards are, we can conclude with respect to his religious beliefs that they do or do not follow from his evidence, in accordance with those standards.

Suppose, however, a study of a man's inductive behaviour leads us (even when we have taken account of the difficulties mentioned above) to conclude that he is using in all his judgements about religion different standards from those which he uses elsewhere. What then are we to conclude from this about his rationality$_1$? We could say either that none of his judgements about religion are rational$_1$ *or* that he has one set of inductive standards for arguing about mundane matters and another set for arguing about religious matters, and that there is nothing irrational$_1$ in this. I think that there are cases where it would be right to say the former, and cases where it would be right to say the latter. It would be right to say the latter, for example, if the man explicitly acknowledged the use of different standards, and was consistent in his use of them, and his arguments about religion were never infected by normal standards. He might for example claim that the only test of religious truth was what was written in the Bible, never attempt to justify this claim in ways which used other inductive standards (e.g. never claim that archaeology or prophecy *showed* that the Bible was true), and never use other standards in religious argument; then it would seem right to say that he just did have one set of standards for arguing about religion, and another for arguing about mundane matters; and so wrong to accuse him of being irrational$_1$. For there would be a coherence about his way of arguing, even if we did not like that way of arguing. On the other hand if the subject makes no explicit claim about what are his inductive standards, but simply seems to argue in a different way about religion, only not consistently so, then it seems right to say that his beliefs about religion are not rational$_1$.

A man's belief is rational$_2$ if and only if it is in fact rendered probable by his evidence, and his evidence consists of basic propositions which he is justified in holding with the degree of confidence with which he holds them. Before we can pass judgement on a man for holding beliefs which are irrational$_2$ we need to know what does make what probable, i.e. what are the true inductive standards. We saw earlier the general way in which we can argue to what are the true inductive standards by extrapolating from most of the particular judgements which we make and then seeing whether we are prepared to stick by any particular judgements which do not conform to the resulting standards. It may be that the inductive standards which we naturally extrapolate from our judgements about history, science, and ordinary life, and which we make sufficiently general to have application to the subject-matter of religion, yield different judgements in that field from those which we are initially inclined to make. Those standards might suggest that the existence of the Universe was some evidence for the existence of God, whereas we judged to start with that it was not—or conversely. We must then just reflect which seems intuitively most obvious—our particular judgement in the religious field, or the general standards extrapolated from other fields. If we conclude that the particular judgement is most evident, then we must modify our account of the true inductive standards. Our account of them may then become more complex by being a conjunction of one set of standards for religious argument, and another set for other fields. Such a set of standards we may well call a split set. I do not believe that anyone who reflects very seriously on the matter is very likely to come down in favour of such a split rationality. For the concepts used for talk in religion, and in particular for talk about God, are concepts which have application in other fields—God, like humans, is said to be 'wise', 'good', 'power-ful', etc., even if only analogically so; and so one would expect *somewhat* the same inductive standards for judging that some being is good, wise, or powerful in the two fields. And certainly any attempt to persuade others by rational means that religious claims are true or that they are false must involve inductive standards which the others share; and that means standards which they apply in other fields, for those are the fields in which our inductive judgements coincide with theirs.

This work of discovering the true inductive standards is of course a co-operative one—other people can suggest alternative sets of principles which an individual must test against his own intuitions; and men may argue about which set of principles is the most natural extrapolation from a given set of judgements. The story of such attempts to codify true inductive principles is the story of inductive logic, sometimes known as confirmation theory, and the work is not easy—as is evidenced by the continuing existence over the years of competing accounts in the field. But I see reason for hope that the task of codifying the inductive standards of at any rate civilized contemporary man is a completable one, and those are the inductive standards which are implicit in most of the judgements which we make and which intuitively seem to us to be correct.

The rationality$_2$ of a man's beliefs is not merely a matter of his using correct inductive standards but of his evidence consisting of basic propositions which he is justified in holding with the degree of confidence with which he holds them.

A man's evidence consists of prior propositions and initial propositions. He is justified in believing his evidence if he is justified in believing those propositions with the degree of confidence with which he does believe them. He is justified in believing prior propositions if they seem to him to be true, intuitively, on grounds of reason, and if he is not too hasty in making such a judgement. Thus if a man's religious belief is grounded in an ontological argument (as the religious belief of most men is not), the premisses of that argument must be ones which seem evident to the believer and on which he has to some extent reflected to see if there is any possible way in which they could be false. (Men may disagree as to the amount of reflection necessary. We saw earlier how argument on the amount necessary can take place.) The same applies if a man's atheistic belief is grounded in a belief that in some way the concept of God is self-contradictory. If a man's beliefs are based on initial beliefs that someone has told him so-and-so or that he has seen so-and-so, his sensations together with his memories of past experiences have to justify the initial beliefs. He must be neither over- nor under-cautious by true standards in his response (in the light of his memories of his past experiences) to sensations. He must not 'jump to the conclusion' that he is seeing a UFO or a man walk on water, when he is not. Nor must he refuse to believe what stares him in the face. Now a man can only describe things as they seem to him at the time. But over the course of time he can investigate whether the judgements which he makes hesitantly almost always turn out to be correct, or whether those of which he is so confident almost always turn out false. By the success or failure of his judgements he can learn to react to sensations appropriately and can pass judgement on the justifiability of his past initial responses to sensations. Also at a given time, others can investigate what are the sensations (e.g. when he seemed to see a UFO) to which a man was exposed and pass their judgement on whether the report which he gives of his experiences is over- or under-cautious, in the light of what seems to them as a result of their own past experience, to be the right response to those sensations.

In so far as a man believes those basic propositions which his experience justifies him in believing, and comes to believe the further propositions which these warrant on true inductive standards, his beliefs are rational$_2$. Some men claim that their evidence makes it probable that there is a God, and some claim that their evidence makes it probable that there is no God. Which beliefs in this field are rational$_2$ is partly a matter of which basic propositions the believers are justified in believing. For some propositions such as 'there is a Universe' or 'there is evil', which are matters of public knowledge, there is no doubt that all men are justified in believing them. For other basic beliefs about what some agent has seen or been told, argument can take place about whether the agent has believed them with too much or too little confidence. The most controversial issue tends to be whether and by how much by true inductive standards any individual piece of evidence or all a man's evidence put together renders it probable that there is a God. I have discussed here the general principles for showing from what evidence a man ought to make his inductive inferences and what are the inductive standards which he ought to use in reasoning about the existence of God.[1]

Rationality$_3$ of Religious Beliefs

Rationality$_3$, rationality$_4$, and rationality$_5$ are a mater of a belief being backed by adequate earlier investigation. A belief is rational$_3$, you will recall, if it is based on evidence resulting from investigation which was in the subject's view adequate and the subject has subjected his inductive standards to criticism which was in his view adequate, and checked in his view adequately that by them his belief was rendered probable by his evidence. We saw earlier that what constitutes adequate investigation depends on the subject's belief at earlier times about the probability of the hypothesis in question, his belief about the probability of investigation affecting the probability of the conclusion, his belief about the importance of holding a true belief about the hypothesis, and his belief about the importance of other actions which he could be doing. If in past times a man was absolutely certain about the truth of his religious beliefs, then there would have been no need for him to investigate their truth; and those

---

[1] For my application of these principles to the issue of whether generally available public evidence makes it probable that there is a God, see *The Existence of God*.

beliefs would automatically be rational$_3$. If, however, he regarded them as dubious or only fairly probable, then, if his beliefs were to be rational$_3$, in so far as he believed the issue important, he ought to have pursued investigations—given that he did not believe that it was more important to do something else or that investigation would achieve nothing. For only if the man pursued investigations would there be any chance of his acquiring beliefs which were very probable.

How a man investigates an issue depends on what he already knows about the field and, in particular, as I stressed earlier, on his beliefs about who are the authorities in the field. To find out the truth about a point of astronomy, the four-year-old will ask his father; the ten-year-old his form teacher, the sixteen-year-old his physics teacher; but the man who already has a Ph.D. in the field will try to persuade some foundation to give him the money to buy equipment which will enable him to find the truth for himself, although, as I stressed earlier, he will need to take for granted results allegedly established by other physicists.

There are fields and cultures where a man has no idea how to set about investigating further the answer to some question. I so interpret my definition of rationality$_3$ that in that case a man's belief, even though he does not believe that it has a probability close to 1 and even though he has done no investigating, is still rational$_3$. In one way the man does not believe that his investigation has been adequate— for there is more which he believes ought to be done; but in another way he does believe that the investigation has been adequate—for he has done all that he can. Since the definition of rationality$_3$ was designed to pick out the rationality which lies within a man's powers to achieve, I shall say that in such a case a man's beliefs are rational$_3$.

It may sometimes be like that with religion; a man may believe on balance that there is a God but have no idea how to pursue further inquiries. In that case the belief is rational$_3$. Yet the first step which will occur to most people, in this as in all fields, is to consult someone who, they have heard, is an expert. An inquirer may well pursue his inquiries by asking the local priest for the answers and taking them on authority. But in so far as he learns that the subject is a disputed one, it will normally occur to the investigator that he ought to cross-check what the priest says by consulting others. Then he will talk to atheists and gradually assemble the arguments which are supposed to be relevant in the field and begin to see how they stand up to objections.

The investigator will try to acquire more evidence than he had before, e.g. discover new historical facts about the New Testament or the religious experiences of his neighbours. He ought also to investigate whether he is justified in believing the basic propositions on which his religious beliefs are based with the degree of confidence with which he does believe them. Suppose that he believes with only moderate confidence the prior proposition that 'God is a most perfect being' is an analytic truth, and that his religious belief was based on this. Then he ought to investigate whether what looked analytic really begged factual questions. He should read some of the philosophical debate on the ontological argument. Or suppose that a religious believer bases his belief in part on an initial belief that his prayers have always been answered. Then he ought to consider further whether they have really. Has he not forgotten the ones that were not answered, or is not his understanding of what constitutes an answer so wide that his initial belief is empty of content? He ought too to look for much more evidence.

Moreover, as we saw, the historical beliefs on which men's religious beliefs depend are received on authority. They can nevertheless be investigated. The believer who was told that St. John's Gospel was written by the apostle John should look at some of the arguments (put forward by writers regarded as competent in his culture) for and against this. Or the believer who accepts everything written in the Bible as literally true should consider the arguments of those who hold that it is not to be believed on scientific matters. Although, as I have stressed, any investigation of such matters can only take place if we assume other things which we have been told on authority, e.g. that the Hebrew Text of the Bible is correctly translated in such and such a way, or that Papias wrote in the second century AD—investigation can nevertheless probe deeper.

The believer should also investigate what are the true inductive standards; we have seen the procedure for doing this. And finally, given those standards which the investigator considers to be correct, he needs to apply them honestly to all the evidence at his disposal, to check what is the evidential force by those standards of his evidence. He needs to take into account the existence of evil, of man's religious experiences, and so on, and not omit anything. As I wrote earlier, how a man will investigate depends on what he already knows. Hence the inquiries which men pursue will be pursued at very different levels of sophistication. The same amount of time devoted by two inquirers to investigating religious truth will be spent in different ways. Those who cannot read books or do not know which books to read, will do their investigation by talking to men of different views. The educated may do their investigating by reading Hume's *Dialogues* and comparing them with Paley's *Natural Theology*. Some may find that the reasons for a position given to them by one expert are so strong that they find no need to consult a rival; or it may never occur to them that it is in any way necessary to check the claims of authorities.

It is hard for those of us who look down from philosophical heights not to deem some of the inquiries which ordinary men make about religion to be so crude as barely to deserve the name of rational. Is the man who talks only to the priest really pursuing rational inquiry? Yes, if he does not realize that the matter is the subject of dispute among experts. But even if he does realize this, so long as he asked the priest for reasons for his belief, the inquirer has conducted some sort of investigation; he has made some check on the priest's claims. The resulting belief may well be rational$_3$ in that the investigation has been in the subject's view adequate. However, if there is any looking down from heights on to the inquiries of others and casting doubts on their rationality, we may perhaps have a dim idea of what superior beings might think of our own rationality in the matter of religious belief. I myself am certainly conscious after years of professional writing and study of the matter, of the paucity of my evidence—of all that I do not know about the religious experiences of the mystics or about Buddhism, for example—of how an enormous amount of further philosophical investigation needs to be done with respect to every point which I make about inductive logic and every point which I make about the inductive worth of arguments for and against the existence of God. To any celestial philosopher who may have spent 2,000 years investigating these issues our inquiries must have such a primitiveness about them that he feels very reluctant to call them rational.

The scope for investigation is endless; one can always go on looking for more evidence and check and recheck the process of utilizing it to form beliefs. All we can do is pursue such inquiries as seem to us adequate within the time at our disposal. The need to pursue investigation is greater, the less the importance of doing other things. In so far as a man has devoted to such investigations the amount of time which he thought to be adequate, and has pursued them honestly, his resulting beliefs will be rational$_3$. If a man's belief that there is a God or that there is no God is rational$_3$, it is established on the basis of as much inquiry as the believer judged it adequate to give to it.

It is noteworthy that the more men seek to have rational$_3$ beliefs about religion (or anything else) and so the more investigation they undertake, the more likely their beliefs are to converge. For the process of investigation will involve a man in learning about the evidence accessible to others and becoming aware of the inductive standards of others and the criticisms which they make of his own standards. Clearly, the greater the sharing of evidence, the closer men will be to having a common basis of evidence whence to make their inference to religious truths. Exposure to each other's inductive standards and criticisms of their own is far more likely to bring them closer together than further apart in their standards. A man must be guided by the truth as he sees it, but the more men investigate the more likely it is that they will see things in the same way.

The rationality$_3$ of a belief is a matter of a man having devoted such time to investigating it as he himself thought adequate. But although a man may think that he has devoted enough time to such investigation, even by his own standards he may not have done. He may have devoted far less time to it than the importance which he believed the matter to have warranted by his normal standards of how much time you ought to devote to investigating things. While believing that religion was a very important matter, he may have devoted far more time to studying football. His resulting belief would then fail to be rational$_4$. For a rational$_4$ belief is one where the believer has by his own standards adequately investigated the evidence, his inductive standards, and the force by them of his evidence.

But whether or not he has followed his own standards, he may not have followed true standards. He may not have devoted the time to religious investigation which the importance of the subject demands. In that case his beliefs will not be rational$_5$. The next chapter will consider the objective factors which determine how much investigation is needed to obtain rational$_5$ beliefs in the field of religion. This depends, we saw earlier, first, on the importance of having true beliefs in the field. We shall consider how important is true religious belief. Then the rationality$_5$ of men's belief depends on how probable the belief is to start with and how probable it is that investigation will achieve anything. We have already considered how the former issue is to be assessed in considering the rationality$_2$ of a man's religious beliefs. Whether there is a probability that investigation will achieve anything, will depend, as all epistemic probabilities do, on the evidence available to the investigator. But superficially, any subject which men discuss and on which books are written can be investigated, and religion is certainly among those subjects. However, there are arguments in vogue to show that religious inquiry is pointless and these I shall need to assess. Finally, since the rationality$_5$ of a belief depends on the importance of securing a true belief in comparison with other claims on a man's time, I shall need to allude to these. A completely general discussion would not be possible without discussing all a man's obligations, viz. the whole of morality. But there have been down the centuries certain arguments to the effect that men ought to cultivate beliefs identified in advance of investigation—that certain beliefs are desirable for reasons other than that they are likely to be true. These arguments are arguments against cultivating rational$_5$ beliefs at all, for they are arguments against investigating beliefs in a way adequate to secure true beliefs.

3

The Value of Rational Religious Belief

WE have seen that the only kind of rationality in belief for which a man can be held to task is rationality$_3$. For that is the only kind of rationality which is under a man's control. While a man cannot, I argued, help having the beliefs which he has at a given time, he can be held to task for not doing something about his beliefs over a period. He can be held to task for not investigating an area to an extent which he considers adequate, to get more evidence and to see what his evidence shows.

Beliefs are rational$_3$ in so far as they are based on investigation which was, in the believer's view, adequate. If it matters that I have a rational$_3$ belief on some issue, it matters because ensuring that I do have a rational$_3$ belief is all that I can do towards ensuring that I have a rational$_5$ belief, that is, one which is in fact backed by adequate investigation. A belief is rational$_3$ if the believer believes it to be rational$_5$. Ensuring that I have a rational$_5$ belief is all that I can do towards ensuring that I have a true belief. For only by acquiring more evidence which is true, representative, and relevant, by checking my inductive standards and what they show (and not suppressing evidence or distorting inductive standards), can I turn my belief into one which really has a high degree of probability on all my evidence. And ensuring that I have a very probable belief is all that I can do towards ensuring that I have a true belief—for a very probable belief is one which is, very probably true.

We saw in the last chapter that beliefs which are rational$_5$ are ones which are in fact backed by adequate investigation. How much investigation is adequate is a function of four things: how important is belief in the field, how probable is the belief to start with, how probable it is that investigation will be fruitful, and the importance of other actions which the investigator may do.

In this chapter I investigate some of the objective factors which determine how much investigation is needed for beliefs about religion to be rational$_5$. I shall again, for the sake of simplicity of exposition, in this chapter understand by 'religious beliefs' simply the belief that there is a God and the belief that there is no God. It will be apparent that many of these results about the duty to pursue religious investigation and the worthwhileness of doing so have application to more specific religious investigation, e.g. to discovering whether God revealed himself in Christ, and I shall make this point briefly later in the chapter. In Chapter 7 I shall argue the point more fully and also argue for the worthwhileness of pursuing religious investigations of other kinds, e.g. into whether the Buddhist eight-fold path leads to Nirvana.

Note that in so far as it matters that a man should hold rational$_5$ beliefs in some field, what matters is not that he should cultivate a certain belief but that he should so investigate as to come to hold a true belief. If there is a duty here, it is a duty to hold beliefs backed by evidence, not to hold certain beliefs identified in advance of investigation. However, it has also often been alleged that it is worthwhile—and perhaps even a duty—to cultivate certain beliefs, and especially religious beliefs which are identifiable in advance of any investigation, and that the value of cultivating them does not derive from the likelihood of their truth. That suggestion I shall consider later in the chapter.

The Importance of True Belief

If it matters that we have true beliefs, we must seek, we have seen, rational$_5$ beliefs. We must now consider why in general it matters that we should hold true beliefs.

Before doing so, I must explain briefly my terminology. Many actions and states of affairs are good in some respects but bad in others. Giving large amounts of pocket money to a child is good in the respect that he will get pleasure out of spending it but bad in the respect that having too much money he will not learn self-discipline. There seems often to be no objective scale on which competing reasons can be weighed so as to say whether it is over-all better to do a certain action then to refrain from doing it or do some rival action. Sometimes, however, that comparison can be made. It is over-all better not to torture children despite the goodness of the pleasure which the sadist might get from torturing. Over-all goodness is moral goodness. A morally good action is one which is over-all better to do than not to do. However, not all morally good actions are duties (that is, morally obligatory). One action might be over-all better than another without one having an obligation or duty to do it. For obligations are actions which we owe it to somebody to do. It may be over-all better that I should read a work of great literature rather than a work of pornography, but unless this has bad effects on others—or I owe my talents to God and so have a duty to use them in the right way—it does not seem very plausible to suppose that I have a moral obligation to read the work of great literature rather than the work of pornography.

In so far as actions are good, they are of importance. It matters that we do them. What matters morally, what is of moral importance, is that a man does the actions (if any) which are over-all better to do than to refrain from doing. In so far as a man seeks to achieve some purpose, he will consider it to some extent a good thing that he achieves that purpose; and for that reason he must hold that his beliefs matter. For only if you have true beliefs will you be able to achieve your purposes. And indeed, since whatever his purposes, it is in some way a good thing that a man achieve them (although sometimes over-all a bad thing), it does matter objectively what a man believes. For this reason alone the old slogan:'it does not matter what you believe; it is what you do that counts' seems to me obviously mistaken. I want to go to London and am confronted by two roads. If I believe that the right-hand road leads to London and the left-hand one does not, I shall go on the right-hand road; and if I believe that the left-hand road leads to London and the right-hand one does not, I shall take the left-hand road. We saw in Chapter 1 that there is this logical connection between belief and action. It then follows that I shall attain my purposes only in so far as I have true beliefs. So of course it matters that I have true beliefs. I cannot give you money unless I have a true belief about which pieces of paper are money or a true belief about what you can do with a signed cheque. I cannot give you information unless I have true beliefs about what words mean. Indeed, I can achieve nothing (except by luck) apart from perform such simple bodily movements as waving my hands,[1] unless I have

---

[1] Philosophers have called such actions which I just do, which I cannot be given a recipe for how to do, basic actions. Opening my mouth, saying certain words, putting one leg in front of another, are basic actions. They are to be distinguished from mediated actions which I do by doing basic actions. I shoot by squeezing my finger, walk by putting one leg in front of another, get you to leave by saying 'go away'. To perform a mediated action intentionally (i.e. meaning to do so) I need true beliefs

true beliefs, including true beliefs about which bodily movements will have which effects.

The more important is something which I seek, the more important it is that I should have a true belief about how to get it. Hence (given that I am not absolutely certain how to get it or absolutely certain that investigation will not bring me nearer to an answer), the more important is is, if I am to be rational, that I should investigate and investigate for longer how that something is to be attained. If I seek a satisfying career, it is very important that I investigate various possibilities in some detail, so that I reach a well-justified belief about where that satisfaction is to be attained. By contrast, if I seek to relax for a few hours by reading a novel, it would be foolish to devote five hours to reading reviews of possible novels in order to come to a true belief about which will prove the most relaxing. If I have a duty to attain some end, I have a duty to ensure that I have a true belief about how it is to be attained; and the greater the duty to attain the end, clearly the greater the duty to acquire the true belief. If, as a parent, I am under a moral obligation to ensure that my children are happily and well educated, then (subject to the qualifications stated earlier) I am morally obliged to investigate possible schools so that I come to a well-justified belief that a certain school will provide happy and good education. Also if I have a duty to provide knowledge for others (e.g. for my children when they cannot obtain it for themselves), then I have a duty to acquire that knowledge in order to do so—and knowledge involves true belief. I may have such a duty either towards my children and others in my care for whom I have a general duty to provide, or towards those in special need for whom I alone can provide. When men are short of food, the man trained in agricultural biochemistry has some obligation to apply his talents to finding out how they can get more food out of the land.

It follows more generally from all this that as we can only intentionally fulfil our obligations if we know what they are, men have a general duty to acquire true moral beliefs. This will (given the earlier qualifications) involve our investigating both what are the primary moral truths (e.g. that men have a duty to pay their debts) and what are the contingent moral truths, that is, the moral obligations which, given that the world is as it is, follow from the primary moral truths (e.g. that since I have bought £10 of books from the bookshop, I have a duty to pay the bookshop £10).

about how to perform it. The distinction between basic and mediated actions is due to A. C. Danto. See his 'Basic Actions', *American Philosophical Quarterly*, 1965, **2**, 141–8.

The holding of true beliefs, I have suggested so far, is of importance, moral or other, because beliefs tell us the means by which ends can be achieved. This does not however seem to be the only reason why the holding of true beliefs is important. The holding of true beliefs seems to be valuable in itself, not merely as a means to something else. For true belief is necessary for knowledge and knowledge is valuable in itself, and especially knowledge of things which concern the nature, origin, and purpose of our particular human community; and the nature, origin, and purpose of the Universe itself.[1] Quite obviously, many men seek such knowledge for its own sake, and obviously the only way to attain the knowledge, if you do not already have it, is to investigate with diligence. We feel that individuals who seek such knowledge are doing something worthwhile and that it is a good that they should acquire the knowledge and communicate it to others. Governments and other benefactors give billions of pounds to men to investigate the structure of the atom, the distribution of the galaxies, the history of science and of culture, and the geological history of the Earth; and they do not give solely because they suppose that such knowledge has technological value. But although it is a good thing that men acquire and communicate such knowledge, is there a duty on them to do so? Under two circumstances, I suggest, there is such a duty. There is such a duty if a man has been given his initial skill at the subject and his opportunity to acquire more by the benefaction of others, and if he has knowingly accepted this benefaction for this purpose. If someone pays my salary for this purpose, of course I have a duty to investigate the structure of the atom and to propagate my knowledge. Also, I have a duty if there is a great need of such knowledge in the community and I alone am capable of acquiring it and propagating it. If I alone have the capacity to acquire knowledge of physics, or psychology, or ancient history, and without my doing so my community would lack this knowledge; then, it seems to me, I have a prima-facie duty to acquire the knowledge and to propagate it. (A

---

[1] The opening sections of Aristotle's *Metaphysics* give a classical exposition of the view that knowledge is of more value for its own sake than for the use to which it can be put, and that the most valuable kind of knowledge is knowledge of metaphysical truth. He writes that we regard men 'as being wiser not in virtue of being able to act, but of having theoretical knowledge and knowing the causes of things' (981b); that this theoretical knowledge is more to be prized than practical knowledge and that the superior science is that which concerns 'first principles and causes'. The view which I am advocating is certainly not as strong as this. I merely suggest that knowledge is valuable for reasons other than its practical utility.

prima-facie duty is one on which a man ought to act in the absence of stronger conflicting duties.) But if these conditions do not hold and I have no wish to understand the structure of the atom or the nature of the mind or the cultural origins of our society in Greece and Rome then, good though that understanding may be, I surely have no duty to acquire it.

The Importance of True Religious Belief

Now let us apply these points about the importance of true, and so of rational$_5$ belief to religious belief. Which of men's purposes are such that true belief about religious matters will enable them to fulfil them? All men want long-term well-being and deep well-being: that is, they want to be for long in a supremely worthwhile situation doing actions of great value. Hence they need to have true beliefs about how such well-being is to be attained. They are confronted from their own experience with the fact that mundane pleasures, though temporarily satisfying, are not permanently and deeply so. They find from experience—and poets, novelists, and dramatists convince them— that not merely do food and drink, leisure and drugs fail to satisfy at the deepest level; but so do family life, careers in public service, belonging to a local community, having an absorbing hobby, and so on. Also, to all appearances, these pleasures last only the span of a human life—at most some seventy or eighty years. And although some mundane occupations—such as helping others to cope with the world and enjoy it—do seem deeply worthwhile, they are on their own frustrating. The only pleasures which you can bring to others seem themselves not to satisfy permanently and deeply, and a man is often beset by desires for lesser goods when he seeks to do what is good.

In this situation men hear the proclamation of different religions (in a wide sense of this term) which offer to those who follow their way a deep well-being which lasts for ever. So it is worthwhile investigating which, if any, of them is most likely to provide it. Among the religions which offer such well-being are theistic religions, such as the Christian religion, which claims that there is a God who will give to men a life after death in which those who have been following the religious way will have the Beatific Vision of God which alone will provide that deep and lasting well-being. Investigation into whether or not there is a God would not go all the way towards settling which, if any, religious way will provide lasting well-being, but it would go quite a bit of the way. For if there is a God, being omnipotent, he can provide such well-being and being perfectly good may well choose to do so. If we find it at all probable that there is a God, it becomes worth while investigating further whether he has revealed that such well-being will be provided for those who follow a certain religious way (e.g. the Christian way). On the other hand, if we find that there is no God, clearly the Christian way cannot provide well-being for there will then be no well-being provided by the means which it describes.

A man's reason for investigating which, if any, religious way will lead to deep and lasting well-being need be in no way self-centred. He may be concerned for the well-being of others and, anxious to give men information as to how to secure salvation, devote much time to finding the answer as well as he can.

Does a man have a moral *obligation* to find the way to his own true and lasting well-being? Only, I suggest, if his ability to discover such a way has been given to him and he has accepted this ability on the understanding that he will use it for this purpose. This however hardly applies. If there is a God, he has given men their talents, but he gave them those talents long before they were aware of what they had received and God's purposes in giving them. However, I suggest that some men have a moral obligation to find the way to true and lasting well-being for others. If they have particular talents in this direction (philosophical, psychological, or literary, together with sensitivity to religious claims), I suggest that they have such a prima-facie obligation. To use my earlier example: when men are short of food, the man trained in agricultural biochemistry has some obligation to apply his talents to finding out how they can get more food out of the land. A similar argument applies when men are short of spiritual food. Further, I suggest that anyone who has a responsibility for the upbringing of others has a duty to ensure, if he can, that they know the way to true and lasting well-being, and so has a duty himself to investigate how that is to be attained. This means primarily parents and to a lesser extent teachers; and of course that means most of us. There is an obligation on most of us to investigate the truth of religion in order to teach our children about whether deep well-being can be obtained, and if so, how. Similarly, of course, if religion is false, the activity of prayer and worship is pointless and certain moral practices are also pointless. A parent's obligations to ensure the well-being of his children will lead him to deter them from such activities if they are pointless, and so there is an obligation on him to find out if they are.

With true religious beliefs we will be able to fulfil our moral obligations in the way of educating our children, and from this too it follows that we have an obligation to cultivate rational beliefs about religion.

However, W. K. Clifford in his famous essay 'The Ethics of Belief'[1] seems to me to have carried this kind of argument rather too far. He argues that all our beliefs and the ways in which we acquire them influence others, and for that reason we have a duty to complete rationality in all matters. He writes that 'no man's belief . . . is a private matter which concerns himself alone' and that men who believe 'unproved and unquestioned statements' for their own 'solace and private pleasure' are a perverse influence. Where a man's influence is very obvious and the responsibility is clear, as with a parent towards his children, or a teacher towards his students, or a priest towards his parishioners, this is fair enough. But surely there is a sphere of private morality in which a man may choose what to do even if some others for whom he bears no responsibility who saw what he was doing *might* possibly be led astray thereby. And of course, outside the parent-child context, where rational adults are viewing a man's behaviour, the influence of his bad actions on them, *may* only be to lead them to avoid such actions in future. Clifford seems to have exaggerated a fundamentally good point.

A further reason why it matters to acquire true beliefs about religion, is that religious beliefs themselves have moral consequences. If there is a God and he has made and sustains the world and issued commands to men, men have moral obligations which they would not otherwise have.[2] The grounds for this are as follows. Men ought to acknowledge other persons with whom they come into contact, not just ignore them—and this surely becomes a duty when those persons are our benefactors. We acknowledge people in various ways when we meet them, e.g. by shaking hands or smiling at them, and the way in which we acknowledge their presence reflects our recognition of the sort of individual they are and the kind of relation they have to us. Worship is the only response appropriate to God, the source of all being. Further, if God has given me particular instructions for the use of the Earth, then of course I have a duty to follow these—for if God made the Earth, it is his. (What greater title can one have to property than having created it *e nihilo*?) And if God has given me instructions

---

[1] In his *Essays and Lectures* (1879).
[2] I summarize here very briefly the argument of pp. 203-9 and of Ch. 15 of my *The Coherence of Theism*.

as to how to use my life and behave towards my fellows, then I have some duty to obey. A system of morality which recognized no duty of grateful recognition and conformity to the wishes of our benefactors is a pretty poor system of morality. Certainly there may be limits to such obligations; but if there are, if, for example, a command by God to me to murder would impose upon me no obligation to murder, then God being perfectly good would not issue such commands, for it would involve claiming a right which he did not possess. Finally, if God is the source of my being and I have failed to use aright the life which he has given me by rendering to him proper worship and obedience, I ought to seek forgiveness from God for having failed to fulfil my obligations. So, in summary, duties to worship and obey God and seek forgiveness from him are contingent moral duties which would follow, if there is a God, from primary moral duties—to acknowledge people, to please benefactors, and to conform to rules laid down by the owners of property which we use. That particular facts create particular obligations has been recognized in all systems of ethics—this would just be one case of that. Among man's duties is the duty to find out what his duties are. He must therefore find out whether the world is his to use as he pleases, or whether it belongs to someone else; whether he is indebted to anyone for his existence, to whom he owes acknowledgement and service. The duty to pursue religious inquiry is a particular case of the duty to check that we owe nothing to any man.

Finally, in considering the general issue of the importance of true belief, I drew attention to the importance of true belief in itself, as involved in knowledge, especially when it concerns the origin, nature, and purpose of our human community and of the Universe as a whole. If history and physics are of importance for this reason, religious knowledge is obviously of far greater importance. For what more central piece of knowledge could there be about the origin, nature, and purpose of man and the Universe, than whether they depend for their being on a God who made them, or whether the Universe, and all that is in it, and the laws of their operation, just are, dependent upon nothing? A true belief here, whether theistic or atheistic, is of enormous importance for our whole world-view. I suggested that men who had talents in this direction might have an obligation to pursue inquiries, particularly for the benefit of others. That other men should have a true belief about whether or not there is a God, is a good thing in itself; but I cannot see that they have any obligation to cultivate such a belief except in order to fulfil correctly the duties discussed earlier.

Further, not merely is the knowledge that there is a God or that there is no God itself of great value but, if there is a God, being omniscient, he will know all there is to be known about the origin, nature, and purpose of man and the Universe, and also about the worthwhile way for men to live. Some religions (including Christianity) claim that he has provided (e.g. in the Church) more detailed knowledge on these matters and a way of life by which men may grow in that knowledge. If we find that there is some probability that there is a God, then that makes it much more likely that knowledge is to be had in these ways, and so much more worthwhile investigating which, if any, creed or way provides such more detailed knowledge.

Some of what I have written so far about the value of true religious beliefs, and so the importance of religious investigation, applies whether or not the resultant belief is that there is a God or whether it is that there is no God. If there is no God and no after-life, it is important that we should believe this because it will prevent us wasting our time in prayer and worship and vain pursuit of everlasting life; it will also prevent us disseminating false information on important matters. Nevertheless, it is, I think, difficult to avoid the view that it is more important to believe that there is a God, if in fact there is a God, than to believe that there is no God, if in fact there is no God. Thus failure to hold a true belief that there is a God could lead to us failing to worship a God to whom worship is due; whereas, if through a false belief that there is a God, we worship a God who does not exist, no-one is thereby wronged. Further, failure to hold a true belief that there is a God could lead to the loss of everlasting life, for if this belief is conjoined with a true belief that, if there is a God, he will give everlasting life after death to those who live a certain kind of life on Earth, a man who has these beliefs is in a position to gain that life. And even if the other religious belief is that if there is a God he will give everlasting life after death to any who try to live a good life on Earth, those beliefs together could encourage a man to persevere with a worthwhile life on Earth and so gain that everlasting life (on this see p. 155 below), whereas failure to hold a true atheistic belief could involve at most the waste of a short finite life. This seems to be one correct point in the argumentation of Pascal's Wager, in which there are a number of incorrect points which I shall discuss later in the chapter.

For the various reasons outlined, it matters greatly that men should have true religious beliefs, and for some of these reasons there is a prima-facie obligation on men to seek such beliefs. It will readily be seen that what goes for the simple belief that there is a God, goes also for beliefs that God has certain properties and that he has done certain actions. Indeed, the belief that there is a God only carries very much in the way of consequence for action about how to seek deep and lasting well-being, or how to worship, or whatever, given further beliefs—e.g. that if there is a God, he wishes to be worshipped in such and such a way, or is to be worshipped for having done such and such actions.

It follows that if a man's beliefs in this field are to be rational$_5$, they will need to be backed up by a significant amount of investigation— unless the man starts with beliefs which are well-nigh certain on his evidence, or it is very probable that investigation in this field will achieve nothing, or he has more important things to do. Some men of course may not realize this. To some men of religious pursuasion it will never even occur that they ought to check up on their beliefs on these important matters. In that case they have rational$_3$ beliefs for they have pursued such investigation as seemed to them adequate— viz. none at all. Nevertheless, I have argued, objectively it is of great importance that men do check up on these beliefs.

Yet, as we have seen, even if it matters that a man should hold true beliefs in some field, it is not worthwhile investigating if investigation will achieve nothing (i.e. not add significantly to a man's evidence or help him to assess that evidence differently). One reason why investigation will achieve nothing, will be if a man cannot get access to the relevant books or other sources of information which he needs to consult in order to pursue the investigation. Clearly, in past centuries there have been many men in closed societies who simply had no access to arguments against their own beliefs or even to arguments supporting those beliefs with any subtlety. Simple men cannot develop sophisticated arguments for themselves; and so if they are situated in such a closed society, they will achieve nothing by investigation. However, there are more general arguments purporting to show that however much access a man may have to sources of information, human inquiry into religious truth will achieve nothing. To the extent that these arguments work, investigation is not necessary in order that a man's beliefs about religion be rational$_5$. (To the extent that a man believes that these arguments work, investigation is not necessary in order for his beliefs to be rational$_3$.)

Reasons for Believing that Religious Inquiry is Pointless

Men have various reasons for believing that religious inquiry will get nowhere. There are to start with, very general philosophical theses about the limits to human knowledge, which many philosophers have put forward. An obvious example is Kant[1] who claimed, roughly, that knowledge of factual matters was confined to knowledge of particular phenomena which we can observe or experience and knowledge of the kinds of possible observable phenomena and connections between them which there can be. Thus, he claimed, we can know about distant stars and their properties, stars being the sort of things that one can observe; and we can know that there must be a cause in some previous (in principle) observable state of affairs of there being those stars and their having the masses, volumes, etc. which they do. But what we cannot know are things beyond possible observation: whether the Universe had a beginning or is spatially finite, or whether matter is infinitely divisible. Hence, he claimed, we cannot know whether the Universe depends for its existence on a Creator God.[2]

There is no space here to discuss Kant's arguments in detail but suffice it to point out that Kant's claim, derived from Hume, that the only causes of things which we can know are precedent observable phenomena, is quite unjustified. It would rule out in advance most of the great achievements of science since his day. For science has been able to explain observable phenomena (e.g. lines in photographs of cloud chambers) in terms of unobservable causes (the movements of such fundamental particles as electrons, protons, and positrons). The science of the last two centuries has told us of fields and forces and strange entities such as quarks and gluons underlying and causing observable phenomena. The grounds for believing the claims of science here are that science postulates entities in some respects simple, whose interactions lead us to expect the observable phenomena.[3] Granted that the scientist has given good reason for believing in the existence of the entities which he postulates, there is no reason in principle to suppose that knowledge cannot advance so far as to explain the whole physical world, observable and unobservable, e.g. in terms of the action of a Creator God.

[1] I summarize here what is in effect the conclusion of the whole of Kant's *Critique of Pure Reason*.
[2] See the chapter in *The Critique of Pure Reason* entitled 'The Ideal of Pure Reason', especially Section 7 thereof.
[3] For elaboration of these points, see my *The Existence of God*, Ch. 3.

Since Kant's day there have been other writers, of religious faith yet very much in Kant's tradition, concerned not so much with the general philosophical theses of the limits to human knowledge as with their application to religious knowledge, who have given arguments purporting to show that good arguments could not be given in support of fundamental religious claims, from which it would follow that it is a waste of time to look for them. I will consider briefly two such arguments. The first is the argument of the Barthian that the God in whom Christians believe is so totally different from things in the world that argument from things in the world by the world's standards won't get anywhere in showing that he exists or that he does not.[1] But God cannot be totally different if he is describable with words which we use to describe mundane things—e.g. 'wise', 'good', 'powerful'. If these words do have, however analogical, an application to him, God must be something like wise, good, and powerful things on earth; and in that case kinds of arguments which are appropriate to prove the existence or non-existence of wise, good, and powerful things in principle have application to proving his existence or non-existence. But if such words did not have application to God, we would have no idea what we are saying when we say that there is a God. And so the claim of theism would be not merely unarguable, but meaningless. But of course the religious believer does not want to say that about his religion and so he must allow that the God whose existence he wishes to assert is not completely improperly described as 'wise', 'good', etc.

The next argument is also a general argument which purports to show worthless both arguments for and arguments against the existence of God. It can be found in a number of places, among them John Hick's book *Faith and Knowledge*.[2] Hick claims that man's most fundamental beliefs are not to be argued about—for example, the belief that there is an external world, or that things will continue to behave as they have been observed to behave in the past (what I called in the last chapter the generalization principle), or that there

---

[1] For a brief exposition of Barth's views and references to his works, see J. MacQuarrie, *Twentieth Century Religious Thought* (revised edn., London, 1971), pp. 318–24.

[2] Another writer who puts forward a similar argument is Clement of Alexandria: 'Should one say that knowledge is founded on demonstration by a process of reasoning, let him hear that the first principles are incapable of demonstration . . . Hence it is thought that the first cause of the universe can be apprehended by faith alone'—*Stromateis* 2. 4. (Writings of Clement of Alexandria, volume 2, translated by W. Wilson, Edinburgh, 1869.)

are certain objective moral truths (e.g. that torture and murder are wicked). Less fundamental beliefs—whether there is a table in the next room or it will rain tomorrow—are possible subjects for arguments, but such arguments utilize the fundamental beliefs, about which we cannot argue with profit.

Thus argument about whether there is a table in the next room already presupposes that there is an external world of tables and chairs, and that things continue to behave as they have been observed to behave in the past (e.g. tables stay where they are put), and that in general what we think we remember happened (e.g. that if I think I remember having put a table in the next room, then probably I did). The fundamental beliefs form a framework within which we can argue about the less fundamental beliefs. But the fundamental beliefs are not things about which we can argue in a rational way. We just do believe these fundamental beliefs, although we have a certain freedom not to believe.

Now, Hick claims, whether the world is created and controlled by God is equally fundamental, and therefore not the proper subject of argument. It must be granted that if a man really did not believe in the external world or the generalization principle, it would be hard to devise a worthwhile argument to convince him. But in fact all men do, and therefore they have common beliefs about the world, and similar inductive standards, which enable them to advance from their present beliefs to new beliefs. However the existence of God seems to me to be in a different category. It is a disputed matter; and also a matter on which some people have certainly come to change their mind after a process of argument, e.g. they have ceased to believe that there is a God, after someone has brought home to them the force of the argument from evil. There is therefore no reason to suppose that in its closedness to rational inquiry the existence of God is as fundamental as the existence of the external world. There is no *a priori* reason to suppose that with common beliefs about the world and common inductive standards, men cannot advance to a rational belief about the existence of God.

These arguments to show that arguments to the existence of God will not work all proceed from general philosophical considerations. There are also arguments which are internal to the Christian religion in the sense that they argue that if the Christian religion is true, it cannot be shown to be true. (Unlike the former arguments they do not have the consequence that if it is false, it cannot be shown to be false; and for this reason they have less force in suggesting that religious inquiry is irrational). One such argument is the argument that the Bible does not contain arguments for the existence of God, and so the God whose existence it asserts is not the sort of God provable by argument. However there is a much simpler explanation than the latter of why the Bible does not contain much in the way of arguments for the existence of God. This is that most people for whom the books of the Bible were written believed in the existence of God and so did not need to be argued into such belief. Yet on matters then disputed the Bible does argue. So it would seem appropriate that those who follow in the biblical tradition should argue, when the supreme belief that there is a God becomes the subject of dispute. Further, the Bible does seem to contain some passages which do argue for the existence of God—e.g. Rom. 1: 18–22 and Wisd. 13–15. It will not do to say that in such passages the author is only arguing to God's nature, e.g. his goodness and power, and not his existence. For arguing that a god is good and powerful is arguing that there is a god who is God (i.e. the omnipotent, omniscient etc. being of mono- theism), and so that there is a God.

Finally, in this latter category there is an argument which seems to me much more powerful. This is the argument that if there were a proof of the existence of God which became known, those who heard and understood it would have no option but to believe, and in that case faith would not be meritorious. John Hick has argued in many places that man needs 'cognitive freedom' in which to choose his religious route; if God were too evident, man would have no choice of route. But, even given the need for cognitive freedom, this can at most be regarded as an argument showing that a God would not allow us to see, without the effort of investigation, an evident and conclusive proof of his existence. It does not show that God would not provide grounds for belief which we could acquire by investigation, for then the voluntari- ness and so the merit of belief would lie in the investigation. Further, one might say that meritorious religious faith is not a matter merely or at all of having a belief that there is a God (and other beliefs also)—what matters is how we act on our belief; what purposes, given that belief, we seek to achieve. (I discussed in Chapter 1 the different ways in which we could act or fail to act on our beliefs.) It is not at all obvious that belief in itself necessarily does have merit, and I shall be returning to this issue later; what matters is how a man acquires his beliefs and what he does with them. So this argument provides no reason for supposing that investigation will not show that it is significantly more probable than not that there is a God, or that there is no God.

I conclude that well-known arguments to show that investigation will not show much in the field of religion do not work. Assuming that no similar arguments work, we reach the position that—given that our beliefs about religion do not have probabilities on our evidence very close to 1 or 0, and that we have no overriding claims on our time—objectively it is important to investigate them, and there is no reason to suppose that it will not be profitable to do so.

Rival Claims on Time

Adequacy of investigation is relative to the time at our disposal and to the rival claims on that time. In a matter as important as religion, perhaps no amount of investigation would be adequate if we had all the time in the world at our disposal. However, the rationality$_5$ of our religious beliefs depends on whether we have done enough investigation, given the rival claims on the very limited amount of time which we humans have on Earth. If I have duties to provide for my relatives, to save my children from death or degradation, or to feed the starving, then clearly it matters less that I should pursue religious inquiry for any great time. It certainly does not follow, however, that there is no duty at all to pursue religious inquiry or that this does not matter at all in these circumstances; the factors which I outlined earlier as to why it matters to acquire true religious beliefs are weighty ones. However, since the major reason why true religious beliefs matter is that thereby we can conduct our lives aright (e.g. seek true and lasting happiness, serve our neighbours in the right way, and worship whatever God there may be), clearly we must not devote so much time to religious inquiry that we have little time left for acting on the resulting beliefs. Religious traditions such as Christianity have always stressed that, though having true beliefs about religion is important, it is equally important to do the right thing with them, act on them with the right purposes.

It is important that the process of investigation shall not prevent worthwhile action, and it can do this, not merely by taking time which could be devoted to the action. There is the possibility that investigation will hamper a man's ability to act when the time comes for that, by producing such confusion of mind that the man is unable to act decisively, and in that case it is appropriate to give very little time to investigation. Newman drew our attention to this danger in the

Grammar of Assent.[1] It is clearly a very real one. There have been many men of strong religious faith who come to have doubts about the truth of their religious beliefs and then investigate them. After investigation their theoretical conviction still remains but the process of investigation has led to such self-questioning that action has become difficult. Clearly in such a case a man should devote only a very small amount of time to religious investigation. For if investigating the way to get to a place is going to damage a man's ability to travel on whatever road investigation suggests is the right one, there is no point in investigating for long. The man should set out on whatever road a brief investigation suggests to be the right one.

So then, the amount of investigation needed to obtain a rational$_5$ belief about religion will depend on the importance of true religious belief, the probability that investigation will achieve something and the rival claims on our time (and, in view of the last paragraph, I should add, of our energy). It also depends on the probability on our evidence of whatever religious belief we have. If on our evidence it is virtually certain that there is a God, or virtually certain that there is no God, investigation becomes less worthwhile.

Non-Rational Grounds for Belief

We saw at the beginning of the chapter that a rational$_5$ belief about religion was of value since to obtain one was all we could do towards obtaining a true belief. I then went on to discuss how much investigation is needed for a man to hold rational$_5$ beliefs, and I have considered the various factors which affect this. I claimed that it was important, in view of the importance of religion, to cultivate true belief about religion through full and impartial investigation. There is no obligation as such to believe that there is a God or to believe any other credal proposition, only to hold whatever belief investigation shows to be probable. We need, however, now to discuss whether there is other reason for getting oneself to believe that there is a God or to believe other credal propositions except that rational inquiry shows that there is. There have been many writers in the history of Christian thought who have suggested that there are reasons for belief in the Christian creed other than the likelihood of its truth; not that they wished to say that it was not true, or even that it could not be known to be true—but only that there were reasons for believing it to be true other than that it was likely to be true. Such reasons for belief

---

[1] See J. H. Newman, *An Essay in Aid of a Grammar of Assent*, pp. 177 ff.

I shall call non-rational grounds for belief. They are grounds for believing which are not concerned with the rationality (in any of the senses which I delineated) of the belief, which was ultimately a matter of the likelihood of its truth. Some of these grounds, it is suggested, give rise to obligations to cultivate a belief; some merely provide good reason for a man to do so.

The suggestion that there are non-rational grounds for belief is not confined to the case of religious belief. Indeed, suggested non-rational grounds for religious belief are special cases of suggested non-rational grounds for belief in general. These suggested grounds are as follows. First there is the suggestion that certain beliefs are such that it is good in itself that men should hold these beliefs. They are basically beliefs which involve thinking well of other people. If people, especially people close to you, behave in ways that look foolish or morally discreditable, you ought, it is often said, to give them the benefit of the doubt, to think no evil of them, and thus to believe that their motives are good. If one's parent or child or spouse is accused of shoplifting, one ought, it is said, to believe them innocent unless the evidence against them is overwhelming. The duty is not merely to treat them as innocent, but to believe it of them. 'You ought not to believe him capable of that', we may be told. One shows respect for persons by thinking well of them, and we have a duty to respect persons, especially those close to us, such as parents and children. It follows from a duty to think well of others that we have a duty to believe people when they tell us what they have done or experienced, even if we are initially inclined not to do so. For otherwise we would be judging them liars, or at any rate fools who do not realize how much in error their memory is or how liable they are to deception. A man who takes a sceptical attitude towards the claims of others shows a lack of trust; and respect for persons involves trust. For both these reasons, if someone assures us that they did not steal the money or break the confidence, then even if we are inclined to believe that they did, we could have a duty to rein in our uncharitable thoughts and to believe them.

Then it is suggested that sometimes the holding of certain beliefs is necessary or at any rate very useful for attaining certain desirable further ends, which would not otherwise be attainable. The ends may be either desirable states of mind of the subject, or his avoiding doing certain undesirable actions, or his doing certain desirable actions. An example of the first is the mother who has to believe that her son is alive unless she is to go to pieces psychologically. An example of the second is the husband who has to believe that his wife is faithful if he is to avoid maltreating her. An example of the third is the lawyer who has to believe that his client is innocent if he is to make a good speech in his defence. Into this third category also come self-fulfilling beliefs—if you believe that you can walk the tight-rope, you will do it; otherwise you will not. Or there is the case where the actor has to believe that something is really the case if he is to act well. (I am not thinking only of the professional actor, but of, say, a con-man; it may be that he can only do a good job if he believes his own story.)

One interesting case of a belief which is needed both for the subject's mental well-being and to enable him to perform desirable actions, is the philosopher's belief in the truth of such claims of common sense, as that there is an external world, there are other people, our normal methods of induction probably work, etc. In a well-known passage Hume described the sad condition of the philosophical sceptic who found himself temporarily losing such beliefs. He wrote

> The *intense* view of these manifold contradictions and imperfections in human reason has so wrought upon me and heated my brain, that I am ready to reject all belief and reasoning, and can look upon no opinion even as more probable or likely than another. Where am I, or what? From what causes do I derive my existence, and to what condition shall I return? . . . I am confounded with all these questions, and begin to fancy myself in the most deplorable condition imaginable, inviron'd with the deepest darkness and utterly depriv'd of the use of every member and faculty.[1]

Now although Hume believed that he was not justified in holding common-sense beliefs, he also realized that the lack of them was causing great mental distress, and also inaction. Having no beliefs about what would lead to what, he would have no reason for doing this rather than that to achieve some end, or indeed for doing anything rather than nothing—and hence paralysis. Now it is a good thing that men should attempt to change the world, rather than just wait upon events. Yet for such an attempt, belief is necessary. A man cannot even attempt to change the world (apart from move parts of his body) unless he has a belief about which bodily movements will produce which changes in the world. Without such beliefs he would not have any idea how to set about changing the world. If he is to succeed in changing the world then, as we saw earlier in the chapter, he will need true beliefs in order to do so. So there are grounds for Hume to induce in himself beliefs, even though he does not at the

[1] David Hume, *A Treatise of Human Nature*, I. 4. 7.

beginning believe that they would be true beliefs. Hume reports that he soon recovered on these occasions by dining, playing back-gammon, conversing and being merry with his friends. It is not clear whether he did these things *in order to* recover, but my argument suggests that if he did, he would in a wide sense have been acting reasonably.

Now, if a man accepts that there are non-rational grounds for his believing some proposition p, he has got to set himself to believe p. We saw earlier that you cannot just decide to believe that p. You have got to get yourself to believe that your evidence makes p probable, and that takes time. You may do that by getting yourself to change your inductive standards by adopting standards which you now believe to be incorrect, or by getting yourself to forget about some of the unfavourable evidence, or by getting yourself to acquire new favourable evidence through looking only where favourable evidence is to be found and then forgetting the selective character of your investigation. If you attempt to change your inductive standards to ones which you now believe to be incorrect, or to ignore in your calculations relevant evidence of whose force you are now conscious, you are seeking to induce an irrational$_2$ belief. There are various ways of doing this. There is Pascal's programme for inducing religious belief: 'You want to be cured of unbelief and you ask for the remedy: learn from those who were once bound like you and who now wager all they have. . . . they behaved just as if they did believe, taking holy water, having masses said, and so on. That will make you believe quite naturally.'[1] Or a man might just concentrate on certain kinds of evidence. Or, perhaps lull himself to sleep with the words: 'It's really true.'

In seeking to induce an irrational$_2$ belief, a man would thereby also be seeking to induce an irrational$_5$ belief (and so an irrational$_3$ belief). For he would be seeking to have a belief about which he had not ensured in any way adequately that his evidence makes it probable by true inductive standards; indeed he would have deliberately sought to ensure that his belief did not have this character. All other methods of getting yourself to believe things specified in advance of investigation are also methods of seeking to induce irrational$_5$ beliefs (but not necessarily irrational$_2$ beliefs). If you seek to forget certain unfavour-able evidence or the selective character of your investigation—which you might do by taking drugs of certain kinds—you are not seeking

---

[1] B. Pascal, *Pensées*, translated by A. J. Krailsheimer (Harmondsworth, Middlesex, 1966), No. 418.

to induce an irrational$_2$ belief; for the belief which you are seeking to have will be a belief probable on your future evidence, even if that evidence is a specially selected set of evidence. Nevertheless you are seeking to have a belief not backed up by much true representative relevant evidence of good quality. Indeed, by attempting to suppress unfavourable evidence, you are attempting to ensure that your evidence is biased (because unrepresentative of the larger sample of evidence which you now have and which you have reason to believe points in the direction of the truth). All these methods of seeking to induce beliefs specified in advance of investigation are methods of seeking to induce irrational$_5$ beliefs. The resulting irrationality in these cases, unlike that of such cases as the idle detective (see p. 50 above), is deliberately sought by methods seen (at the beginning though not at the end of the process) to be biased against truth.

Non-Rational Grounds for Religious Belief

So much in general on non-rational grounds for belief. Let us list one by one the various non-rational grounds which have been suggested for religious belief, and see how they are examples of the kinds of general ground which I have outlined. First, one might claim that the duty to believe the Gospel when one hears it follows from the general duty to believe people when they tell us what they have done or experienced. Those who preach the Christian Gospel belong to a community which purports to have had a revelation. They claim our belief in virtue of a community experience which the unbeliever has not shared. Those who deny that there is a God do so on the basis of evidence which all can see and assess; they do not claim our unbelief because of what they, unlike we, have seen and experienced. So there is no corresponding duty to believe them. Maybe the duty to believe informants does not exist when what they tell us is very improbable, but if it is not very improbable there is perhaps that obligation. A major difficulty here is that there are around a number of rival claims to have experienced a religious revelation, of which the Christian Gospel is only one. Sometimes these revelations are incompatible, and so if you believe one you cannot believe the others. (If God gave his fullest revelation to Mohammed, he did not reveal himself most fully through Jesus Christ; and if you believe the former you cannot believe the latter.) Since however it is, as I have suggested, plausible to suppose that the probability of the belief has something to do with the duty to believe it (there being no duty to believe anything *too* improbable), the obvious thing to say is that the duty is to believe the most probable claim to Revelation, so long as that is not too improbable.

I next consider various suggestions that the holding of a religious belief is necessary or at any rate very useful for the attainment of desirable further ends, which would not otherwise be attainable. A number of different suggestions of this kind have been made, and I shall consider the most important of them. First there is the suggestion that belief that there is a God (and perhaps other religious beliefs as well) is a necessary condition of attaining Heaven; only by believing shall we attain the most worthwhile thing in the Universe. (Of course every advocate of this suggestion admits that a believer has in some way to act on or to be ready to act on his belief in order to get to Heaven.[1] But the point claimed is that belief is necessary.) One should distinguish here different views on why belief is necessary for attaining Heaven. A crude view is that belief is necessary for getting to Heaven because God rewards belief with Heaven (and unbelief with Hell). A less crude view would maintain that you can only get to Heaven if you do certain actions and it is impossible in practice to do those actions unless you believe. I shall consider the less crude view in considering shortly whether belief is necessary for the performance of worthwhile actions; but, meanwhile, the crude view. It is not altogether clear to me whether Pascal was advocating the crude view or the less crude view, but I shall take him as an example of the crude view (though I may be being grossly unfair to him). He wrote:

Let us then examine the point and say 'God is', or 'He is not'. But to which side shall we incline? Reason can decide nothing here . . . A game is being played . . . heads or tails will turn up. What will you wager?[2]

If you bet on God and win, you win 'an infinity of infinitely happy life'; whereas if you bet on God and lose, you lose at most a mere finite amount. If you bet on no God, or, which amounts to the same thing, refuse to bet openly, then, if you win, you gain at most a mere finite amount, mere temporary happiness, whereas if you lose, you obtain 'an eternity of miseries'.[3] Hence you ought to bet on God, and the context reveals that the bet, the wager, is to believe; you ought to bet on God because the possible gain if you are right is so great and the possible loss, if you are wrong, is so small.

---

[1] See Chapter 4 for what such action might amount to.
[2] *Pensées*, No. 418.
[3] Ibid., No. 429.

A well-known difficulty with Pascal's Wager is that he has stated the alternative states misleadingly. If the alternatives are meant to be 'there is a Christian God'[1] and 'there is no after-life', then Pascal has ignored other possible states of affairs—e.g. 'There is a god who consigns Christians to eternal Hell and non-Christians to eternal Heaven'.[2] Alternatively, Pascal may have intended his alternative states to be simply 'There is a Christian God' and 'There is not a Christian God'. But in that case it is unclear what are the outcomes and so the gains and losses on the second alternative of the two policies—Heaven remains a possible outcome for Christian or non-Christian even on this alternative.

Now clearly we can represent the alternative states as two or many or infinite. Yet perhaps the most useful way to represent them is threefold:

(A) There is a Christian God (and so an after-life)
(B) There is no after-life
(C) There is an after-life but no Christian God.

The outcomes of the two alternative policies, becoming or not becoming Christian, are then, we may suppose for the moment, as Pascal stated them for alternatives (A) and (B); but there are a variety of possible outcomes under the third alternative, and we cannot say much definite about them. The outcomes under the alternative policies will therefore be as follows:

	(A)	(B)	(C)
(1) Becoming Christian	Christian life of worship and service followed by eternal heaven	Christian life of worship and service	Christian life of worship and service followed by ?
(2) Not becoming Christian	Worldly life followed by eternal Hell	Worldly life	Worldly life followed by ?

So, even granted that (A_1) is infinitely worth having and (A_2) is to be avoided at all costs, whether policy (1) is to be preferred to policy (2) clearly depends on how probable it is that under state (C) belief rather than unbelief will get a large reward; and how probable it is that state (C) is the true one. If there is very little chance of the latter, then the position is as Pascal stated it. But if there is quite a chance of the latter,

---

[1] i.e. 'a God who has (roughly) the properties and has done (roughly) the actions affirmed in Christian creeds'.

[2] This point has been well made by (e.g.) Antony Flew. See his *God and Philosophy* (London, 1966), 9. 9 ff.

everything turns on whether it is probable that Christian belief as such, however acquired, is rewarded or penalized in that state. On some possibilities under (C) Christian belief would be punished or at any rate not rewarded (whereas some incompatible belief would be much better rewarded)—e.g. if there is a God hostile to Christians. Pascal needs to show that such possibilities are remote if his argument is to work. As Pascal presented the wager nothing seemed to turn on exact probabilities (e.g. just how probable it was that there is a God); unfortunately the probability of the Christian religious system being the true one in contrast to the probability of some other system being the true one crucially affects rational conduct. The probabilities of different religious systems affect rational conduct under this argument, as they did under the argument concerned with the duty to believe. Roughly, we may say that belief in the Christian God will be the rational policy only if the Christian religious system (with its rewards and penalties as understood by Pascal) is more probable than any other system which postulates an after-life.

A further difficulty is to whether Pascal has correctly stated the gains and losses under the Christian system. It may be that rewards are offered to those who trust God and that in order to trust God you do not have to believe that he exists. Is the threat of punishment the threat of a punishment which literally lasts for ever? And is the reward offered to those who force themselves to believe things which their reason tells them to be false and then in some way act on those beliefs? Or is the reward offered only to those who do not force themselves to adopt irrational$_2$ beliefs? Contemporary religious opinion, both Catholic and Protestant, does not in general accept Pascal's account of the gains and losses. In subsequent chapters I will give moral reasons and reasons of New Testament exposition for supposing that Pascal has mis-stated the gains and losses.

Further, there is the difficulty that, quite apart from moral considerations and biblical evidence, Pascal is claiming that God has made a world in which a supremely worthwhile goal is to be attained by cultivating an irrational belief (by setting yourself to believe that something is probable when in fact you believe now that it is not). I find it implausible to suppose that God would have made a world of this character, for the following reason. You can only come to see that arguments such as that of Pascal work, by the careful exercise of reason, and that means not merely by following the steps which Pascal set out but, as we have seen, by following steps to show, for example, that the Christian religion is more probable than any other religious system. If a' man just abandoned his rationality, he might draw some very different conclusions from Pascal's Wager from the ones which Pascal wishes him to draw. So if God values our making Pascalian moves, he values our exercise of reason. It would be odd in the extreme if he then valued our making the final move of acquiring the belief that he exists by our denying our reason. I conclude that it is rather unlikely that God has set up a world in which both God rewards belief that he exists highly and the only way to acquire it is on Pascalian-type grounds. For this reason alone it seems not very likely that the world is such that applying Pascal's Wager will get us to heaven.

There are however other desirable ends (other than the direct reward of Heaven) which might be forwarded if a man has a religious belief. It may be a good thing—for reasons to be discussed in Chapter 5—that we should act on, live by, the assumption that there is a God, and such action may be rewarded with heaven. I made the contrast at the end of Chapter 1 between acting on a proposition and believing the proposition (and I shall discuss in the next chapter something of what this 'acting on' the assumption that there is a God, amounts to). You can in theory act on propositions which you believe to be very improbable. However in practice it may be that many of us can only act on, live by, the assumption that there is a God, if we actually believe that there is a God. We cannot live the Christian life without having the belief to back it. In that case for those of us of whom this is so, we have another argument providing a non-rational ground for belief—believe in order that you may act-as-if. (Note the contrast between this view that believing will help you to act-as-if with Pascal's suggestion which I discussed in Chapter 1 that acting-as-if will help you to believe.)

Next, it may be suggested that for many of us religious belief is a necessary condition of much moral action, the desirability of which, unlike that of the action of acting as if there is a God, is in no way connected with the truth or falsity of religion. A man may believe that he ought to pursue an honest and upright course of life and believe that he cannot do this without a religious belief (including, perhaps, the belief that honesty is rewarded in the world to come). So to secure an honest course of life he may try to persuade himself that religion is true. Or it may be some one heroic moral action which a man feels that he ought to perform but cannot perform without religious belief; and to secure the performance of which he tries to persuade himself into religious belief. Clearly this argument, like the last one, has force only for men of a certain psychological make-up. There are those who can do heroic moral actions without religious belief, but I would think that there are also those who need religious belief if they are to do heroic moral actions.

Pascal did not claim that men had an obligation to seek Heaven, and so cultivate a belief not backed up by reason. The reasons that religious belief will enable us to act on the assumption that there is a God or to do heroic moral actions which we would not otherwise be able to do could be presented either merely as good reasons for an agent to cultivate such belief by irrational means or as indicating an obligation on him so to do.

Next, we have suggestions put forward by a number of writers that some belief in some propositions of religion is a necessary condition for the acquisition of further religious knowledge or of really coming to know that the original propositions are true, or even of under-standing the original propositions.

Basil Mitchell has urged that a high degree of commitment to an ideology is needed in fields such as politics or education if we are to pursue the consequences of our ideology far enough to feel its force or criticize it adequately. 'A man who is prepared to change his mind about any of his beliefs whenever it appears to him that the evidence tells against them will not be able to hold on to them long enough to work them out and test them properly.'[1] The same point applies with greater force, Mitchell urges, to religion. The difficulty with Mitchell's suggestion is that it runs up against my earlier claim that belief is a passive matter; that you can only believe something if you believe that the evidence supports it. If that is right, the only way in which you can save your belief in the face of negative evidence is by disguising from yourself the negative force of the evidence. But I do not think that Mitchell really wishes to recommend this, because he recommends that if there is too much negative evidence over a long period, people should give up their belief. But if people systematically disguise from themselves the existence of negative evidence when it first appears, they will never know when there has been much negative evidence over a long period. I suggest that we understand Mitchell's recommendation in the light of my argument about the passivity of belief as a recommendation that people who are most of the time believers should hang on to the practice of religion, should act as if it was true (not, should *believe* it), on their off-days (when on balance the evidence seems to be against it). The latter seems an

---

[1] Basil Mitchell, *The Justification of Religious Belief* (London, 1973), p. 130.

eminently sensible recommendation. One should not give up something which has seemed to one of supreme value and which has dominated one's way of life without considerable serious thought—this from respect to one's former intuitions, spiritual wrestlings and allegiance, and acknowledgement of the importance of the issue. Mitchell is, I know, really far too committed to rational belief and behaviour to merit discussion in our present category at all.

Anselm makes a claim apparently somewhat similar to that of Mitchell. Anselm commends belief in order to deepen our understanding of spiritual reality: 'I do not seek to understand that I may believe, but I believe in order to understand. For this also I believe,—that unless I believed, I should not understand.'[1] But Anselm is, I think, of a less rationalist spirit than Mitchell. If Anselm were to agree that to believe something, you have to believe that the evidence supports it, he might still commend belief despite the evidence (which would involve getting yourself to believe that the evidence in fact supported you). Anselm's grounds for belief in the passage which I quoted was that belief was a necessary condition for understanding the faith. We cannot take this quite literally, for clearly you cannot believe something unless you understand what you believe. But what I think he is saying is that some belief to begin with in the propositions of religion is necessary in order to acquire a deep understanding of what is involved in those propositions. In this Anselm could well be right, but presumably having the original belief does not guarantee subsequent deep understanding. And it may be that if the belief is acquired in a way which involves self-deceit, that irrational act hampers the progress of the soul towards any subsequent depth of understanding. There is, after all, some plausibility in supposing that resistance to truth in a certain field will not help in the process of subsequent acquisition of truth. Anselm needs to provide us with some sort of argument to show that, *however* the belief is acquired, it will help in the process of understanding.

Further, and crucially, understanding of the consequences of a false proposition is not particularly desirable—at any rate at the cost of having a totally false world-view. Yet making oneself acquire a belief which evidence suggests to be false is likely to get one to hold a totally false world-view, and so to be avoided. The understanding would be acquired at too high a price if it is gained by inducing oneself to believe a false world-view.

Finally we have the view that to have a religious belief gives a man

---

[1] St. Anselm, *Prosologion* I (translated by S. N. Deane, Chicago, 1903).

happiness and should be cultivated for that reason. A variant on this is the view that to have any sort of *Weltanschauung* is conducive to happiness, and if evidence does not favour theism against atheism or conversely, a man can take his choice. Just as for Hume it was perhaps a good thing to avoid general scepticism on non-rational grounds, partly because beliefs conduce to happiness, so, more specifically, the suggestion here is that it is a good thing to avoid scepticism about religion, because beliefs in this area conduce to happiness. Given empirical evidence that theistic (or, as the case may be, atheistic) belief would conduce to happiness for a given individual, that seems in itself a good reason for him to cultivate it. It could not however plausibly be regarded as giving rise to an *obligation* to cultivate theistic (or atheistic) belief.

So much for various grounds for non-rational belief that there is a God. Note that the arguments for these grounds fall into two groups. Some of them commend goals which would be forwarded by religious belief, the desirability of attaining which is quite independent of whether or not there is a God. Peace of mind is a good thing, whether or not there is a God. And even if the way to get the peace of mind is to believe that there is a God, it is the belief that there is a God and not directly God that produces that peace of mind. Whereas acting as if there is a God is presumably only desirable if there is a God— although of course we may think it worthwhile to act as if there is a God, even if the probabilities seem against it. And the Heaven which Pascal (on my interpretation) claims that God gives to the believer, is clearly only attainable by the believer if there is a God—even if it is worth the believer's while to assume that there is a God, when the evidence is against it.

Is the Likelihood of its Truth the Sole Reason for Cultivating Religious Belief?

Ought we to cultivate religious belief on any of these non-rational grounds? I argued earlier that for various reasons men had a moral obligation to cultivate rational belief about religion, and also that men had various good non-obligatory reasons for doing so. If there is no God, there is a moral obligation to cultivate a true atheistic belief in order to have a right influence on those dependent on us—children and pupils (and if a man is especially qualified to pursue inquiries in this field, to have a right influence on the unlearned). If there is a God, there is a moral obligation to cultivate a true religious belief for the same reasons. If there is a God, there is also an obligation to worship and in other ways to please our Creator. There is a moral obligation to find out what our moral obligations are and so to cultivate rational belief about religion in order to know how to teach those dependent on us, and whether to worship and to perform other acts which would be right only if there was a God who wanted us to perform them.

One might claim that all these obligations to cultivate rational religious beliefs are only prima-facie obligations, ones which hold in the absence of obligations to do some contrary action. Just as perhaps there is an obligation to look after a neighbour if he is ill, there is an even stronger obligation to look after one's own child if he is ill; and if both obligations cannot be fulfilled together, the obligation to look after the child takes precedence over the obligation to look after the neighbour. The obligation to look after the neighbour is only a prima-facie obligation; it holds in the absence of stronger incompatible obligations. But if there are such, the former obligation lapses. So do any of the non-rational grounds for belief constitute stronger obligations to cultivate an irrational belief?

We saw that only some of those grounds could plausibly be regarded as giving rise to obligations. There was some plausibility in supposing that there was a duty to believe the most probable claim to revelation, so long as that was not too improbable; and perhaps some obligation to induce religious belief if this was necessary for a man to act as if there was a God or do moral actions, when he would not otherwise be able to do these things and there was an obligation to do them. Against this there is a clear obligation described above to pursue some religious inquiry in order to ascertain whether we have a duty to worship and how to influence those dependent on us. If such an inquiry concludes that it is likely that there is a God, then the non-rational grounds for cultivating belief need not operate, for we would believe. If the inquiry concludes that it is unlikely that there is a God, then there will be an obligation on the inquirer to influence in an atheistic direction any dependent on him. He will not be able to do that if he induces in himself a religious belief. How are any obligations to do the latter to be weighed against the obligation to influence correctly? I cannot here see any knock-down argument. One may argue that the final obligation will depend on the strength of the competing obligations—e.g. just how strong is the duty which a man cannot perform without a religious belief, and how close to a man are those whom he influences. Alternatively one may argue that the obligation not to deceive is always paramount. I am myself inclined to suggest that the obligation to teach the truth to children, whether that truth be atheistic or religious, is very considerable and very little could override it. If religion is false, it matters greatly that children should not waste their lives in prayer, worship, and evangelism, and in conforming to moral codes which derive their point from religion. If religion is true, it matters desperately that children should learn to practice it in order to attain deep and permanent well-being. Very little could, I suggest, override the obligation to ascertain the truth about religion and to hand it on to those whom we greatly influence, in particular to our children.

But not all of us are in positions of parental responsibility. If one has no obligation to influence others aright then obligations to induce religious belief have no priority. Further, in the absence of such obligation to influence others aright, there seems nothing wrong in the atheist inducing in himself religious belief (for any of the reasons which we have considered)—for he would owe it to no man not to do so.

If, however, religious inquiry leads to belief that there is a God, there would be something grossly immoral in a man trying to persuade himself out of religious belief. For if a theistic religion is true, man owes his whole being to God, and to neglect to worship and in other ways to please God would be an act of enormous ingratitude. Yet a man who persuaded himself out of religious belief would no longer recognize an obligation to do these things and so would be far less likely to do them. By cultivating unbelief the believer would be making himself unlikely to perform those powerful duties which he now recognized. The only possible obligation to hold an atheistic belief parallel to those which we considered for theistic belief, would arise if a man could only do certain moral acts if he believed that there was no God; and hence in order to do those acts, he might have an obligation to cultivate atheistic belief. But it is hard to think of a plausible case where atheistic belief would make a moral act possible, let alone a case when an obligation to cultivate that belief in order to do the moral act would outweigh the duty to worship and in other ways to please God.

It follows from all this that all men, quite apart from considerations which relate to their positions as parents and teachers, who believe that there is a God, are highly culpable morally, if they try to persuade themselves out of this belief, or even allow themselves through negligence to slide into unbelief. They owe it to God, to whom they believe that their being is due, to ensure that they worship and obey him (which they are only likely to do if they continue to hold true belief in the field), and so to ensure that they do not on this crucial matter mutilate their rational nature which, they believe, God has given to them. The Christian religion has always claimed that on a matter of this importance, there are no non-rational grounds good enough for such mutilation of our rational nature, a view which is, I suggest, highly plausible. Men have no doubt down the centuries cultivated unbelief or allowed themselves to slide into atheism on various bad non-rational grounds—e.g. in order to be able to commit other sins without a bad conscience. But this is surely one kind of unbelief which the Christian religion has rightly stigmatized as a great sin.

I conclude that the primary obligation on a man is to pursue religious inquiry with diligence, and to hold whatever religious belief that inquiry suggests. There are possible rival obligations to cultivate a belief that there is a God, where the evidence suggests that there is not; although these would only operate either in special circumstances (e.g. where a man could not do an important moral act without religious belief) or with very limited force (e.g. the duty to believe the most probable claim to revelation if it is not too improbable). However, for any one in a position to influence, it would in general be immoral to cultivate an irrational belief that there is a God, though the obligation not to do might be lessened by the considerations of the last sentence. But there is a strong obligation not to cultivate a belief that there is no God where the evidence suggests that there is a God; and it is not plausible to suppose that that obligation could be overriden. Any obligations to hold theistic belief and to hold atheistic belief are not symmetrical.

I believe that my conclusion is very much in the spirit of Aquinas, although in process of expounding his view he makes what I have argued earlier is a philosophical error. He seems to assume, as I shall show in my discussion of his account of faith in the next chapter, that if it seems to one that the evidence in favour of a proposition is not overwhelming, one can choose there and then whether or not to believe it. This, I argued in Chapter 1, is a mistaken view. One's beliefs about whether the evidence favours a proposition determine one's beliefs about that proposition. All one can do about one's beliefs is to pursue investigations over a period, which may lead to a change of belief; or set oneself to change one's beliefs by less rational means.

Given his assumption, Aquinas claims that one's duty is to believe what is supported by evidence. The duty to believe in God and Christ and so (on his view of faith—see Chapter 4) to have faith, arises, according to Aquinas, from the fact that men (normally) see that the evidence points in that direction—when they hear the Gospel preached to them (possibly after hearing the arguments of philosophers).

One must not, according to Aquinas, seek to avoid the pointing of reason, and if, for example, one's reason suggests that Christ is not God, it would be wrong to believe that he is and conversely. Aquinas is quite explicit about this. He wrote that

> to believe in Christ is good in itself and necessary for salvation; all the same this does not win the will unless it be recommended by reason. If the reason presents it as bad, then the will reaches to it in that light, not that it really is bad in itself, but because it appears so because of a condition that happens to be attached by the reason apprehending it . . . We should state quite simply that every act of will against reason, whether in the right or in the wrong is always bad.[1]

Given that one cannot choose one's beliefs at the time, the natural amendment to Aquinas is to read him merely as holding that one should seek to have beliefs which are backed by honest and adequate investigation. And indeed Aquinas does also claim this in addition to the earlier claim, when he makes the point that there are truths which men ought to discover and if their failure to do so arises from negligence, they are culpable for not knowing those truths. He wrote that if a man follows an erring conscience when the conscience is 'mistaken through voluntary error, whether directly or from negligence',[2] and the matter is one about which the man ought to know, he is culpable. 'If, however, it be an error arising from ignorance of some circumstances without any negligence that makes the act involuntary, then it excuses, so that the corresponding act of will is not bad.' If, as Aquinas held (see the next chapter), faith consists in believing that certain propositions are true, then, given this amendment, the obligation to have faith is in effect an obligation to pursue honest religious investigation and to hold whatever beliefs result from it. I have considered in this chapter the factors which determine the amount of investigation needed for this purpose, i.e. in order to have rational$_5$ beliefs. Aquinas expected that the resultant beliefs would normally be Christian beliefs but if, unfortunately, they were not, there would be no obligation to hold Christian beliefs; indeed, there would be a positive obligation not to do so. Subject to the various qualifications which I have made in the course of this chapter, this seems basically correct. Thomist faith is only to be had for Thomist reasons.

[1] St. Thomas Aquinas, *Summa Theologiae*, 1a, 2ae, 19. 5 (Blackfriars edn., London, 1966, translated by Thomas Gilby OP).   [2] Ibid., 1a, 2ae, 19. 6.

4

The Nature of Faith

So far in this book I have been concerned with propositional belief. I have analysed what it is to have a belief that so-and-so is the case, when belief is 'rational' in various senses of 'rational', when it matters what we believe, and what we ought to do about our beliefs. I claimed that it matters greatly that one should have a true belief about whether there is a God, and what he is like and what he has done. However, the virtue which the Christian religion commends is not belief but faith. What is faith, and what is its relation to belief? The faith which the Christian religion commends is basically faith in a person or persons, God (or Christ) characterized as possessing certain properties and having done certain actions; and secondarily perhaps in some of the deeds which he has done, and the good things which he has provided and promised.[1] Thus in the Nicene Creed, the man who pledges his allegiance before being baptised or in the course of worship, affirms (in the Latin) *credo in* ('I believe in' or 'I have faith in') '. . . one God, the Father Almighty, maker of Heaven and Earth . . .; and in one Lord Jesus Christ . . . and in the Holy Spirit, the Lord, the Giver of Life . . .; the Holy Catholic Church . . . the Resurrection of the Body . . .'. But there have been different views in the Christian tradition as to what this 'belief in' or 'faith in' amounts to. I shall spell these views out and show their relation to each other. We shall find

---

[1] In his analysis of the New Testament uses of πίστις ('faith') and πιστεύω ('believe' or 'have faith in') W. Cantwell-Smith (*Belief and History*, Charlottesville, Virginia, 1977) has pointed out that the most common use is where no object of faith is specified. Faith is stated to exist or is commended, without our being told that it is faith in God or Christ or whatever. Cantwell-Smith argues (p. 93) that faith is 'a quality of human living', quite independently of what (if anything) the faith is in, and he suggests that it is perhaps such a quality that is being stated to exist or being commended. I do not myself find this convincing, since the context of such occurrences would seem to imply that it is attention to God or neglect of him that is at stake. However, even Cantwell-Smith (in his later work *Faith and Belief*, Princeton, N.J., 1979) seems to allow that in the early church and in its subsequent life, the faith which was commended was normally faith in some object.

that, despite appearances, advocates of the different views are not necessarily commending very different conduct or affirming very different doctrines from each other.

The Thomist View of Faith

First then, there is what I shall call the Thomist view of faith. It is a view which is found in St. Thomas Aquinas and was developed fairly explicitly by the Fathers of the Council of Trent. It is a view which has been held by many Protestants and many outside Christianity, and by many Christians long before Aquinas. Indeed it is by far the most widespread and natural view of the nature of religious faith. This is the view that, with one or two additions and one qualification which I shall state, to have faith in God is simply to have a belief-that, to believe that God exists.[1] Although to speak strictly, the object of faith is the 'first truth', God himself, to have that faith it is alone necessary that you believe a proposition, that God is.[2] The man of religious faith is the man who has the theoretical conviction that there is a God.

The first addition which Aquinas adds to this simple doctrine is that to have faith in God, you have to believe not merely that there is a God, but certain other propositions as well, and you have to believe these latter propositions on the ground that God has revealed them. If you are to have the faith of which the New Testament and Christian Church speak, you have to believe that there is a God who has the properties and has done the acts which the Christian creeds describe. Your faith must be a faith in a God of a certain kind, not just any god. The belief which is affirmed in the Nicene Creed in God as having done certain things (e.g. as 'Maker of Heaven and Earth') is the belief that God did these things (e.g. 'made Heaven and Earth'); the belief in the good things which God has promised and provided (e.g. 'the resurrection of the dead') is the belief that they are or will be (e.g.

---

[1] This normal interpretation of Aquinas has been denied by W. Cantwell-Smith. (See his *Faith and Belief*, pp. 78–91). Cantwell-Smith claims that Aquinas's *fides* and *credo* is (p. 87) 'a quality of personal life' involving commitment. Cantwell-Smith's interpretation seems to me to be an interpretation of Aquinas's 'formed faith'. But Aquinas is very careful to distinguish 'faith' from 'formed faith'. For Aquinas, devils have faith (see later), and it is an intellectual act concerned with the same kinds of things as knowledge (*scientia*) and conjecture (*opinio*). He seems to me very clear on this point—see especially *Summa Theologiae*, 2a, 2ae, 2. 1 (and also 2a, 2ae, 1. 2).

[2] Aquinas adds that 'the only reason for formulating a proposition is that we may have knowledge about the real'—*Summa Theologiae*, 2a, 2ae, 1. 2, ad. 2.

'there will be a resurrection of the dead'). Aquinas claims that unbelievers (*infideles*, e.g. presumably pagans or Muslims) may in a way believe that there is a God (*deum esse*), but because they do not believe 'in the way which faith determines', they do not truly believe *in* God (*non deum credunt*).[1] Aquinas also writes that 'the things of faith surpass man's understanding, and so become part of his thought only because God reveals them. For some, the Prophets and Apostles for example, this revelation comes from God immediately; for others the things of faith are proposed by God's sending preachers of the faith.'[2] The First Vatican Council also taught that 'it is required for divine faith that revealed truth be believed on the authority of God who reveals it.'[3] We shall see the need for this clause in Chapter 7.

A second addition is to be found in Aquinas, but not in many others who in general follow in the Thomist tradition. Aquinas describes 'belief' as 'faith's inner act'[4] and claims that public confession is the outward act. He claims that inward belief and outward confession belong together, which seems to imply that one who did not publicly acknowledge his beliefs would not be a man of faith. However, others in this tradition seem to write as if outward confession was a work enjoined on the man of faith; but its practice was not part of having faith. In expounding the Thomist tradition in future I shall take the latter view.

The qualification on this view that faith is basically belief is, that the belief that is involved is a belief which does not in general amount to knowledge. Aquinas says that 'to believe' (*credere*) is 'to think with assent' (*cogitare cum assensione*),[5] a definition which he derives from Augustine. As Aquinas uses the terms, belief is a state inferior to, and incompatible with, knowledge. If you believe that *p*, you do not know that *p*, and conversely. I do not think that this is our modern use, where in my view and that of most philosophers who have analysed knowledge in recent years, knowledge entails belief—if you know that *p*, you believe that *p* (although of course not necessarily conversely). In this book I am using 'believe' in this modern sense. Belief which does not amount to knowledge, which alone Aquinas calls belief, I will call *mere* belief. Aquinas holds that at least

---

[1] *Summa Theologiae*, 2a, 2ae, 2. 2, ad. 3.

[2] Ibid., vol. 31 (translated by T. C. O'Brien), 2a, 2ae, 6. 1. (I replace O'Brien's translation of *cognito* as 'knowledge' by 'thought' which seems more correct, and so I am able in future to translate *scientia* as 'knowledge' without confusion.)

[3] Vatican I, *De Fide*, canon 2.   [4] *Summa Theologiae*, 2a, 2ae, 2. 2.

[5] Ibid., 2a, 2ae, 2. 1.

some of the beliefs (in our sense) involved in faith are mere beliefs. He holds that 'faith is midway between knowledge and opinion'[1] and thus endorses the definition given by Hugh of St. Victor that 'faith is a form of mental certitude about absent realities that is greater than opinion and less than knowledge'.[2] For Aquinas, as for many other medieval writers, men can come to *know* (by philosophical demonstration) that there is a God, although for most men, this too is a matter of mere belief. But some particularly Christian truths about God, such that he became incarnate in Christ, can only be, for all men on Earth, objects of mere belief, although belief which is justified on adequate grounds; and yet to believe some of these truths is necessary for Christian faith. The man who has 'the heavenly contemplation, the vision of supernatural truth in its own being',[3] however is no longer, according to Aquinas, a man of faith.

This view that faith is not sight does of course echo a long tradition of Christian thought, beginning with the famous Chapter 11 of the Epistle to the Hebrews, where the author describes faith as 'the assurance of things hoped for, the proving of things not seen'.[4] But do not some Christians on Earth claim to 'know' that there is a God who became incarnate in Christ? Yet if they know, how can they be men of faith, as we would be inclined to suppose? The border line between mere belief and knowledge is not always a very clear one. Recent philosophical discussions of knowledge seem to indicate that if S knows that p then S has a very well justified strong true belief that p.[5] But if my belief is true, just how well justified does it have to be in order to amount to knowledge? Do I know or only believe truly that it is not yet 5.30 p.m., etc., etc.? There are too, many things which I am rightly said to know, yet which I could have been wrong about (though I am not), which I know, though not with incorrigible certainty through a means like sight. I know that I am now writing Chapter 4 of my book—but I just could be wrong. So, even if, unlike Aquinas, we allow that there may be Christians who know the truth

---

[1] Ibid., 2a, 2ae, 1. 2.

[2] *De Sacramentis* I. X. 2. Quoted by the editor of the edition of *Summa Theologiae* referred to at p. 106, n. 2, in a footnote to the passage from the *Summa* just quoted in the text.

[3] St. Thomas Aquinas, *Summa Theologiae*, vol. 31, 2a, 2ae, 5. 1, ad. 1.

[4] Heb. 11: 1.

[5] Also, to meet the objection of Gettier, we must say that to amount to knowledge, the belief must be justified in a certain kind of way. See Edmund L. Gettier, 'Is Justified True Belief Knowledge?', *Analysis*, 1963, **23,** 121–3; and the discussion leading to this qualification, in Keith Lehrer, *Knowledge* (Oxford, 1974), Ch. 1.

of all the propositions of their faith, we should, I suggest, claim that they do not know them incorrigibly with a certainty like that of those who have the beatific vision. The common Christian understanding is that faith rules out sight, and if, unlike Aquinas, we say that it does not rule out knowledge, we must nevertheless say that it rules out the kind of knowledge which is incorrigible, analogous to that given by sight, which is more or less the point which Aquinas is making. The Blessed do not live by faith.

So then this is the Thomist view that the man of faith is a man who holds certain beliefs-that. Now in Chapter 1 I drew attention to the relativity of belief. To believe that *p*, I argued, is to believe that *p* is more probable than any alternative; and what belief amounts to depends on which alternatives are being considered. The normal alternative to a belief is its negation; and then one who believes that *p* believes that *p* is more probable than not-*p*. But sometimes there are alternatives, *q*, *r*, etc., other than the negation, and then to believe that *p* is to believe that *p* is more probable than *q*, and more probable than *r*, etc. Now what are the alternatives with which the propositions which Aquinas's man of faith believes are being contrasted? It is not clear. Guidance can be obtained by considering the historical circumstances in which controversies about each of these propositions took place, and by seeing with what they were being contrasted. 'There is a God' is no doubt being contrasted with 'there is no God', but some of the propositions of faith may be being contrasted with particular detailed heresies. In so far as there is uncertainty about the alternative or alternatives with which a proposition is being contrasted, it is unclear about what 'belief' that those propositions are true amounts to. In Chapter 6 I shall consider what are the alternatives with which any credal belief necessary for the practice of a religion *ought* to be contrasted.

In itself the Thomist view of faith seems to be a perfectly coherent one (although a somewhat unclear one). On this view, to have faith is basically to have certain beliefs-that, and clearly people can have those beliefs. It does however look an odd view, but this is because we tend to suppose that faith as such is meritorious (and we may even go so far as to suppose that faith alone gains salvation). Yet the Thomist man of faith may be a complete scoundrel, one who does his best to defy God.

However this is no problem for Aquinas, for he does not hold that faith as such is meritorious, and he is careful to distinguish faith from meritorious faith. Indeed he explicitly allows that devils (who have enough true beliefs about God) have faith. In support of his view he quotes St. James—'thou believest that God is one; thou doest well: the devils also believe, and shudder',[1] and he interprets the claim about their belief as a claim about their faith.[2] However, although the devils have faith, there are, on the Thomist view, two things lacking to them, which they would need to have if their faith was to be meritorious. The first thing which the faith of the devils lack, in Aquinas's view, is that it does not come into being in the right way. It is not meritorious faith, because it is not a voluntary faith. Aquinas writes that 'the devils' faith is, so to speak, forced from them by the evidence of signs. That they believe, then, is in no way to the credit of their wills.' For the devils 'the signs of faith are so evident that they are forced to believe'.[3] By contrast, Aquinas holds men can choose whether or not to have faith—the signs are not for them so evident that they have to believe; in that case, if they do believe, it is to their credit that they do. However I argued in Chapter 1 that all belief as such is a passive matter. We cannot help having the beliefs that we do at the time at which we have them. All that we can do is to set ourselves to submit them to impartial investigation or change them in less reputable ways over a period. Hence if we are to maintain that Thomist faith is a voluntary matter, we must maintain that the voluntariness of it is a matter of its resulting from investigation over a period or from our setting ourselves over a period to cultivate it. (By contrast, we could say that the faith of devils is involuntary because, whatever they do, they cannot but have that faith.) Aquinas does however seem to write as though, at any rate normally, the merit of faith resulted from one's choosing there and then to follow the dictates of reason; yet this, I have argued, cannot be. He is however aware elsewhere, as I pointed out in the last chapter, that a mistaken conscience can be the result of negligence and it would be natural for him to allow that lack of faith could result from negligence. With this caveat, the arguments of the last chapter give us reason to accept Aquinas's view that to be meritorious, Thomist faith, i.e. belief-that, has to result from religious inquiry of some sort.

However, there is another and more substantial reason why, in Aquinas's view, the faith of devils is not meritorious. This is that their

---

[1] Jas. 2: 19.

[2] This interpretation is prompted by the fact that *credo* is the obvious Latin translation of the Greek word for 'believe' $\pi\iota\sigma\tau\epsilon\acute{\upsilon}\omega$, and that the natural Latin name for the state denoted by *credo* is *fides*. There was no obvious noun in medieval Latin etymologically close to *credo*, to denote 'belief'.

[3] *Summa Theologiae*, 2a, 2ae, 5. 2 ad. 1, and ad. 3.

faith is not 'formed by love',[1] i.e. that it is not joined to the firm purpose of bringing about the works which the love of God ought properly to bring about, which are presumably the works involved in committing oneself to God's service. The Council of Trent put the point in similar terms.[2] It was not, I think, insisting that actual good works were needed for salvation, for a man might acquire perfect love and then die before he had any opportunity to do any,[3] but only complete readiness to do them.

So, although Thomist faith by itself is a very intellectual thing, a faith of the head and not the heart, a faith which may be held without any natural fruit in Christian living, the meritorious faith which the Thomist commends involves the whole person. It remains to be seen just how different this view of faith is from other Christian views of faith.

The Lutheran View of Faith

The second view of faith which I shall consider is that faith involves *both* theoretical beliefs-that (Thomist faith) *and* a trust in the Living God. The man of faith, on this view, does not merely believe that there is a God (and believe certain propositions about him)—he trusts him and commits himself to him. The 'believe in' of the Creed is to be read as affirming a belief that there is a God who has the properties stated, and that the good things stated (e.g. 'the resurrection of the dead') have occurred or will occur; and also a trust in God who has the properties stated, and a trust in the means of salvation which he has provided (e.g. 'the Holy Catholic Church') as a route to the good things to come (e.g. 'the life of the world to come'). In my analysis of trust, I shall concern myself mainly with trust in God; trust in the good things would, I suggest, be susceptible of a similar but somewhat more complicated analysis.

I shall call this second view of faith the Lutheran view of faith; for Luther stressed this aspect of faith as trust[4] to such an extent that

---

[1] *Summa Theologiae*, 2a, 2ae, 4. 3, 4, and 5.

[2] Council of Trent, *De Justificatione*, Decretum cap. 7, and canon 11.

[3] This is not of course a very likely situation. Normally the development of good character is a process which takes place through the doing of a lot of good actions. On this see pp. 148 ff.

[4] See his 'The Freedom of a Christian', § 11, in *The Reformation Writings of Martin Luther*, translated by B. L. Woolf, vol. i (London, 1952). The Lutheran view is found in the *Book of Homilies*, commended in the Thirty-nine Articles: 'A quick and living faith is not only the common belief of the articles of our faith, but it is also a true trust and confidence of the mercy of God through our Lord Jesus Christ, and a steadfast hope of good things to be received at God's hands.' (Sermon of Faith, Part I.)

the Council of Trent was moved to declare: 'If anyone shall say that justifying faith is nothing else but trust in the divine mercy, which pardons our sins for Christ's sake, or that it is by such trust alone that we are justified, let him be anathema.'[1] Later, Lutheran theologians distinguished three parts of faith (*fides*): knowledge (*notitia*), assent (*assensus*), and trust (*fiducia*), and declared that the first two were subordinate to the trust. Trust is, on this view, the central element in faith.[2] The *notitia* is, presumably, roughly the Thomist belief-that; and the *assensus* is something like Thomas's public confession. A similar threefold division of the parts of faith occurs in the opening chapters of Barth's *Dogmatics in Outline* where, after an introductory chapter, there are three chapters on faith entitled 'Faith as Trust', 'Faith as Knowledge', and 'Faith as Confession'.[3]

However, this notion of trust in God needs careful examination. To start with, what is it to put one's trust in an ordinary person? To trust a man is to act on the assumption that he will do for you what he knows that you want or need, when the evidence gives some reason for supposing that he may not and where there will be bad consequences if the assumption is false. Thus I may trust a friend by lending a valuable to him when he has previously proved careless with valuables. I act on the assumption that he will do what he knows that I want (viz. treat the valuable with care), where the evidence gives some reason for supposing that he will not, and where there are bad consequences (viz. the valuable gets damaged) if he does not. An escaping British prisoner of war may have trusted some German by telling him of his identity and asking for help. Here again, he acts on the assumption that the German will do for him what he knows that he wants (viz. provide help), when many Germans are ill-disposed towards escaping British prisoners and liable to surrender them to the police. Or again, a patient who trusts a doctor to cure him acts on the assumption that the doctor will do for the patient what he knows that he needs him to do, where there is some possibility that he may not (because attempts to cure are not always successful), and where things will stay bad unless the doctor is successful. We saw in Chapter 1 that to act on the assumption that *p* is to do those actions which you would do if you believed that *p*. The prisoner of war may not on balance believe that

---

[1] Council of Trent, *De Justificatione*, canon 12.

[2] In his *Faith and Belief*, Ch. 6, and *Belief and History*, Ch. 2, W. Cantwell-Smith argues that up to the seventeenth century the English word 'believe' used to mean 'trust'. The quotation from the *Book of Homilies* in note 4 on page 110 casts some doubt on this, but Cantwell-Smith has accumulated many quotations to illustrate his view.

[3] Karl Barth, *Dogmatics in Outline* (London, 1948).

the German will help him; but he believes that there is some
probability that the German will help, and trusting the German
provides his only hope of getting out of Germany. To act on the
assumption that *p* is to use *p* as a premiss in your practical inferences,
whether or not you believe *p*. But why *should* you act on the
assumption that *p* if in fact you do not believe *p*? Because you have
the purpose to achieve *X*. You can, you believe, do so only by
doing action *A*, and action *A* will achieve *X* only if *p* is true. If
your purpose to achieve *X* is strong enough (is far stronger than
your other purposes) then you will still do *A* even if you believe
that *p* is not very probable. As we saw in Chapter 1, the belief that
in fact guides you is the belief that there is at least a small, but
not negligible, probability that *p*. But we can describe you as acting
on the assumption that *p*, because you would do the same action
if you believed strongly that *p*. Within limits, the degree of *p*'s
probability does not make any difference to your action. So a
simplified description of what you are doing is 'acting on the
assumption' that *p*. We saw that to trust a man is to act on the
assumption that he will do for you what he knows that you want
or need, where the evidence gives some reason for supposing that
he may not, and there are bad consequences if the assumption proves
false. This, it now follows, is to do those actions which you would
do if you believed the stated assumption strongly, where in fact
the evidence gives some reason for doubting the assumption
(and there are bad consequences if it is false).

So much for trusting an ordinary person. What about trusting
God? We have seen that on the Lutheran view trusting God is
something additional to believing that he exists and to believing
propositions about him. It is presumably to act on the assumption
that he will do for us what he knows that we want or need, when the
evidence gives some reason for supposing that he may not and where
there will be bad consequences if the assumption is false. Yet one who
believes that God exists and believes the propositions of the Christian
creeds about him already believes that God will do for us what he
knows that we want or need; that follows immediately from those
propositions. Indeed, on some definitions of 'God' and some moral
views, all this will follow from God's goodness. However, whether or
not this does so follow, plausibly it is a central Christian doctrine and
so one which a man of Thomist faith also believes. One who believes
this will necessarily, in the primary sense distinguished in Chapter 1,
act on that belief. Luther himself commended this additional *belief*

(*not* just acting on the assumption).[1] He wrote: 'let no one be content with believing that God is able, or has power to do great things: we must also believe that he will do them and that he delights to do them. Nor indeed is it enough to think that God will do great things with other people, but not with you.'[2] Yet one who does not believe this may still, as we have seen, act on the assumption, by doing those actions which he would do if he did believe.

The trouble with the Lutheran account of faith, as I have expounded it so far, is that it has in common with the Thomist account the feature that the perfect scoundrel may yet be a man of faith. For what you do when you act on an assumption depends on what your purposes are. One who acts on the assumption that there is money in a till and who has the purpose of stealing will break open the till; one who acts on the same assumption and who has the purpose of protecting the money will lock the room carefully. A man may act on the assumption that God will do for him what he wants or needs, with purposes good or evil. Acting on that assumption, he may try to conquer the world, believing that God will help him in his task. Shall we call such a man a man of faith? Does he not trust God? Or the antinomian whom St. Paul attacks for suggesting that men should 'continue in sin, that grace may about'?[3] Does he not trust God, to see him right?

The Lutheran, like Aquinas, may be prepared to allow that the scoundrel can be a man of faith. But historically Lutherans have wanted to claim, against Aquinas and with the historical Luther, that faith alone suffices for salvation. If the Lutheran also claims this, he seems committed to the view that the would-be world conqueror and the antinomian are exhibiting the sort of trust which alone a man has to exhibit in order to obtain from God (unmerited) salvation. If he wishes, as he surely does, to deny that they exhibit such trust, he will have to put some further restriction on the concept of faith. He will have to say that those who act on the assumption that God will do for them what they need or want, have faith only if their purposes are good ones. A man must be ready to please God or do his duty or benefit his fellows, if his trust is to amount to faith.[4]

---

[1] Though whether he distinguished adequately between 'believing' and 'acting on an assumption' I have some doubt.

[2] M. Luther, *Magnificat*, in *Reformation Writings of Martin Luther*, vol. ii (London, 1956), p. 199.

[3] Epistle to the Romans 6: 1.

[4] Calvin claimed that faith can 'in no way be separated from a devout disposition' and he attacked 'the Schools' for distinguishing between 'formed' and 'unformed' faith

But if the Lutheran holds that to have faith a man must have good purposes, be ready to do good works, that means that he must have, in the Catholic sense, Love. And in that case the Reformation controversy about whether faith alone would secure salvation, would seem no real controversy about matters of substance, only a dispute resulting from a confusion about the meaning of words. The Lutheran and Catholic could agree that love was needed on top of Thomist faith, while admitting that Lutheran faith (since it included love) was sufficient for salvation. The parties only quarrelled, on this view, because they misunderstood each other's use of the word 'faith'. In so far as one thinks that the Reformation controversy was not merely a result of verbal confusion, one must think of the reformers as insisting on points implicit in the Catholic position, but not always made explicit—as denying that one's works need to be successful (i.e. that one's attempts to bring about good should come off), or that one needs to have been doing many or even any good works. What is needed for salvation (in addition to beliefs) is a basically good character, that is, a mind full of good purposes, set to bring about good results as opportunity arises, to guide the beliefs on which one acts. Failure to attempt to do good works in appropriate circumstances shows, however, the lack of such good purposes.

I shall argue in Chapter 6 that Christianity does indeed require (in addition to belief of some sort) that a man have a good character if he is to attain salvation. But I shall point out that the development of a good character often takes a long time and is achieved by attempting to do good works over a long period. I shall suggest in Chapter 6 that the good purposes involved in the good character need to become rather more specific before a man can finally attain salvation. They need to be the purposes to attain the goals of religion, i.e. salvation for oneself and others, and the rendering of due worship and obedience to God.

Luther himself was conscious of the close tie between faith and good works. In one passage he writes as though the tie was a logical one. In the Preface to his commentary on the Epistle to the Romans, he writes that faith 'cannot do other than good at all times. It never waits to ask whether there is some good work to do. Rather, before the question is raised, it has done the deed and keeps on doing it. A man not active in this way is a man without

and supposing that 'people who are touched by no fear of God, no sense of piety, nevertheless believe what is necessary to know for salvation'. (J. Calvin, *Institutes of the Christian Religion*, III. 2; translated by F. L. Battles, London, 1961, vol. i, p. 553 and p. 551.)

faith.'¹ Elsewhere, however, he seems to write as though the tie was less strict, perhaps merely contingent. 'Faith without good works does not last', he wrote in his 'Sermon on Three Sides of the Good Life',² implying that for a time one could exist without the other.

So then, to summarize, the man who has Lutheran faith is a man who believes that God exists and believes certain propositions about him; and who trusts him, in the sense of acting on the assumption that God will do for him what he wants or needs, when evidence gives some reason for supposing that he may not, in which case bad consequences would follow. Belief in such things as 'The Holy Catholic Church', and 'one baptism for the remission of sins', which the Nicene Creed affirms, is a matter of believing that the Church is one, holy, and Catholic, and that remission of sins comes through a first baptism alone; and also acting on the assumption that such institutions provide the way to Heaven (when there is some reason for supposing that they do not, in which case bad consequences would follow from trying to use these institutions as providing a way to Heaven). Again belief in such things as 'the life of the world to come' is a matter of believing that there is such a life and of acting on the assumption that one can attain it (given similar qualifications to those in the last sentence). Also it is necessary, if a man is to have Lutheran faith, that he should have good purposes in his actions on these assumptions—e.g. seek remission of sins or the life of the world to come. As with Thomist faith, what the belief-that involved in Lutheran faith amounts to, depends on the alternatives with which the credal propositions are being contrasted. Again, in so far as there is uncertainty about what these alternatives are, there is unclarity about what 'belief' that these propositions are true amounts to and so as to what Lutheran faith amounts to.

The Pragmatist View of Faith

While Lutheran faith involves both belief-that (however interpreted) and trust, Luther stresses that the trust is the important thing. Is a third form of faith possible where one can have the trust without the belief-that? I think that it is and that many recent writers who stress the irrelevance to faith of 'belief-that' have been feeling their way towards such a form of faith. I shall call such faith Pragmatist faith.³

¹ *Reformation Writings of Martin Luther*, vol. ii, pp. 288 f.
² Ibid., vol. ii, p. 124.
³ I find traces of this third view in much modern writing on the subject of faith; but,

As we have seen, one can act on assumptions which one does not believe. To do this is to do those actions which you would do if you did believe. In particular, you can act on the assumption not merely that God, whom you believe to exist, will do for you what you need or want, but also on the assumption that there is such a God (and that he has the properties which Christians have ascribed to him). One can do this by doing those actions which one would do if one believed these things. In Chapter 1 I quoted Pascal who replied to a man who said 'But I can't believe' with a recipe of how to acquire belief. The recipe was that the man should act as if he believed, do the actions which believers do, 'taking holy water, having masses said', etc. and that would produce belief. Although Pascal did not hold that acting-as-if it was the essence of faith, he saw it as a step on the road. But it is natural enough to develop this third view of faith according to which the belief-that is irrelevant, the acting-as-if is what matters. After all belief is a passive state; merit belongs only to actions. Surely if a man does those actions which a believer would do and for which he is to be esteemed, then the man should be esteemed whether or not he has the belief.

As we have seen, trusting God may be not just acting on assumptions; but doing so where one has good purposes. Those who have wanted to define faith in terms of trust alone would, I think, wish such a restriction to be included in the understanding of trust. So, on the Pragmatist view, a man S has faith if he acts on the assumptions that there is a God who has the properties which Christians ascribe to him and has provided for men the means of salvation and the prospect of glory, and that he will do for S what he knows that S needs or wants—so long also as S has good purposes. He

as I also find most modern writing on this subject almost unbelievably unclear, I find it very difficult to find an unambiguous expression of it in any one author. I have however called it Pragmatist faith, since in 'The Will to Believe' William James seems to commend a faith which is a matter of acting-as-if. (The trouble with James, however, is that he commends this because he seems also to hold a view which I have argued to be mistaken, that all belief is simply a matter of acting-as-if—see *The Will to Believe and Other Essays in Popular Philosophy*, first published 1897; New York, 1956, p. 29 n.) Yet clearly much of the responsibility for the traces of this view in modern theological writing derives from Kierkegaard. Kierkegaard frequently inveighs against those whose religious 'belief' is a matter of reason and balance of probability. Thus: 'the probable is so little to the taste of a believer that he fears it most of all, since he well knows that when he clings to probabilities it is because he is beginning to lose his faith. Faith has in fact two tasks: to take care in every movement to discover the improbable, the paradox, and then to hold it fast with the passion of inwardness' (*Concluding Unscientific Postscript*, translated by David F. Swanson, Princeton, N.J., 1944, pp. 208 f.)

will thus seek not his own fame, but long-term and deep well-being for himself and others. Seeking these things, he may believe that they are only to be had if there is a God who provides such well-being in this world and in the world to come. Hence he may act on the assumption that there is a God—for unless there is, that which is most worthwhile cannot be had. He will do the same things as the man with Lutheran faith will do. He will, for example, worship and pray and live a good life partly in the hope to find a better life in the world to come. He prays for his bretheren, not necessarily because he believes that there is a God who hears his prayers, but because only if there is can the world be set to right. He lives the good life, not necessarily because he believes that God will reward him, but because only if there is a God who will reward him can he find the deep long-term well-being for which he seeks. He worships, not necessarily because he believes that there is a God who deserves worship, but because it is very important to express gratitude for existence if there is a God to whom to be grateful and there is some chance that there is.

The Common Structure in the Three Views

Pragmatist faith is not, however, that far distant from Lutheran faith. The man of Pragmatist faith need not believe that there is a God, but he must have certain other beliefs. He has to have moral beliefs, e.g. that any God ought to be worshipped and that he ought to help others to happiness; beliefs about his long-term well-being, e.g. that it would consist in having the Beatific Vision of God rather than living a Lotus-eater life on Earth; and beliefs about the best route to attain that well-being, e.g. by seeking a life after death or a life of service in the African jungle (though he may believe that it is improbable that even the best route leads to that well-being). And he needs the belief that there is some (maybe small) finite probability that there is a God. It is no accident that Pragmatist faith as I have described it does involve such beliefs. These could not be detached from it and anything both rational and faith-like be left. For any advocate of a way of life, such as the Christian way, which prescribes for man certain conduct and has any pretence to rational justifiability, must have a belief as to why this conduct is to be pursued (e.g. because there is some chance that it is a duty, or because there is some chance that it will lead to happiness for oneself or others here or hereafter); and a belief as to why the goal cannot be attained more easily in some other way. The difference lies not in a fact that Pragmatist faith lacks belief-that, but simply that it involves less in the way of belief-that than does Lutheran faith. You need not believe that there is a God and that in consequence you will obtain deep and long-term well-being if you do certain actions (which will bring you deep and long-term well-being if there is a God); only that there may be a God and so that you are more likely to obtain happiness by doing these actions than you are if you assume that there is no God. Some sort of creed is difficult to avoid.

Also, as we have seen, Lutheran faith is not very different from Thomist 'meritorious faith' (i.e. faith 'formed' by a voluntary process and combined with a readiness to do works of love), although it is different from Thomist faith by itself. Also, as we have seen, in so far as belief (rather than assumption) is involved in faith, the faith will vary acccording to the beliefs with which credal propositions are being contrasted. It is by now, I hope, beginning to become clear that, on all three views of faith, the sort of faith which is meritorious involves belief of some sort and a good character, normally shown in good actions. On all these views of faith the actions which a man is ready to do include those which involve achieving good purposes, relying on the belief, or at any rate assumption, that God will do for us what we want or need. Given that the claims about God's nature and existence are not absolutely certain,[1] there is some danger that he may not. If God does not do for us what we want or need then, unless there is no God but is some other way to attain the goals of religion (to be discussed in the next chapter), such as salvation, there will be the bad consequence of our not obtaining those goals. Hence men's actions in relying on the cited belief can be described as putting trust in God. Hence faith involves trust on all three views. The real difference between kinds of faith (one which cuts across the Thomist/ Lutheran division) seems to lie in just how strong the credal beliefs which faith contains have to be. This is a matter partly of whether the propositions of the Creed are believed (e.g. the belief is that God is the Father Almighty, Maker of Heaven and Earth); or whether they are simply assumptions which guide action, and so the belief is simply that our goals are most likely to be attained if we do act on the assumption that the Creed is true. The strength of belief that a proposition is true is also a matter of the alternatives with which the proposition is contrasted.

---

[1] Even on the view (see p. 179, n. 2) that the existence of God is provable with absolute certainty, what God will do for us lies within the sphere of revelation and can be known only with a high degree of probability.

I brought out this latter point in the first chapter, and have referred to it at important points in this chapter. Here I must emphasize it again.

To believe a proposition is to believe it more probable than any alternative. So what the belief amounts to depends on what are the alternatives. The normal alternative to a proposition is its negation. To believe that *p* is to believe that *p* is more probable than not-*p*. But the alternatives to a proposition may be narrower than the negation. In that case to believe that *p* is to believe that *p* is more probable than each of these alternatives *q, r, s*, etc., but not necessarily more probable than their conjunction. It follows from this that there are really two different things which believing a creed such as the Nicene Creed might amount to. It may be a matter of believing each item of the Creed to be more probable than its negation. Thus, understanding 'I believe *in* God the Father Almighty, maker of Heaven and Earth and of all things visible and invisible' as 'I believe that there is a God who is Father Almighty, Maker of Heaven and Earth and of all things visible and invisible', we may in turn understand this as 'I believe that it is more probable that there is a God who is Father Almighty, Maker of Heaven and Earth, and of all things visible and invisible, than that there is not'. And so on for each item of the Creed. This interpretation makes it crucial just how one divides up the Creed into items. For, as we saw in Chapter 1, it does not follow from *p* being more probable than not-*p*, and *q* being more probable than not-*q*, that (*p* and *q*) is more probable than not-(*p* and *q*). Although it is to some extent clear how the Nicene Creed is to be divided up into items (for example, belief in 'God the Father Almighty' is belief in a different item from belief in 'One Holy Catholic and Apostolic Church'), it is by no means always obvious exactly where the line is to be drawn between different items. Is belief in 'God the Father Almighty, Maker of Heaven and Earth' belief in one item or belief in two separate items?

Alternatively, believing a creed such as the Nicene Creed might be a matter of believing each item of the Creed to be more probable than each of a number of specific heretical or non-Christian alternatives. A man in affirming his belief in 'the resurrection of the body' may be claiming that it is more probable that men rise embodied than that (as some other religions claimed) they rise disembodied, and so on. In affirming his belief that Christ was 'begotten, not made', a man may only be affirming a belief that it is more probable that the pre-Incarnate Christ was brought into being *e nihilo* than that he was made from pre-existent matter. And so on. This view has the difficulty of the previous view about how the Creed is to be cut up into items, and the further difficulty of how we are to know what are the alternatives to each item. The historical circumstances of the formulation of the Creed provide guidance on the latter issue, and indeed on the former one too. By studying the reasons which led men to put a certain clause in the Creed we can see what it was designed to deny. But it remains the case that on either of these views there is very considerable uncertainty as to what believing the Creed amounts to. On the second view a man who believes a creed consisting of p, q, and r, believes p to be more probable than p_1, p_2, etc.; q to be more probable than q_1, q_2, etc., and so on. In that case he will believe his total creed to be more probable than alternative heretical or religious systems, e.g. (p, q, and r), to be more probable than (p_2, q_2, and r_2). Conversely, if he believes p-q-and-r, to be more probable than alternative religious systems (including both systems which form bases of actual religions and systems which can be constructed by combining parts of the latter), then he will have belief of the second kind. He will believe p to be more probable than p_1, p_2, etc. and so on. So the second view can be expressed by saying that a man believes a creed if he believes it to be more probable than any alternative rival system.[1] One who believes the Christian Creed on this view believes it to be more probable than the creeds of Buddhism, Islam, etc., or any amalgam of parts of such creeds. I shall call belief of the first kind in a creed a strong belief, and belief of the second kind a weak belief. Theoretically, there is a third possibility that the creed as a whole is being contrasted with its negation. On this view, to believe the creed is to believe that the conjunction of propositions which form it is more probable than the negation of that conjunction. Yet although this is theoretically possible, I find it difficult to accept that religious men have supposed that belief in a creed is as strong a thing as that. For this view carries the implication that the believer believes that it is

---

[1] If p is more probable than p_1, p_2, etc., q is more probable than q_1, q_2, etc., and r is more probable than r_1, r_2, etc., it normally holds that (p, q, and r) is more probable than any other combination of p's, q's, and r's, such as (p_1, q_1 and r_1). There are however odd cases where it does not hold. These are cases where p, q, and r count against each other (e.g. where not all three can be true together). However, in view of the fact that religious creeds normally fit neatly together to give a coherent world-view, we may in this context ignore such cases. It also holds normally that if (p and q and r) is more probable than any other combination of p's, q's, and r's, e.g. (p_1, q_1, and r_1) that, for suitable ways of picking out the constituent propositions which make up the whole (e.g. for picking a proposition p_1, as an alternative to p rather than as an alternative to q), p is more probable than p_1 and q than q_1, etc.

more probable that his creed is true in all its details than that there is any mistake anywhere in it. Yet by comparison, most of us who believe complex historical or scientific claims allow the possibility of some error somewhere. So I confine myself to the two kinds of belief which a man may have in a creed and which I called strong belief and weak belief.

So the crucial issue with respect to faith is, given that meritorious faith involves good action springing from trust in God or commitment to Him, what sort of belief in the Creed is involved? Strong belief that it is true, or weak belief that it is true, or merely the belief that if one acts on the assumption that it is true, one is more likely to achieve the goals of religion (e.g. Heaven, forgiveness of sins, etc.) than if one makes any other assumption. Whichever view we take of credal belief, the results of the last chapter surely hold with regard to it. The main duty in this matter of belief is to investigate and to yield to whatever reason suggests to be true.

In both the New Testament and early Christian writing both belief-that of some kind and trust in God, involving acting on assumptions, is commended. The long sermon on faith in Hebrews 11 seems to contain an understanding of faith both as belief-that and as action on-the-assumption-that. On the one hand, 'He that cometh to God must *believe that* he is, and that he is a rewarder of them that seek after him.'[1] Yet on the other hand the faith of Abraham is seen in his obedience to God 'to go out into a place which he was to receive for an inheritance; and he went out, not knowing whither he went'.[2] And the faith of many other heroes of the Old Testament is seen by the writer as a matter of their doing actions in hope rather than belief.

The response required to the preaching of the Gospel by St. Peter in Acts was that his hearers should 'repent and be baptised'.[3,4]

[1] Epistle to the Hebrews 11: 6. In *Belief and History*, pp. 73–80, W. Cantwell Smith has argued that in this and two similar New Testament passages (Jas. 2: 19 and John 13: 9) πιστεύω is best translated 'recognize' rather than 'believe'. He claims this on the ground that the writer presupposes the existence of God and that the modern English 'believe that' does not presuppose the truth of the clause that follows it, whereas 'recognize' does presuppose the truth of the clause that follows it. That may be. But although the New Testament writers presupposed the existence of God, the verb πιστεύω (whether used by them or anyone else) does not carry this presupposition, and so I suggest that 'believe' is the better translation. But in any case 'recognize that' entails 'believe that'. The greater claim involves the lesser.

[2] Heb. 11: 8.

[3] Acts 2: 38.

[4] W. R. Inge in his study of the understanding of 'faith' in Bible and Church, summarized his account of the New Testament understanding by saying that 'believers' at the end of the first century AD 'were conscious that the word included

Yet although both belief-that and acting-on-the-assumption-that are commended in early Christian thought, it seems clear to me that by far the greater number of uses of the words normally translated into English as 'faith' and 'believe in' (e.g. πίστις, πιστεύω, *fides*, *credo*) are better translated as 'trust' and 'put trust in' than as 'belief' and 'believe that'. In a very well documented chapter of his *Faith and Belief*[1] W. Cantwell Smith illustrates this with respect to the lectures at baptism given in the fourth century, traditionally attributed to St. Cyril of Jerusalem. He argues persuasively that the commitment involved in baptism and in the creeds originally used at baptism (by the word πιστεύω) involves doing an action (putting trust) rather than expressing a passive conviction. However, as Cantwell Smith also emphasizes, the baptisands recognized that there was a God who had certain properties and had done certain actions, and their commitment to him took for granted this background. And recognition, like knowledge, involves belief. To recognize something involves coming to believe that it is so. Cantwell Smith supposes that to say of a man that he believes something implies that he has very considerable doubt about it. That just seems false, as a point about ordinary English—I believe that I am writing this on a Friday, and I have no doubt about it. Cantwell Smith seems to use 'belief' in the sense (see pp. 106–7 above) of 'mere belief'. However his discussion gives rise to a crucial question which he does not face, whether those who had mere belief were eligible for baptism. Do you have to be sure of the existence of that in which you put your trust, or is mere belief sufficient? Cantwell Smith does not explicitly consider this crucial point of just how much belief-that those to be baptised need in order to make the commitment. For those who were following other religious paths (e.g. the old pagan ways) presumably lacked both the belief that God had certain properties and had done certain actions, and the trust in him. Their conversion involved changing both their beliefs-that and the object of their trust. But how strong did their new beliefs-that need to be?

I do not think that the early Church was in the least clear about this. It had not faced the issue as a doctrinal problem. However,

moral devotion and self-surrender to Christ, a firm conviction that by uniting themselves to Him they would find remission of sins and eternal salvation, and intellectual conviction that certain divinely revealed facts are true.' (W. R. Inge, *Faith*, London, 1909, p. 23). Speaking more particularly about St. John's use of πιστεύω he wrote that 'the two meanings of intellectual conviction and moral self-surrender are about equally emphasised' (ibid., pp. 22 f.).

[1] Op. cit. pp. 70–8.

although it would need much historical research to substantiate my conjecture, I suggest that implicitly, in earlier centuries, men tended to assume that Christianity was being contrasted with various other religions and philosophical systems; and that in expressing belief in Christianity you were expressing a belief that it as a whole was more probable than each of those other systems. Those, like Augustine, who agonized over religious allegiance in the first centuries AD, were concerned with a choice between Christianity, Judaism, Mithraism, Manichaeism, Epicureanism, Stoicism, etc. Their concern in making a choice was with which was most likely to be true; and so among religions which offered salvation, which was most likely to provide it. There was not in those days a vast pool of 'agnostics' who owed allegiance to no system. Yet if in order to believe a system you had to believe each item of its creed to be more probable than its negation, then since you might expect most people to think that no system had all its items each more probable than its negation (although they would think that systems differed among each other in probability), you might expect most people to believe no one system and to belong to a vast agnostic pool. Religious belief then does seem to have been relative to fairly specific alternatives. In later centuries there seems to be a change. The post-Renaissance centuries saw the emergence and steady growth, among intellectuals to start with and then more widely, of a vast pool of 'agnostics'. Of course there was more than one reason for the growth of agnosticism, but many of these agnostics must have felt that one religion was more probable than others, and yet they still felt themselves unqualified for entry to it. We hear the great cry of 'I would like to believe, but unfortunately I cannot'. Clearly men supposed that there were stronger conditions for belief than those which, I have claimed, existed in early centuries. It was, I suspect, partly as a reaction to this situation, that some men developed an understanding of faith which did not involve any belief-that the propositions of the Creed were true, viz. the Pragmatist understanding of faith. Yet it seems fairly clear to me that for the New Testament and the early church *some* sort of belief that the propositions of the Creed were true was required of the Christian.[1] However, although the historian may read an implicit understanding of what faith is assumed to involve in

---

[1] Inge (*Faith*) claims this explicitly; and Cantwell Smith (*Faith and Belief*) claims that the commitment involved in faith includes 'recognition' of the existence of its object, God, with stated properties. I have argued that recognition entails belief-that things are as recognized.

various centuries, to my knowledge the Church has never made any dogmatic pronouncements about the kind of belief which is involved in faith. In the next two chapters I shall consider on more aprioristic grounds what kind of belief is needed for pursuit of the aims of religion, and what kind of belief a church ought to demand of its adherents.

Before coming to this question, I must mention one minor matter. All the kinds of faith which I have discussed involve attitudes towards, behaviour in the light of, *propositions*. They are not necessarily always so phrased, but my claim is that talk about believing in God or trusting God can without loss of meaning be analysed in one of these ways. John Hick however seems to claim that faith is not concerned with propositions. He entitles his view of faith as 'non-propositional' and claims rather that the man of faith is one who experiences the world as God's. He writes: 'faith consists of a voluntary recognition of God's activity in human history, consists in seeing, appreciating, or interpreting events in a special way'.[1] The man of faith 'sees' not merely disease, but the hand of God. But this view of faith seems easily expressible in propositional terms. The man of faith is one who sees the world and in so doing automatically and naturally *believes that* the world is God's creation; does not merely see disease, but in so doing automatically and naturally *believes that* God has brought it about. Is not to experience X as Y in this kind of case simply to experience X and in so doing automatically and naturally to *believe that X is Y*? The 'non-propositional' aspect of Hick's view of faith is simply a matter of the way in which he has expressed it.[2] There is nothing essentially non-propositional about it.

---

[1] John Hick, *Philosophy of Religion* (Englewood Cliffs, N.J., 1963), p. 71. He is developing here ideas from his *Faith and Knowledge* (1st edn., 1957; 2nd edn., London, 1967).

[2] The same may be said about Cantwell-Smith's attacks on propositional accounts of belief. See his bold claim: 'No one . . . has ever believed a proposition'—*Faith and Belief*, p. 146. Statements of belief can always be expressed as statements of belief in propositions. Aquinas saw Hick's position (see *Summa Theologiae*, 2a, 2ae, 1. 2, obj. 2) and claimed that his view was in no way incompatible with it (2a, 2ae, 1. 2, ad. 2).

5

The Purpose of Religion

ON all the views of faith considered in the last chapter, meritorious faith, the faith which men ought to pursue and are to be commended for pursuing, involves both having good purposes and having some sort of belief, but on different views of faith different kinds of belief-that are needed. On one view it is belief that each of the propositions of some creed is more probable than its negation. On another view it is belief that Heaven or a worthwhile life or some other goal of religion is more likely to be obtained if the creed is true than if some other rival religious system is true.

Way, Creed, Religion, and Salvation Defined

The Christian religion, like other religions, involves two elements—a way and a creed. By a 'way' I understand a life-style, a collection of kinds of action. (Often in *The Acts of the Apostles* the Christian religion is called 'The Way'.[1]) The Christian religious way is characterized by doing the actions of service and worship enjoined and refraining from the actions forbidden in the Sermon on the Mount and St. Paul's Epistles. These are sometimes made more detailed and explicit in the teaching of different Christian denominations, especially the Roman Catholic Church.

The actions of service include some actions which would, on a natural view, be morally obligatory anyway, quite apart from whether they are commended by the Christian religion—e.g. paying your debts, and not causing pain just for fun. It would be wicked to torture just for fun, whether or not there is a God. But the Christian religion also commends more demanding actions, some of which one might reasonably suppose would not be morally obligatory if there were no God (although they might still be good to pursue), and some of which would be a futile waste of time if there was no God. It

---

[1] e.g. Acts 9: 2.

commends a life of generous love to one's fellows—giving up many of the pleasures of life to see that others have food and shelter, joy and companionship, and to encourage those others themselves to pursue the Christian way. It also commends worship of God in the fellowship of the Christian Church, asking forgiveness from God for one's sins, prayer to God for one's own needs and the needs of the world, and prayer of meditation on the nature and actions of God and an attempt to contemplate that nature. It commends living the particular way of life (performing the particular kind of service and worship) which seems to the one praying after his prayer to be the way which God in his wisdom wants him to pursue, this being to follow a vocation—e.g. become a monk, set up a leper hospital in Africa, found a school, etc.

Many of these actions, according to all Christian theologians, are obligatory. Worship is obligatory—it is the proper response of respect by man to his creator. Some Christian theologians hold that all the above actions are obligatory—for God has commanded them and it is man's duty to obey his creator in all things. Other Christian theologians hold that there is no obligation on man to give his life totally to the service of God and his fellows; but they would add that a man who does not, is less likely to secure the great benefit which the Christian religion offers—the joy of Heaven; and that God wishes men for their sake to do these things which will secure the perfection of their nature, and to get them to Heaven. Actions which are not obligatory but which are good and the doing of which helps men towards salvation are known as supererogatory, or works of supererogation. Protestants on the whole have denied that there are any supererogatory actions—whatever is good is binding.[1] Catholics have affirmed the existence of supererogatory actions.[2] Both groups, however, share the view that it is obligatory on a man to do whatever is necessary to secure his salvation (while Catholics hold that there is no obligation to do what is merely likely to forward, helpful in forwarding, that salvation). The grounds for this common view are that as man owes his existence to God, he has a duty to do what God commands him to do. But that assumes that God commands rather than merely commends the pursuit of salvation. One might urge that no one has any right to impose so large an obligation—the total direction of his life—on anyone else; and so a good God would not command this. But then, no one has any right to an after-life, nor can

---

[1] See e.g. Article 14 of the Thirty-nine Articles of the Church of England.
[2] See e.g. St. Thomas Aquinas, *Summa Theologiae*, 1a, 2ae, 108. 4.

anyone reasonably expect God to provide a happy after-life for anyone who does not try to make of himself something worth preserving for an after-life.

Some Christian theologians may so understand the trust involved in faith as itself involving all aspects of the pursuit of the way. For them there are no good works additional to the manifesting of faith. For other theologians the pursuit of the way involves doing some actions which do not manifest faith, but some other virtue, e.g. charity. Not much more than a verbal point is at stake here unless, like the Lutheran, we tie faith to salvation and say that faith alone suffices for salvation. In that case, I shall be arguing in Chapter 6, the trust involved in faith must itself involve seeking the goals or purposes of religion which, I shall be arguing in this chapter, are one's own salvation, that of others, and the rendering of due worship and obedience to God.

Non-Christian religions commend different ways. These include some of the actions which the Christian religion commends, and some different actions.

The other element in a religion is its creed. A creed, such as the Nicene Creed of Christianity, typically contains various very general metaphysical claims about the nature of the Universe (e.g. that it depends for its existence on God who has himself such-and-such a nature), claims about how God has intervened in the Universe in various ways, and also claims that certain actions ought morally to be done or need to be done if a man is to obtain salvation. A man who adheres to a religion and is on the way to the salvation which it offers will both be following the religious way and also have some sort of belief in the religious creed.

In this chapter I shall investigate the point of pursuing a religious way. This will, I believe, lead us to see what is the point of a creed. The answer which I shall suggest to the latter question in Chapter 6 is basically that a creed provides a rationale for pursuit of a way, and that without some sort of belief in a creed, pursuit of a way would be irrational. Although creeds have been of more central importance in Western religions—and above all in Christianity—than in other religions, for this reason no religion could do without some sort of creed. The difference between Christianity and other religions has been rather that in the former individuals are required to give public assent to creeds and that disagreement about creeds leads to church divisions.

The answer to the question of the last paragraph should make clear what is the justification for exercising the virtue of religious faith and what sort of belief is involved in a justified faith.

Christianity is one among many religions. I could simply investigate the point of pursuing the Christian way. I would however like my results to be susceptible of somewhat more general application, and so I would like to investigate somewhat more generally the point of pursuing a religious way. But I shall consider in detail only the point of pursuing the Christian way. To investigate the point of pursuing a religious way, we need some understanding of what is a 'religion'. This concept may be understood in ways varying from a very narrow understanding to a very broad understanding. One may understand a religion as a pursuit which involves worship of a God and an attempt to conform to his will. But such an understanding would rule out some forms of Buddhism, in which worship of a God has little importance. Or one can understand a religion as any pursuit which dominates the life of many men and cements them together in common dedication to an aim. On this understanding not merely Christianity and Buddhism, but Marxism and Fascism become religions. I shall adopt an understanding of religion which includes Buddhism as a religion but excludes Marxism. I believe that such an understanding conforms best to ordinary usage. It sounds odd to call Marxism a 'religion'; religion is supposed to have some concern with extra-mundane entities and goals. It will be useful to me to conform to normal usage because the points of pursuing a Christian way and a Buddhist way have certain similarities, whereas the point of pursuing a Marxist way is rather different.

I propose to understand by a religion a system which offers what I shall term salvation, a word which I have used several times already in this book. I shall understand that a religion offers salvation if and only if it offers much of the following: a deep understanding of the nature of the world and man's place in it; guidance on the most worthwhile way to live, and an opportunity so to live; forgiveness from God and reconciliation to him for having done what we believed morally wrong; and a continuation and deepening of this well-being in a happy after-life. Christianity is one of a number of rival religions which offer a package with most of these elements. It tells us that the world is dependent for its existence on God, and that he is dependent on nothing; and it tells us something about God's nature. And it assures us that as we grow in the pursuit of the Christian way, on earth and after this life, we shall grow into a very deep understanding of these things.[1] Like Islam and liberal Judaism, it offers forgiveness, reconciliation, and guidance on how to live an abundantly worthwhile life and the opportunity to live such a life of worship and service; and a continuation and deepening of this well-being in the joy of Heaven where the Blessed shall 'see God'. Hinduism and Buddhism, however, also in their own way offer salvation. They do not in all their forms offer forgiveness from God and reconciliation to him, but they do always offer the other elements of salvation. They give man an understanding of the world and show man the worthwhile way to life (e.g. pursue the noble eight-fold path of Buddhism) available to him; and they assure him that if he follows that way, then by a series of reincarnations in this world he will eventually escape pointlessness and attain a deeply worthwhile state (e.g. of Nirvana).[2] Marxism, by contrast, offers relatively little of the package. True, it offers an understanding of the world. But it offers no forgiveness and reconciliation, no guidance as to the most worthwhile way to live (for a typical Marxist, values are subjective), and certainly no long-term well-being (since the Marxist holds that one life on this Earth is all that a person has). I conclude that my understanding of a religion includes those systems which we most naturally include as religions, and excludes those which we most naturally exclude.

First Good Purpose for Pursuing a Religious Way—To Obtain Salvation

So then what is the purpose of pursuing a religious way? I suggest that there are three good purposes for a man to pursue such a way—to secure (in so far as in him lies) the deepest well-being of himself, of his

[1] See St. Paul's First Epistle to the Corinthians 13: 12. 'Now we see in a mirror darkly; but then face to face: now I know in part; but then I shall know even as also I have been known.'

[2] I am interpreting Nirvana here as a permanent state of a man which (although it begins in this life) continues after death. This, as I understand it, is (despite all sorts of qualifications about not taking 'permanent', 'state', etc. too literally) the normal Buddhist understanding. If, however, Nirvana is supposed to be a temporary state of psychological well-being which a man may come to possess at the end of an earthly life, after which he ceases to exist, then Buddhism seems to me to offer so few of the elements of salvation as not properly to be classed as a religion. Trevor Ling, in his *Buddhism* (Harmondsworth, Middlesex, 1976, p. 136) seems to interpret Buddhism in this latter way: 'The original Buddhist goal *Nirvana* was the restoration of healthy conditions of life *here and now* rather than in some remote and transcendent realm beyond this life. It will be seen that the Buddhist way is essentially a therapy.'

fellows, and of God (in the sense of due reverence being given to him). They are all purposes for which advocates of religions have commended pursuit of their religious way. The pursuit of a religious way is normally[1] a very demanding thing; it demands a man's whole life. There would be no point in pursuing a religious way, except for a very worthwhile goal. I shall argue in this chapter that the three purposes are very worthwhile purposes. They are all purposes which will be attained by pursuit of the religious way only if the religion's creed is basically true. I shall show in the next chapter, in the case of the Christian religion, how its creed explains how pursuit of the way will achieve its purposes.

The first good purpose for a man to pursue a religious way is that suggested by my definition of a religion—to achieve his own salvation. A man seeks to understand the world, to acquire forgiveness from God and reconciliation to him, guidance on the most worthwhile way to live, and an opportunity so to live, and a continuation and deepening of this well-being in a happy after-life. The first and third of these elements of salvation are surely abundantly worth pursuing. As I argued earlier (p. 76) knowledge is good. A deep understanding of the world is abundantly worth pursuing. Likewise man needs the opportunity to live a greatly worthwhile life. Forgiveness from God and reconciliation to him are clearly only goals worth pursuing if there is a God. But if there is, men owe their existence to God. Yet they spend their lives in trivial and unworthy pursuits, ignoring their creator, generally making a mess of their lives. If there is a God, men abundantly need such reconciliation and forgiveness; and if there is a God, as I shall argue shortly, deep happiness will inevitably include such forgiveness and reconciliation.

Although clearly enough, a continuation and deepening of well-being in a happy after-life would seem abundantly worth pursuing, it is important that the sort of after-life which is offered should be deeply worth having and should provide a permanent happiness. For the after-life as depicted in some religious traditions looks somewhat

---

[1] There are exceptions. Some religions have ways which are not too demanding, and some religions have different ways, one for 'high-fliers' and one for ordinary men. But I think that it is true to say that religions of the former type offer much less in the form of salvation, than do other religions (e.g. no life-after-death in ultra-conservative Judaism), and religions of the latter type offer much less to those who pursue the inferior way (e.g. Hinduism which offers to those who live an averagely good life the same sort of life again). It remains true that those religions which offer much in the form of salvation require the pursuit of a very demanding way to obtain it.

trivial and the living of such a life forever would seem a goal not worth pursuing.

I shall now attempt to show that the life of Heaven which the Christian religion offers is a well-being greatly worth pursuing and one which will bring great happiness to him who has it. The greatest well-being belongs, I suggest, to a man who performs greatly worthwhile actions in a situation where it is very good to be and who knows that he is in such a situation doing such actions and who wants only to be in that situation doing those actions. What are the most worthwhile actions, the most worthwhile tasks to pursue? I suggest that they are: developing our understanding of the world and beautifying it, developing our friendship with others, and helping others towards a deeply happy life. And what are the most worthwhile situations? The having of pleasurable sensations is desirable, but they are the better for coming from the doing of worthwhile actions. It is better to get the sensations of sexual pleasure through the development of a personal relationship, not by themselves. It is better to drink alcohol in company than alone. And so on. And a worthwhile situation will be one in which a man has much understanding of the world, where the good triumphs in the world and a man's own contribution towards this is recognized.

If all this is correct, the occupations of the inhabitants of the Heaven depicted by traditional Christian theologians would be supremely worthwhile, and so would their situation be. If the world depends for its being on God, a personal ground of being, the fullest development of understanding will be growth in the understanding of the nature of God himself. Friendship is of great value to a man when his friends are good people, enjoyable company in virtue of their kindness and ability to keep us interested. Friendship with God would be of supreme value, for he is (by definition) perfectly good, and being (by definition) omnipotent and omniscient, will ever be able to hold our interest by showing us new facets of reality, and above all his own nature. According to Christian theology the principal occupation of Heaven is the enjoyment of the friendship of God. This has been traditionally described as the 'Beatific Vision' of God. Aquinas stresses that this 'vision' is an act of ours, not just something that happens to us.[1] Since God is a being of infinite wonder, it will take finite beings an eternity to comprehend him. Knowledge in Heaven will be more sure. On earth men depend on

---

[1] 'By a single, uninterrupted and continuous act our minds will be united with God'—*Summa Theologiae*, 1a, 2ae, 3. 2, ad. 4.

their sense-organs and nervous systems which may lead them astray or let them down. Christian theology assures men of a more direct grasp on reality in the hereafter. God will be present to the inhabitant of Heaven as intimately as his own thoughts. Friendship with a person involves acknowledgement of their worth. So friendship with God, the supremely good source of being, involves adoration and worship.[1] According to Christian tradition, Heaven will also involve friendship with good finite beings,[2] including those who have been our companions on Earth. The task of comprehending and worshipping God will be a co-operative one, one in co-operation with those who have shared a man's lesser tasks on Earth. Christian theology has always stressed both that Heaven will involve a renewal of earthly acquaintance, and that the enjoyment of such acquaintance will not be its main point. And of course one always enjoys acquaintance the better if it serves some further point—if one and one's fellows are working together for a goal. Even friendship with God would involve his helping us towards understanding himself and fulfilling other heavenly tasks. The main other such task, according to traditional theology, is helping others towards their deepest happiness, (and perhaps also beautifying the world). According to Christian tradition, the saints have work to do (by intercession or other means)[3] in bringing others into the sphere of God's love. These others may be, like many on Earth, half-developed beings ignorant of their capacities for these tasks, with wounds of body and soul to be healed. But the relation of those in Heaven to those others will be of a different kind from the bodily relation which we have to our fellows on Earth. A man seeks friendship with others not only for his own sake but for theirs, as part of helping others towards a deeply happy life. The most worthwhile such helping would be helping others towards their own deepest happiness; and thus seeking this sort of friendship also indirectly contributes to the seeker's own happiness.

A man in Heaven would be in a situation of supreme value, for he will already have much understanding of the world, his own worth (such as it is) will be acknowledged, and good there will be triumphing. Further, traditionally, the man will get bodily pleasure

---

[1] On the importance of such worship, see *The Coherence of Theism*, Ch. 15.

[2] Aquinas claims that in the blessedness of Heaven 'the society of friends adds a well-being to blessedness'—op. cit. 1a, 2ae, 4. 8.

[3] And see also Christ's words to his disciples: 'Ye which have followed me, in the regeneration when the Son of Man shall sit on the throne of his glory, ye also shall sit upon twelve thrones, judging the twelve tribes of Israel.' (Matt. 19: 28.) 'Judging' may mean here 'ruling over'.

out of being in Heaven. Aquinas[1] quotes Augustine[2] as saying that blessedness involves 'joy in the truth' and that the happiness of Heaven will involve the body.[3]

So, in the Heaven depicted by Christian theology a man will be performing actions of supreme worth and be in a situation of supreme worth. Also he will know that he is doing such actions and in such a situation. However, he will only want to be there doing those actions if he has a certain character. The man who wants to be applauded for what he has not done, who wishes to see the good humiliated, and to get pleasure out of the company of similarly malevolent persons, would not want to be in Heaven. The man who has the wrong character, for whom the life of Heaven is not natural, would clearly, even if he got to Heaven, not have the well-being possessed by those who want to be there.

Would the life of Heaven give to him who lives it a deep happiness? To answer this question, we must discuss briefly to consider wherein consists happiness.

Happiness is not basically a matter of having pleasant sensations. Certainly it involves the absence of unpleasant sensations and may be found in having pleasant sensations, but all this is not its essence. There are no pleasant sensations had by the man who is happy in reading a good book, or playing a round of golf with a friend; nor by a man who is happy because his son is making a success of the business which the father founded. Basically, a man's happiness consists in his doing what he wants to be doing and having happen what he wants to have happen. The man who is happy playing golf is happy because he is doing what he wants to be doing. A man who is having pleasant sensations may indeed be happy for that reason; but he will not be happy if he does not want to have these sensations, e.g. if he wants to try and do without such things for a period.

Unfortunately, men so often have conflicting wants, e.g. a man may want to have the pleasurable sensations caused by heroin, and want to avoid heroin addiction. Sometimes these conflicts are explicitly acknowledged; sometimes they are ones of which we are only half-conscious, and sometimes they are suppressed from consciousness altogether. A man will only be fully happy if he has no conflicting wants; if he is doing what he wants and wants in no way to be doing anything else. A man who does have conflicting

---

[1] *Summa Theologiae*, 1a, 2ae, 4. 1.
[2] *Confessions*, 10. 23.
[3] St. Thomas Aquinas, *Summa Theologiae*, 1a, 2ae, 4. 5.

wants may nevertheless still be on balance happy, especially if he is doing what he really thinks to be most worthwhile.

However, although a man may be fully happy doing some action or having something happen, his happiness may arise from a false factual belief or from doing an action or being in a situation which, objectively, is not really a very good one. Happiness is surely more to be prized according to whether the happy man has true beliefs about what is happening and according to whether what is happening is in fact of great value or only of little value. A man who is happy because he believes that his son is making a success of the business, when in fact he is not, has a happiness which is not as worth having as the happiness of the man who has a true belief that his son is making a success of the business. We can see this by asking ourselves which we would choose if faced with a choice of much happiness with a false belief that something marvellous was so, or small happiness with a true belief that some small good thing was so. Further, a man who is happy because he is watching a pornographic film by himself, or because he has made men sneer at some companion, has a happiness which is less to be prized than the happiness of a man enjoying a drink in company or watching the performance of a great work of art. That this is so can be seen by those of us capable of enjoying all such pleasures, comparing them for their worth.[1] In so far as happiness is to be prized, I shall call it deep, and I shall contrast deep happiness with shallow happiness which is to be prized less.

It follows that a man's deepest happiness is to be found in pursuing successfully a task of supreme value and being in a situation of supreme value, when the man has true beliefs about this and he wants to be only in that situation pursuing that task. Hence the life of the Christian Heaven would provide deep happiness for the man who wants to be there and wants nothing else, that is, for the man with the right character, but not for those who have other wants.[2]

---

[1] Even Utilitarians have had to make the distinction between lower and higher pleasures, although it seems to be somewhat against Utilitarian principles to do so — for there is scant reason to suppose that those who rejoice in lower pleasures are less happy (have less quantity of pleasure) than those who rejoice in higher pleasures, although their pleasure is less valuable, less deep. See J. S. Mill, *Utilitarianism* (first published 1861; 12th edn., London, 1895): 'some kinds of pleasure are more desirable and more valuable than others' (p. 15), and 'it is better to be a human being dissatisfied than a pig satisfied; better to be Socrates dissatisfied than a fool satisfied. And if the fool, or the pig, are of a different opinion, it is because they only know their own side of the question. The other part to the comparison knows both sides.' (pp. 18 f.)

[2] And not merely is happiness in the work of Heaven unavailable to those who have the wrong character, but much of the work *may* not even be able to be done by those of

I suggest that only that sort of life would be worth having for ever. Only a task which made continued progress valuable for its own sake but which would take an infinite time to finish would be worth doing for ever; only a situation which was ever more worth having would be worth living in for ever. The growing development of a friendship with a God who, if he is the sort of God pictured by Christian theology, has ever new aspects of himself to reveal, and the bringing of others into an ever-developing relationship with God, would provide a life worth living for ever; and a man who desired only to do the good would want that sort of life for ever. Most earthly occupations indeed pall after a time, but the reason why they pall is that there are no new facets to them which are greatly worthwhile having. A man who has moulded his desires so as to desire only the good and its continuation would not, given the Christian doctrine of God, be bored in eternity.[1]

Other theistic religions have often depicted a Heaven somewhat similar to the Christian one. Such a Heaven is only available if there is a God, for its activity is centered on the development of friendship with him. As I noted earlier, the non-theistic form of Buddhism also claims that there is a kind of after-life; yet there is to my mind considerable plausibility in maintaining that an after-life without God would not be as happy as the theistic Heaven. For friendship is with persons. If there is no God, the only friendship to be attained is with persons with limited ability to satisfy our needs, limited natures to reveal to us, limited abilities to do things for us and satisfy our curiosity.

Christian theology emphasizes that the life of Heaven is something which begins on Earth for the man who pursues the Christian way. This is because the pursuit of that way on Earth involves starting to do the tasks of Heaven—for a short time with limited tools and understanding, with many obstacles to success, and desires for other

the wrong character. To understand the nature of God, a man needs certain concepts such as 'just', 'loving', 'compassionate', 'generous'. H. H. Price has argued that one may need to be to some extent just, loving, etc. in order to understand what these characteristics amount to in others. (See his *Belief*, London, 1969, pp. 471-3.) There is some plausibility in this, but I do not find here or elsewhere a convincing rigorous argument to show this. That the impure cannot perceive the pure, and so that purity of life was needed for spiritual discernment was a theme of Clement of Alexandria. See the discussion in E. F. Osborn, *The Philosophy of Clement of Alexandria* (Cambridge, 1957), pp. 128-31.

[1] Bernard Williams affirms the necessary undesirability of eternal life in 'The Makropoulos Case' (in his *Problems of the Self*, Cambridge, 1973, Ch. 6). But those whom he pictures as necessarily bored in eternity seem to me persons of limited idealism.

things. The Christian on Earth has begun to understand the divine
nature (by Bible reading, receiving religious instruction, etc.) to
worship (in the Eucharist with music, poetry, art, etc.) and to show
the divine love to others. But his tools are poor—his mind and his
instructors provide weak understanding of the divine nature; his
organs and choirs are poor things; and he has many wants to do other
things, which need to be eradicated before the Christian way can be
enjoyed.

The kind of deep, permanent, and happy well-being, which on the
Christian doctrine reaches its fullness in Heaven, in fact encompasses
all the other elements of salvation. We have seen that that happiness
involves deep understanding of the nature of the world and man's
place in it. Since, as we have seen, it involves having true beliefs about
what is worthwhile, it will involve obtaining an understanding of the
most worthwhile way to live. It involves too, having the opportunity
to live such a worthwhile life. Since friendship with God is only
possible if we obtain forgiveness from God and reconciliation with
him, it involves this too. Aquinas taught that man's ultimate goal is
beatitudo, literally 'blessedness' but often translated 'happiness'. The
latter translation is a bad one. The English word 'happiness' denotes
a subjective state, a man doing and having done to him what he
wants—even if what he is doing is not of great worth and he has false
beliefs about what is going on. I argued that happiness is most worth
having when the agent has true beliefs about his condition and gets
his happiness from doing what is worthwhile. It is the deep well-being
which provides such worthwhile happiness which is *beatitudo*.[1]

The Pursuit of one's own Salvation is not Selfish

I have been suggesting that it is a worthy aim for a man to pursue the
religious way in order to secure salvation for himself; and I sketched

[1] See St. Thomas Aquinas, *Summa Theologiae*, 1a, 2ae, 1–5. Aquinas argues that
full *beatitudo* consists in the 'activity' (3.2) of 'laying hold of our ultimate end' which is,
he claims, God, the supreme good. He has arguments to show that it does not consist in
riches, honour, fame, power, bodily well-being etc. It is necessary for *beatitudo* that one
should seek to get the right thing—God, although the attainment of that thing
depends on God himself giving it to us. Aquinas holds (1. 7) that all men desire
beatitudo, but that some men have false ideas about where it is to be found.

In 'Two Conceptions of Happiness' (*Philosophical Review*, 1979, **88**, 167–97)
Richard Kraut brings out how similarily Aristotle had an objective understanding of
εὐδαιμονία, which differs from our modern subjective understanding of happiness. See
also Robert W. Simpson, 'Happiness', *American Philosophical Quarterly*, 1975, **12**,
169–76; and Elizabeth Telfer, *Happiness* (London, 1980), for this contrast and for the
connections between εὐδαιμονία and happiness.

the Christian view on what salvation consists in. But would it not be selfish for a man to pursue a religious way to secure his own salvation; and so a religion of generous love such as Christianity would surely not encourage pursuit for this motive? According, for example, to D. Z. Phillips, a man who pursued a religious way in order to gain salvation for himself would have missed the point of religion:

> Construing belief in the immortality of the soul as the final state which gives men good reasons for acting in certain ways now falsifies the character of moral regard. It certainly allows no room for anything that might be meant by the spirituality of the soul. It seems to me that if people lead a certain kind of life simply because of the final set of consequences to which it leads, they are indifferent to that way of life.[1]

It seems to me that Phillips is wrong here; although there are other good motives for pursuit of a religious way, its pursuit to gain one's own salvation is also a good motive. In pursuing salvation, I am seeking to make the best of myself. If it is good that I should improve my capacities (my knowledge of history or my ability to run)—as surely it is; and if it is good that I should seek to prolong them (to keep mentally and physically active when I am old, instead of letting myself sink into an arm chair)—as surely it is; *a fortiori* it must be good that I should seek to make myself a saintly and generous person and to preserve such a being to eternity. But, Phillips might say, my main goal ought not to be my own well-being—just as the mother ought not to seek to improve her own health before her child's. Yet that parallel does not hold, for the reason that my own salvation can never be in competition with any one else's well-being. On the Christian view (as I shall show in the next chapter) and on most other views too, I pursue my salvation by showing generosity to God and man, seeking their well-being (seeking God's well-being in the sense of seeking that he receives the worship and obedience due to him), and thus make myself a person fitted for salvation. The pursuit of the religious way is not a competitive examination, such that if you gain the prize, others will not. To seek to make the very best of oneself is not an unworthy aim.[2] In pursuing it one will inevitably learn total generosity, even to the extent of being prepared (if that

---

[1] D. Z. Phillips, *Death and Immortality* (London, 1970), p. 30.

[2] The Council of Trent declared that it was not wrong for a man to hope for and seek to gain his eternal salvation (*De Justificatione*, canons 26 and 31). In the seventeenth century there was some opposition to the official Catholic position from the Quietists. On the history of disputes about whether the pursuit of the Christian way must be disinterested, see K. E. Kirk, *The Vision of God* (London, 1931), pp. 441–72.

were possible—which it is not) to lose one's salvation for the sake of others.

The Second and Third Purposes for Pursuing a Religious Way

The second good purpose for pursuing a religious way is to secure salvation for others. Clearly it is good that others should attain salvation. But how is it that my pursuit of the way can gain it for them? A more detailed account of the Christian answer to this question will be given in the next chapter. But in general the answer is threefold. First, by ministering to the earthly needs of others—by providing company, worthwhile work, and mundane pleasure generally for them, I can provide them with a happy life on Earth for a short period and of limited worth. Secondly, by following the way, I can give others an example of how to live and am in a position to teach them about the religion, so as to help them towards a deep and long term well-being. And thirdly, by praying for others, I may move God to help them towards both temporary and long-term well-being.

The third good purpose for pursuing a religious way is to render due worship and obedience to God, who has called us to friendship with himself. If there is a God, he is the source of all being. We owe honour to those who benefit us. So we owe enormous honour to a God who has made us and kept us in being and given us all the good things of life (and, according to most religions, the hope of a gloriously happy life in a world to come). As the source of all things, dependent on nothing, he is mysterious and vastly different from created beings, and so we owe him a peculiar honour. As he has given us our being and lent us the use of the Earth, we owe him obedience in using ourselves and the Earth in the way he wishes.[1] We owe him also penitence for our failures of worship and obedience. If he who made us and whose creation we have spoiled, calls us to friendship with himself, we have indeed a duty to respond. The rendering of due worship and obedience to God, if he exists, is therefore a good purpose to fulfil.

These three purposes for the pursuit of a religious way provide the reason for which preachers try to draw men into their religion. They constitute the point of the religion. The point of practising religion is to secure one's own deepest well-being, or that of one's fellows, or that of God (in the respect that he is properly honoured and obeyed).

---

[1] For much more detailed argument on this, see *The Coherence of Theism*, Chs. 11 and 15.

The three purposes of course overlap enormously. It does not automatically follow for all religions that man who pursues a religious way to achieve one purpose will forward the achievement of the others also, but it does follow, given most creeds, including the Christian Creed. According to the latter, by rendering due worship and obedience to God, you will become the sort of person to whom God gives salvation; and indeed doing what God wants you to do involves seeking your own salvation. You seek your own salvation partly by forwarding that of others. And so on.

Other Purposes for Pursuing a Religious Way

There are of course other purposes, some of which we came across in Chapter 3, for which men follow religious paths. Men go to church to get more business for their trade, join a religion in order to marry a believer or have immediate peace of mind, worship God in the hope that he will answer their prayers for wealth, and so on. None of these are purposes for which the advocates of a religion seek to propagate it, purposes which a church is in business to encourage. Religion seeks greater goods than these for men. In general, a man who pursued a religion seriously would soon find that it involved pursuing greater goals, and seeking the lesser ones only if they were compatible with the greater ones. A man who pursued a religion to attain lesser goals would find that he was paying a high price for a small gain.

Thus a man who followed the Christian way with all its serious demands in order to get more business for his trade, might find himself having to give generously of his time and money, so that on balance he lost money. It might seem sensible to perform some of the public acts involved in the Christian way, such as going to church on Sundays in order to get business for one's trade. But if one did only this, one would certainly not attain the greater goods which the Christian religion offers—e.g. salvation. There is no Heaven for those who worship only to increase their trade. Heaven is a place for the generous and a man who sought only to increase his trade would not get there. Worse, if the Christian religious system is true, he will suffer for his hypocrisy. For he could only gain business for his trade by worship if he pretended to have other purposes for worshipping; and if there is any truth in the Christian doctrine of judgement, he will be punished therefore.

Marrying a believer or getting immediate peace of mind might seem more worthy purposes for following a religious way. But serious pursuit of the way will mean that other purposes must become dominant in the pursuer; and these involve a high price. They too could lead to a man losing that for which he joined the religion. He might lose his spouse through having to die for his faith; or find that taking his religion seriously led to greater moral sensitivity—and so (at least on Earth, while he was working out his salvation), led to more agonies of conscience.

To pursue a religion for reasons such as these would seem foolish in view of the seriousness of the commitment involved.

It is sometimes suggested that one should pursue a religious way either for its own sake or for the sake of obviously morally desirable and attainable earthly goals. The life of prayer, worship, and service to others, it is argued, has its own value on Earth—whether or not there is a God or whether or not there are other transcendent realities beyond this world.

Now certainly a good man may pursue some of the paths of a religious way for their own sake. Certain kinds of conduct such as truth-telling and promise-keeping which the religious way commends, have their own value, quite apart from any further goals which pursuing them may forward. Other paths of the religious way forward obvious earthly goals. Feeding the hungry and clothing the naked produces good on Earth, quite apart from any good which it produces hereafter. And even meditation on the transcendent may produce the good of peace of mind for the meditator, whether or not there is a transcendent realm. However the pursuit of some paths of the Christian religious way (and the same applies to other religious ways) can only have a point if there is some supernatural reality. Petitionary prayer for the bodily needs of others does indeed serve an earthly purpose, but it can only do it if there is a God who can intervene in human history in response to it. The activity only has a point if there is a God. Other paths of the religious way seem to have no value either in themselves or in forwarding earthly goals (whether or not there is a God). Saying 'God forgive me' would seem to have no value unless thereby the utterer is seeking God's forgiveness, an aspect of salvation.[1] Worship and encouraging others to worship

---

[1] D. Z. Phillips' *The Concept of Prayer* (London, 1965) is a sustained attempt to argue that prayer for forgiveness and petitionary prayer do have a point if there is no transcendent God. Thus, 'The prayer of petition is best understood, not as an attempt at influencing the way things go, but as an expression of, and a request for, devotion to God, through the way things go . . . In prayers of confession and in prayers of petition, the believer is trying to find a meaning and a hope that will deliver him from the elements in his life which threaten to destroy it: in the first case his guilt, and in the second case, his desires' (op. cit., pp. 120 f.). This seems to me a totally false account of the meaning of the

serve no earthly goal, and have value only if thereby God is glorified and men are nearer to their salvation. Worship and asking God for forgiveness have their point only if there is a God apart from man, and that point is to cement the relationship between God and man. Only some of the paths which form the religious way have an earthly justification. And although some paths do have an earthly justification, advocates of Christianity would urge their pursuit also for the sake of the goals of salvation for oneself and others.

Summary

Some of the goals for which a religious way is to be pursued are worth pursuing for their own sake—e.g. deep understanding of the Universe; others are worth pursuing only if there is a God—e.g. forgiveness from God. A pursuer does not need to believe that there is a God in order to pursue goals of the second type. He needs only to believe that there may be a God, and to wish to avoid the situation of the non-satisfaction of those goals if there is a God. A man may believe that God may have made him and wish at all costs to avoid a situation of an unthanked God, and so be moved to thank God.

A man will pursue the goals of religion either because he wants those goals or because he believes that they are worth pursuing.

It is good that a man seek great goals, seek to make the most of his life and that of others, and to ensure that if there is a God he is properly worshipped and obeyed; above all, that if there is a God who calls men to friendship with himself, that call is answered. It is good that a man should seek for himself and others deeper and longer term well-being than this Earth can provide. Realizing the shallowness of the satisfactions that Earth can provide—the limited and temporary understanding of the world and friendship with others which it gives —men seek for greater good. Indeed only a man with that kind of ambition is a great man; and, if the arguments of this chapter are correct, only a man who wants such things without having any conflicting wants is capable of the deepest happiness. It has been a primary task of the preachers of the great religions to bring this message home to men: 'Here is no enduring city, but we seek one to come.'[1] It follows

prayers of most who have prayed in the Christian and other theistic traditions over many centuries, including the present century. Phillips's account of prayer is, I think, best regarded as a suggested reinterpretation of prayer for those who feel that, even if there is no transcendent God, there is still a point in pursuing an activity, which is not prayer, but which, in the words and gestures used has some outward similarity to prayer.

[1] Epistle to the Hebrews 13: 14.

that a man must seek these things if he is to be fitted for the deepest happiness which the Christian Heaven allegedly provides; if faith alone secures salvation, faith must involve the pursuit of these goals.

Is there an obligation on any one to pursue a religious way? We saw that many paths of a religious way which concern our relations with our fellow men—such as keeping promises, paying debts, etc.—are obligatory anyway, quite independently of whether or not there is a God. I have suggested that, if there is a God, there is an obligation to worship; and also an obligation to treat others as God's children and the world as God's world. We must use it as tenants and not as owners.[1] Yet duties which exist objectively are only binding on those who recognize their existence. A man can only be praised or blamed for his moral worth or lack of it, in respect of those actions which he believed that he had an obligation to do or not to do. Now a man can only justifiably believe that he has an obligation to worship God and so treat others as God's children and the world as God's world, if he believes that there is a God, i.e. that it is more probable than not that there is a God. Yet when a man believes that there is a God, he may justifiably conclude that there is an obligation upon him to pursue many of the paths of the religious way. Whether, if there is a God, a man has an obligation to pursue all the paths of the religious way, viz. to give his whole life to the service of God and others, depends on whether he has an obligation to seek salvation. That, I suggested earlier, is not too evident. However, although a man who does not believe that there is a God can hardly be blamed for not worshipping and serving, there is, I argued in Chapter 3, (given certain conditions) an obligation on him as on all men, to pursue inquiry as to whether or not there is a God; and if he recognizes this latter obligation, he is blameworthy if he does not pursue inquiry. If he does pursue inquiry, he may come to believe that there is a God and so come to recognize the obligation to worship and serve him.

So then, a man will only rationally pursue a religious way if he seeks the goals which it offers. He will only seek the goals of religion if he has a reason for doing so, and that can only be that he wants those goals or considers that they are overall worth pursuing (e.g. because he is morally obliged to seek them). And he will only pursue the way to obtain the goals if to some extent he believes that the pursuit of the way is likely to lead to the attainment of the goals. I will discuss in more detail what sort of belief he needs in the next chapter.

[1] On all this, see *The Coherence of Theism*, Chs. 11 and 15.

6

The Role of Creeds

I ARGUED in the last chapter that there are three purposes for which preachers advocate pursuit of a religious way, and that they are good purposes worth a man giving much to achieve. But there is only point in pursuing a certain religious way to fulfil these purposes if there is some chance that pursuit of the way will achieve the purposes. That is where the creed of a religion comes in. The creed explains how it is that pursuit of a particular way will probably achieve the purposes, and why pursuit of other ways will probably not achieve the purposes.

The Christian Explanation of how Pursuit of the Christian Way Leads to the Achievement of Salvation for the Pursuer

I shall now show, with regard to the Christian religion, how the creed provides this explanation. I understand by a creed a theological system in a wide and vague sense, in which there are some central claims agreed by followers of the religion and other disputed less central claims. I am not using the term 'creed' in the narrower sense of a collection of propositions to which a church member is required in some sense to assent. I shall however later illustrate how the Christian Nicene Creed, to which the assent of Christians is often required, encapsulates an explanation of this sort. I am not now attempting to show that the creed (in the wide sense) is true; but only that, if it is true, it does explain why pursuit of the Christian way will lead to salvation for the pursuer and for others, and to the rendering of due worship and obedience to God; and why pursuit of other ways is unlikely to achieve those purposes.

How is it that pursuit of the Christian way will attain salvation for the pursuer? Evidently the Christian religion offers in its creed an initial understanding of the world. This understanding is, it claims, a true and profound picture of the world, showing the dependence of all things on God, the nature of his purposes for men, how he has intervened in history, etc. The religion is, it claims, in a position to provide this picture, because it is enshrined in the Church;[1] and that knowledge has come to the Church partly by the revelation of God to Israel and, more fully, in the teaching of Jesus Christ. The Christian religion offers to those who reflect with prayer on its doctrinal statements and try to 'live out their consequences in the world, a deepening of understanding. To be thus the gateway to a deep understanding, the initial doctrinal statements must of course be true, but they need also to be of central religious significance. The Christian Creed asserts that the statements at its centre do have this significance. Again, it claims divine authority for this assertion. It is not certain that study of these statements will lead to conviction of their truth; but the Creed claims that those who pursue the other paths of the way also (service and worship) will often grow in such conviction on Earth. However, Christian theology also affirms that understanding reaches great depth and conviction in Heaven for those who succeed in getting there. We saw in the last chapter how there is happiness to be attained in such growth of understanding.

The Christian Creed also provides guidance on how to live. According to it, the Christian way described earlier is in fact the supremely worthwhile way to live. It is a way of generous action, generous to God and generous to men. The generosity to God involves giving him deserved worship and obedience.The Christian Creed declares what constitutes true adoration (e.g. on Earth, the celebration of the Eucharist rather than human sacrifice) and for what God is to be worshipped. The way includes developing a friendship with God. For the latter, an understanding of God's nature is necessary; for to be friends with anyone you have to understand what they are like. Generosity to man involves caring for man's needs of body and deeper needs of soul. The Creed explains what constitutes such generosity (i.e. what man's needs are, which need care). The Christian way, according to the Christian Creed, is the living of the right sort of generous life, for it consists in giving to others what is right for them. Man has the opportunity to begin to live this sort of life on Earth for, whatever our situation, we can all be generous.

According to the Christian Creed, forgiveness and reconciliation to God is available to all who ask for it with proper penitence. Forgiveness can only take place where there is penitence. I can

---

[1] I avoid the denominational issue of just how it is enshrined in the Church— whether by Bible or Pope or Church Councils or 'consensus of the faithful'.

forgive your bad conduct towards me if you express your regret and if you show this regret by a changed life and by some token of sorrow; but if you do not, all I can do is to ignore the bad conduct, not be offended by it, i.e. not take it seriously.

Now, according to Christian tradition, the problem of sin is a very weighty one. Down the ages men have sinned badly by failing to render to God their creator due worship and obedience, to show love to their fellows, God's children, and to use the created world in the way which its owner has laid down. They have influenced each other for evil. Because men are a community of beings of similar nature who are what they are because of the enormous influence which they exert on each other, the whole human race, as well as each individual, needs forgiveness. Yet because of the bad influence of his fellows, man grows up corrupt, that is, suffers from Original Sin,[1] and so is not able to show the proper penitence even for his own actual sins. For the more serious the sin, the more evident and long-lasting needs to be the change of life and the larger the token of sorrow. A casual 'sorry' shows no penitence for a serious offence.

The only solution would be for one man born without the corruption of original sin to offer on behalf of others to God a penitential life in lieu of ordinary men, and for God to treat his penitential life as our token of sorrow, the token of sorrow of each individual who was prepared to acknowledge it as such and to join his own half-hearted penitence to that fuller token of penitence. Thereby there would be no 'overlooking' of sin; it would be taken seriously. But God has no right to make one man take such a burden on behalf of others; and anyway what was needed was a man freely and gladly to take this burden on himself if the token of penitence was to be worth having. If God was to ensure that this token was offered and so reconciliation be effected and forgiveness be made available, what he must do was in some sense or some form to become a man and make the offering of a penitential life himself. So, according to the Christian

---

[1] I distinguish Original Sin, the corruption of nature, our being burdened by strong desires for lesser goods, about the existence of which all theologians are agreed, from Original Guilt, the individual's responsibility for the sins of others and in particular of the first sinner ('Adam'), about which theologians differ. In writing that 'Original Sin' is transmitted by the 'influence' of men on each other, I do not need here to assume that the 'influence' is transmitted socially rather than (e.g.) genetically, as has sometimes been held. It seems fairly obvious however that there is a large element of social conditioning in the spread of Original Sin. Its being spread socially provides a plausible explanation of why a good God allows men to be burdened with Original Sin—it is the result of God giving men great responsibility for other men. See *The Existence of God*, Ch. 10, especially p. 195.

Creed, seeking to forgive men, God in Christ came to Earth as man, let men do to him the worst that men do to men, suffered, died and was buried. This allowed God to forgive man, a forgiveness symbolized and made evident by God's giving back life to Christ who had freely given it up.[1] It is all this which gives reason for believing that God provides forgiveness and reconciliation to those who ask for it by joining themselves to the new humanity which Christ formed in his body, the Church, and so for believing that forgiveness becomes available through 'one Holy Catholic and Apostolic Church, one baptism for the forgiveness of sins', to all its members who ask for it (however half-heartedly).

Yet how could Christ be both God and man? Is not there some logical incompatibility here? Christian theology made an attempt to make sense of this claim by its doctrines of the Trinity (God being three persons—Father, Son, and Holy Spirit who are one God—in one substance) and the Incarnation (Christ being one person with two natures, divine and human). Once again I am not concerned to argue that these doctrines are true, or even coherent; but only to point out that if they are true, they explain why the pursuit of the Christian way will attain one of the goals of religion, viz. forgiveness from God and reconciliation to him.

Finally, how is it on the Christian view that pursuit of the way will bring greatly valuable long-term and deeply happy well-being to the pursuer? The well-being will be long-term because God will give to those who pursue the way a life beyond death on Earth continuing in

---

[1] There are a number of different versions of the doctrine of the atonement in Christian theology. Untypical is the 'subjective' version which claims that the only value of the life and death of Jesus was that it served as an example to others. This version has been seen almost unanimously by Christian tradition as unorthodox. The 'objective' versions claim that the life and death of Jesus made by itself an objective difference to man's status in the sight of God in providing him with a means of reconciliation which he would not otherwise have. They express what was effected in different ways—the paying of a ransom for men; the paying of a judicial fine for men; the paying of a token instead of the fine which God has remitted; the offering of a sacrifice. Christian orthodoxy has often seen value in more than one such theory. It was, however, difficult to show in the text the explanatory relevance of the doctrine of the atonement without expressing it in a way which shows a preference between these versions in one respect. The first two versions claim that Jesus paid on behalf of men the ransom or fine which they owed and would otherwise have to have paid themselves. The latter two versions claim that the offering made by Jesus was no substitution of this kind; God forgives without the full penalty or ransom being paid. It will be apparent that I have opted in the text for the latter view. It seems to me the view of the New Testament and to represent God as merciful. But if anyone prefers the other view, the points in the text about the explanatory power of the doctrine of the atonement (in showing that forgiveness is available) can easily be made in terms of it.

Heaven. We saw in the last chapter how it is that the well-being of the Christian Heaven will be greatly valuable and deeply happy. What remains to be explained is why pursuit of the Christian way is more likely to attain the goal of Heaven than pursuit of any other way, or no way at all. Does God give the well-being of Heaven only to those who pursue the Christian way, and if so does not this seem ungenerous of him? Will not a generous God reward good and bad alike with Heaven? One might answer that man has no right to Heaven, and God wrongs no one by not giving it to some men; but he has offered it to those who pursue the Christian way, and he will fulfil his promise. Man has the choice of whether to pursue the way or not; but he must take the consequence of not doing so. It is good that men should pursue the way, and by his promise God encourages them to do so. Those who pursue the way in the face of uncertainty deserve a reward. God is not here pictured as totally irrational. It would not be very unreasonable behaviour on the part of God, to reward worthwhile action; whereas it would, I argued in Chapter 3, seem to be very unreasonable behaviour of God to reward belief, irrespective of the methods by which it was obtained. However, it does seem a rather shallow answer, giving rise to further problems. Not all men have heard the Gospel, and so know the offer and the conditions on which it is made (let alone have reasonable grounds for believing that the offer announced by the Church comes from God). Why through ignorance should they be deprived of the reward? Further, if Heaven is simply a reward for good action, it seems a reward out of all proportion to the actions done. A few years of good action rewarded with an eternity of Heaven. But not enough good actions, and you lose the eternal reward?

The Christian Explanation of how the Good will Attain Heaven

The solution to these problems must be that Heaven is not primarily a reward for good actions but a home for good people. What determines whether a man gets to Heaven is not what he has done but what sort of person he is. This follows from both the Catholic and Protestant accounts of who will be saved, to which I referred in Chapter 4. What is needed is the right character, the readiness to perform the right sort of actions, not actually having done them.[1] It

---

[1] This view receives abundant biblical support in the parable of the Labourers in the Vineyard (Matt. 20: 1-16). Entry to the Kingdom of Heaven is compared to a situation where the same reward is given to those who have worked the whole day and to those

follows also from the Christian doctrine of Heaven given in the last chapter that such a character is necessary. For the inhabitants of a Christian Heaven will be performing actions of supreme worth and be in a situation of supreme worth; and they will know that they are doing such actions and in such a situation. Hence they will have the deep happiness which it provides so long as they want to be in that situation, doing those actions, and do not want in any way to be anywhere else or doing anything else. That is, they need a certain character. I argued in the last chapter for the plausibility of the Christian view that the traditional occupations of Heaven—the adoration of God in company with our fellows, leading to progressive understanding of the divine nature, and the bringing of others into the sphere of God's love—were supremely worthwhile actions; and that a man's situation in Heaven would be one of supreme value. A man who wants to live this sort of life and to be in Heaven, is fitted for Heaven, for he alone can gain happiness out of pursuing it. A good God might well be expected to put such a person in Heaven, for he would wish to give deep happiness to those capable of having it. The claim of Revelation that he does so is highly plausible. If a man sees the supreme goodness of the life of Heaven and wants to live that life and wants to be doing nothing else, his purposes will be to be in Heaven seeking the goals of the activity of Heaven. Since the activity of Heaven consists in forwarding the well-being of God (in the sense of rendering to him true worship and obedience) and the deepest well-being of himself and his fellows, it follows that the purposes needed by a man for the attainment of Heaven are the three purposes for pursuing a religious way. Hence, as I claimed in Chapter 4, the trust involved in the faith which is needed for salvation must involve seeking to achieve the purposes of religion.

The life of Heaven which is so desirable is, as we saw earlier (p. 195), the same sort of life as the pursuit of the Christian way on Earth—though with the difficulties and obstacles to success, and desires for lesser goods, removed. Hence a man can begin to live the life of Heaven on Earth. But how is a man who sees the goodness of that life to get himself to want to pursue it, and so obtain the happiness which Heaven provides? The answer is by living that life in the unfavourable conditions of Earth.

A man is so made that by the actions which he does over a lifetime

who have worked only one hour. What determines whether they get their reward is their status as workers, that they are developing the vineyard (having accepted the challenge to work when it came), not how many hours' work they have done.

he determines his character. We start life with opportunities to pursue various paths; by choosing to do certain sorts of action and allowing himself to respond to situations in certain ways, a man gradually becomes the sort of person for whom a certain sort of action and response is natural. In the circumstances of man's life there are always opportunities to do good or evil. A man who chooses the good will find more opportunities to pursue good ways. He may not do good actions naturally to start with; but determined pursuit will make for eventual natural pursuit. And a man will want to do what he both does naturally and also judges to be good. Just as a man can through effort make a certain sort of action natural, so he can make a certain sort of reaction natural. If he judges a certain kind of situation (e.g. the situation of worship) a good one, so, by dwelling on its merits and reflecting on the demerits of other situations, seeking the good situation and avoiding the bad, he can make himself want to be in that sort of situation. The process of character-formation normally takes many years. It is good that it should do so. For a continuing choice over a period of time guarantees the serious intention of the agent. There may however be those who can change themselves (or allow themselves to be changed through a conversion) in a very short space of time. All they have to do subsequently is to remain the same. In the process of character-formation a man is of course helped by the society in which he moves, and clearly in general the Church is an organization which, through its life of worship and instruction, helps men to do the right actions and have the right attitudes. Hence pursuing the way involves church membership.[1] It is however the case that sometimes man is so beset by bad desires (the legacy of Original Sin—see p. 145) that all the effort in the world may not enable him finally to eliminate them and so make himself fully suited for Heaven. The Christian Creed, in assuring such a man of good will of a place in Heaven, in effect assures him that in the next life, if not in this, God will eliminate the bad desires.

However, not all men who seek to do what is good pursue on Earth the Christian way; for, on the Christian view, they have a false idea of

---

[1] Christianity has usually insisted on the doctrine that (because of Original Sin—see p. 145, n. 1) no man can attain salvation without the help of God's grace. Clearly a man needs the help of his fellow Christians both to know about the Christian way and to begin to follow it; and help of the Church in order to continue to follow it (since following it involves practising it within the Church). Christianity can therefore give content to this doctrine by holding that other Christians and the Church are the channels of grace. On the desirability of a man being helped or hindered by his fellows in the development of his character, see *The Existence of God*, pp. 187–96.

what the good life consists in. It may not ever have occurred to such a man that he has any duty to pursue religious investigation; or if he does pursue it, through acquiring misleading evidence or incorrect inductive standards, he may come to think that some other way, e.g. the Muslim one, is that which most probably will achieve the goals of religion. In following that way he will (in the Christian view, through error) have become a different kind of person from what he would have become, had he followed the Christian way. He learns to worship in a way which in fact does not honour God perfectly, by worshipping him for having qualities which are in fact second-rate ones; he learns to treat other people in ways which show inadequate respect and love, etc. If you think that God walked on Earth, you are likely to have a different kind of reverence for him than if you think of him merely as a philosopher's first principle; and also a different kind of reverence for men of whom God became one. A man's character being a matter of how he behaves, such a man will have a different character from the Christian's. Sincere practice of different religions (and even, to a small extent, sincere practice of different versions of a religion such as Christianity) produce different kinds of character. It follows that the sincere Muslim and Buddhist will be ill-fitted for life in the Christian Heaven; for they will not pursue naturally or want to pursue the occupations of the Christian Heaven.

Let us call a man who seeks to do only what is good, whether or not he has true beliefs about what is good, a man of good conscience; and a man who yields instead to desires which he believes to be bad, a man of bad conscience. Similarly, for the rest of this chapter I shall call a desire good if it is a desire for something believed to be good, whether or not that thing is good; and a desire bad, if it is a desire for something believed to be bad; and a choice good or bad in so far as it is a choice of something believed to be good or bad.

In the history of Christian theology there have been different views about the fate of men of good conscience with false religious beliefs. The view which seems finally to have prevailed is that a man who has tried to pursue the good but through ignorance has failed to do so, has implicit faith, *fides in voto* in Catholic terminology, which suffices for salvation. Where the Christian Gospel has not impinged on a man's conscience, such faith is enough. The slogan, *extra ecclesiam nulla salus* ('outside the Church there is no salvation') must be understood so as to include those of implicit faith as members of the Church.[1]

---

[1] This view would, I believe, be accepted by the majority of Protestants. It gained final Catholic recognition in the decree of the Second Vatican Council, *Lumen*

A loving God might indeed be expected to allow men to achieve salvation if they have sought the good but through no fault of their own failed to find the way which makes men best fitted for Heaven. However, it follows from earlier arguments that such persons would only enjoy Heaven when they had come to do naturally and to want to do the occupations of Heaven, e.g. to worship God for the right sort of qualities in the right sort of way. If they are to do this, they must first be informed of credal truths—what is the right way to worship, etc.; their search for religious truth which reached the wrong answer on Earth must be allowed to reach the right answer hereafter. Since, *ex hypothesi*, such men seek the good, as they begin to acquire true information about how to worship and serve, they will seek to worship and serve in that right way. But changing a way of behaving is not easy. There is, and must be, a certain stickiness about character. If a man has made himself the sort of person who does something naturally, to do anything else is going to be unnatural—to start with. Hence, changing a man's character involves a continuing choice over a period of time. In this case it involves his trying to bring about the good at which he was previously aiming in the ways in which he now realizes that it is to be achieved.[1] The faith which suffices for salvation requires true belief as well as right purpose.

An extreme example of a man of good conscience who had made himself thoroughly unfitted for the Christian Heaven would be a conscientious Buddhist. If Buddhism really involves the killing of all desire,[2] then clearly the Buddhist is not going to fit into the Christian Heaven. For he will not be happy in the activities of

Gentium, 16. This declared that all men who strive to live a good life and who through no fault of their own 'do not know the Gospel of Christ and his Church . . . can attain to everlasting salvation'. This possibility is open not only to theists but to those who, through no fault of their own 'have not yet arrived at an explicit knowledge of God'.
This view is, I believe, that best consonant with the New Testament. See the saying of Jesus in Luke 12: 48, that the servant which did not know his master's will and did things worthy of a beating 'shall be beaten with few stripes', in contrast with the servant who knew the master's will and still did not do it, who 'shall be beaten with many stripes'. The point of the saying must lie in the contrast, not in the fact that the ignorant servant would have a small beating. The teaching of the parable of the Talents (e.g. Matt. 25: 14-30) seems also to be that what is required of man is to make what he can from what has been given to him, and it is natural to interpret it so as to include in what has been given to a man his religious knowledge.

[1] Aquinas writes that no one can attain to the vision of God 'except by being a learner with God as his teacher' and that 'a person becomes a sharer in this learning not all at once but step-by-step in keeping with human nature.' *Summa Theologiae*, 2a, 2ae, 2. 3.

[2] And I may have misunderstood it here.

knowledge-acquisition, worship, and service which are the occupations of the inhabitants of Heaven. For happiness involves being glad that you are doing what you are doing, i.e. doing what you want to be doing; and the Buddhist does not want to be doing anything. For a man to come to see that it was good that he should get himself to want things and then to get himself to want them might be very hard.

But granted that men of good conscience go to Heaven, what about men of bad conscience? Why should not a generous God give at their death to men of bad conscience, not merely true beliefs, but good desires, so that they too go to Heaven? And if God did this, there would be no need for a man even to try to pursue the good on Earth in order to go to Heaven, for a generous God would ensure that you get there anyway.

The answer to the question, why men of bad conscience do not go to Heaven, requires an understanding of the nature and desirability of human choice.

Although young children have often not reached this situation and (as we shall see later) the old may sometimes have passed beyond this situation, there is a stage in a normal man's life at which he reaches what I may call the normal situation of choice. In this situation he has moral perceptions—he sees some actions as morally good (and some of those as obligatory), other actions as morally bad (and some of those as obligatory not to do). Of course his moral judgements may not always be the right ones—he may fail to see of some morally worthwhile acts that they are morally worthwhile. But nevertheless he does have moral perceptions. If a man believes that it is a good thing that he do some action, to some degree he will want to do it. If a man really thinks that some action is a good thing (and does not simply think that it is good by normally accepted criteria), he will to some extent want to do it. He may on balance prefer to be doing something else; but he will in a wide sense to some degree want to be doing it. For its goodness gives him reason for doing it and in recognizing its goodness he recognizes that he has such a reason.

A man will, however, also have other wants for lesser goods. In so far as a man wants to do some action, he will believe that it is in some way a good thing that he do it. For if he wants to do the action, he will want it because (he believes) there is something good about it. The man who wants to steal a car, (rightly) regards it as in some way a good thing that he possess the car. For possession of what gives pleasure is good. The trouble is of course that it is more good for other reasons that he refrain from stealing.

A man has to choose between what he sees as over-all the best action to do and what he regards as lesser goods. In this situation, it is often said, the strongest desire wins. But if one calls a desire strongest if and only if it is the one on which the man eventually acts, that is a very uninformative tautology; and on any other criterion of 'strongest desire', it is often false. A natural way of measuring strength of desire, is that a desire is strong in so far as it needs much effort to act against it. Sexual desires are often strong, whether or not men often act on them, because men have to struggle hard not to act on them. In this latter sense of strength of desire, a man's situation is indeed one in which there are desires of different strengths to do actions; and also one where he sees the actions as having different degrees of worth. The ordering by strength and the ordering by perceived worth may not be the same. The man has to choose whether to resist strong desires in order to do the morally good action, or to yield to them.

Now men come into existence with a limited range of choice, a limited set of good and evil actions which are for them live possibilities. By our choices (encouraged or frustrated by our bodily condition, mental state, environment, upbringing, friends, and enemies) we shift the range of possible choice. By good choices this time, there come within our range possibilities for greater good next time and some evil choices are no longer a possibility. Conversely, by bad choices this time there come within our range possibilities for greater evil next time and some good choices are no longer a possibility. Further, many of men's strongest desires are for lesser goods, i.e. for the bad. (This is part of what is involved in Original Sin.) Without effort men will slide towards the bad.

So a man who chooses the good may not do the good action naturally; he may have struggled against his strongest desire in order to do it. But, as we saw earlier, we are so made that what we have to struggle to do to start with will eventually become natural. That is, a man's desire to do it will become his strongest desire (as measured by the strength of resisting it).

However, a man may yield to bad desires against his better judgement. Now those who (by yielding to such a bad desire) reject a good desire, will have such good desires again. But if they systematically resist desires of a certain kind, they will gradually become the kind of person to whom such desires do not occur with any force. Those who refuse to give to charity once, may have a fit of conscience and give more next time. But those who systematically refuse to give, come no longer to regard it seriously as a good thing to give. Giving passes out of the range of their possible choice. A man who never resists his desires, trying to do the action which he perceives over-all to be the best, gradually allows what he does to be determined entirely by the strength of his desires (as measured by the difficulty of resisting them); that is, he eliminates himself (as an agent doing the action of greatest perceived worth or allowing himself to be overcome by strong desire to do an action of lesser worth, or simply choosing between actions of equal perceived worth). There is no longer a 'he'; having immunized himself against the nagging of conscience, the agent has turned into a mere theatre of conflicting desires, of which the strongest automatically dictates 'his' action.

Now far be it from me to say that that has happened to any man whom I have ever met; there is a lot more latent capacity for good in most people than appears on the surface. Nevertheless it is a possibility that a man will let himself be so mastered by his desires that he will lose all ability to resist them. It is the extreme case of what we have all often seen; people increasingly mastered by desires so that they lose some of their ability to resist them. The less we impose our order on our desires, the more they impose their order on us.

We may describe a man in this situation of having lost his capacity to overrule his desires, as having 'lost his soul'. Such a man is a mere collection of bad desires. He can no longer choose to resist them by doing the action which he judges to be overall the best thing to do. He has no natural desire to do the actions of Heaven and he cannot choose to do them because he sees them to be of supreme worth. There is no 'he' left to make that choice. Perhaps God could make the choice for him, give him a strong desire to do the good, and annihilate all other desires in him. But that would be imposing on an agent something which, while he was still capable of choosing between actions in virtue of their worth, he had in effect chosen not to do—by yielding so continually to temptation. Free will is a good thing; and for God to override it for whatever cause is to all appearances a bad thing.

It might be urged that no man would ever be allowed by God to reach such a state of depravity that he was no longer capable of choosing to do an action because of its overall worth. But in that case God would have prevented men from opting for a certain alternative; however hard a man tried to damn himself, God would stop him. It is good that God should not let a man damn himself without much urging and giving him many opportunities to change his mind, but it is bad that a man should not in the all-important matter of the destiny of his soul be allowed finally to destroy it. Otherwise the situation would be like that of a society which always successfully prevented men who would otherwise live for ever, from committing suicide. A society certainly has no right to do that; and plausibly even God has no analogous right to prevent men destroying their own souls.

It may be said that God should not allow a man to damn himself without showing him clearly what he was doing. But a man who simply ignored considerations of worth and gave in continually to his strongest desire, could hardly fail to realize that he was becoming merely a theatre of conflicting desires. He might not know the depth of the happiness which he was losing, nor that it would be prolonged for ever in Heaven; he would however know that he was choosing not to be a worthwhile kind of person.

Strangely, it would not necessarily help a man to attain the happiness of Heaven if God did make it crystal-clear to him that Heaven existed and provided happiness for the good. For, as we saw earlier, in the Christian view the life of Heaven is a way of life which (although crowded with difficulties) begins on Earth. Now if a man did not in any way seek such a life on Earth, why should he seek it if he comes to learn that it can go on for ever and provide deep happiness? Either because he wants to live forever or because he wants the happiness. But while a man is seeking to live the good life for those reasons, he will not find the happiness of Heaven. For the happiness of Heaven is not just happiness. It is, as we have seen, a special kind of happiness. It is a happiness which comes from doing actions which you know to be supremely good because you want to be doing those supremely good actions. A man who sought the happiness of Heaven for *its* own sake could not find it, while that was his goal; for it is the happiness which comes from doing certain actions for *their* own sake. The happiness of Heaven is a happiness which comes to those who are seeking not it[1] but the well-being of the life and situation on which it is based. This, I suggest, is the truth at which those men were getting who claimed that it was wrong for a man to seek his own salvation (see pp. 137 ff.). There is nothing wrong in seeking one's own salvation; what is wrong, is trying to seek the happiness apart from the pursuits of Heaven.

True, the news of the happiness of Heaven might provide an initial incentive for a bad or weak-willed man to pursue the good way, which he might later come to pursue for better reasons. (Heaven and

---

[1] See Christ's saying: 'He that findeth his life shall lose it; and he that loseth his life for my sake shall find it.' Matt. 10: 39.

Hell have often been preached for this purpose.) But clearly, if you encourage a man to pursue happiness (or everlasting life), there is quite a chance that he will continue to do so. In this way, by pursuing happiness (or everlasting life) he might fail to find the happiness which we might otherwise have got.[1] Also, there are good reasons other than to provide an incentive for the bad why God should tell men about Heaven. The news of Heaven could, for example, show men that God was good and so provide further reason for giving particular content to the good life—that is, for worshipping God. It could also provide encouragement for those who to some extent sought to live the good life anyway, to know that they could go on doing so forever under circumstances where the obstacles to living that life had been removed, and in a situation where it was supremely worthwhile to be. It would also provide good reason for men to encourage other men to pursue the way that leads to Heaven.

Perhaps the best compromise would be for God to let men know that there is *some chance* of their going to Heaven if they lead a good life (and of 'losing their soul' if they lead a bad life), but only some chance—so as to avoid to some extent the danger of men pursuing Heaven for the wrong reason and so losing it. And indeed the knowledge-situation of most men in most societies has been just this. True, in our secular society a man might not know even that. Yet, as we have already seen, that is not necessarily a bad thing; and also there is the most important point that if one insists that agents have to know that there are such chances before they can be deprived of Heaven, this would have the consequence that God would have to promulgate the Gospel independently of the activities of men. If men, in particular a church, are to make known the possibility of Heaven, there must be those who otherwise (if men fail in their duty to make known that possibility) would live in total ignorance of the possibility. It is good that the fate of men should depend in small part on the activity of other men, that men should carry the enormous responsibility of the care of the souls of others.[2]

I conclude that the Christian Creed has the resources to explain

---

[1] Recall the concluding verses of Christ's parable of Dives and Lazarus. Dives, in Hell, asks Abraham to send Lazarus to warn his five brothers to change their life-style lest they go to Hell. He says to Abraham: 'If someone goes to them from the dead, they will repent.' But Abraham replies: 'If they hear not Moses and the prophets, neither will they be persuaded if one rise from the dead.' Luke 16: 29 f.

[2] On this see *The Existence of God*, pp. 187–96.

how a good God might well allow a man to put himself beyond the possibility of salvation, of attaining Heaven.[1]

So much for the Christian account of how pursuit of the Christian way will lead to salvation for the pursuer, and failure to pursue it (except through non-culpable ignorance) will lose it.[2] The pursuit of the way will make a man in the Lutheran sense a man of faith, in the Catholic sense a man of faith formed by love, and so the sort of man to whom God gives salvation.

The Christian Explanation of how Pursuit of the Christian Way Leads to the Achievement of its Other Purposes

How will pursuit of the Christian way attain the second goal of religion, salvation for others? Part of a man's pursuing the Christian way will involve his ministering to the earthly needs of others— helping to give them health and company and worthwhile work. A man concerned for the well-being of others will seek these things for them, and his doing so will be helping to provide them with a temporary, very limited, but nevertheless important aspect of salvation. But a man truly concerned for the well-being of others will seek for them above all that deep and long-term well-being which is the core of salvation and which is the natural extension and deepening of their earthly well-being. Hence another part of a man's pursuing the Christian way will involve his preaching the Gospel to others, i.e. telling them, after study, what the Universe is like, how to live a worthwhile life, how to obtain forgiveness, and how thereby to obtain salvation; and giving them, after study, reasons for believing

---

[1] Some traditional answers as to why a good God might allow this, seem to me unsatisfactory; see, for example, St. Thomas Aquinas, *Summa contra Gentiles*, 4. 93. My own answer is, I hope, more satisfactory. Because of the unsatisfactory nature of past answers to this question, some Christians in this century have adopted the universalist view that in the end all go to Heaven. See, for example, John Hick, *Death and Eternal Life* (London, 1976). This view has been held in other centuries too, e.g. by Origen in the third century AD. The universalist view seems to be unsatisfactory for the reason given on pp. 154 f.

[2] There are problems about the plausibility—given the goodness of God—of traditional Christian doctrines about the fate in the after-life of those in categories intermediate between the good and the bad, e.g. the fate of those who pursue the good but with limited dedication. There is the connected issue of the ultimate fate of those who attain or lose Heaven. Can the inhabitant of Heaven lose his good character, and does the man who has lost Heaven suffer endless physical pain? These problems are not so central to my concern in the main body of this chapter, of making plausible (within the framework of Christian doctrine) the claim that pursuit of the Christian way would lead to Heaven. I discuss the other problems briefly in the Appendix to this chapter.

what he tells them. Further, a man's pursuit of the way will be an example which will encourage others to follow. Men sometimes begin to practise religion when they become parents, in order to set an example to their children; presumably often in the hope that their children copying them may acquire salvation. Believing that pursuit of the way is likely to attain salvation for the pursuer, and knowing that ways of life are contagious, that children are likely to imitate parents, a man pursuing the way will believe that as others are likely to copy him, his pursuit of the way will (indirectly) lead to their salvation. Also it seems to be a fairly central Christian belief that God hears the prayers of those who follow the way; and that he will answer them if they accord with his will, that is if he judges them desirable.[1] God seeks the salvation of all; but he will not pressure any, and so he will at most give encouragement and opportunity for men to seek their salvation. Although he desires that men seek their salvation, he will not necessarily give the maximum encouragement to some without prayer from others, for he desires to be guided by the prayers of others.[2] So the prayer of others will lead him to provide encouragement to men to pursue the way. But making petitionary prayer for the salvation of men is part of pursuing the way, and maybe God is more likely to listen to our prayer if we are pursuing the way in other respects also. Some Christian doctrine explicitly affirms this, and there are independent grounds within Christianity for supposing it. God is anxious to have friendship with man. Friendship involves giving special consideration to the friend. God is likely to give special consideration to the prayers of those who by their lives give special consideration to his wishes. (There is of course no guarantee that a man who pursues the religious way to secure the salvation of others will achieve his purpose. Whether that is achieved depends in part on those others. All that a man can do is by his teaching, life, and prayer, to ensure that the goal of their salvation is presented to those others as something worthy to be sought.)

It is evident how pursuit of a religious way will fulfil the third goal of religion—rendering due worship and obedience to God, who has called us to friendship with himself. The religious way involves such worship and obedience, and it shows what worship and obedience consist in. The Christian way involves certain kinds of worship (e.g. through the Eucharist) and obedience in keeping certain commandments etc. The claim is that it is revealed how to worship and obey.

---

[1] See e.g. Matt. 7: 7–11.
[2] On the point of petitionary prayer, see Eleonore Stump, 'Petitionary Prayer', *American Philosophical Quarterly*, 1979, **16**, 81–91.

The Nicene Creed

So far in this chapter I have been showing that the Christian theological system, the Christian creed in the wide sense, explains how pursuit of the Christian way will achieve the purposes of religion. My appeal has been to the tradition of Christian doctrine down the years, and where there have been conflicting elements in that doctrine, I have sometimes shown preference for one rather than another element as providing better explanation. The creeds to which Christians have been required in some sense to 'assent' are clearly of narrower scope. But most of the items in many such creeds are ones which explain how it is that pursuit of the Christian way will achieve the purposes of religion. I illustrate this by reference to the best known of all Christian creeds, the 'Nicene Creed', the creed approved at the Council of Chalcedon in AD 451 as the faith of the earlier councils of Nicaea and Constantinople. I shall take it as affirming propositions.

It begins with affirming that God is the Creator of all things—'God the Father Almighty, maker of Heaven and Earth and of all things visible and invisible'. That explains worship and obedience being owed to God, and so pursuit of the Christian way involving seeking to render such worship and obedience.

It then goes on to affirm the oneness of the incarnate Jesus Christ with God ('one Lord Jesus Christ, only begotten Son of God, begotten of the Father before all ages, Light from Light, True God from True God, begotten not made, One in substance with the Father, by whom all things were made'). That oneness helps to show us the kind of God to worship and on whose nature to meditate, and gives abundant additional grounds for worship, and gives reason to suppose that God in Christ could redeem the world. The Creed then goes on to affirm that Christ did become man and so did redeem the world—that 'for us men and for our salvation he came down from Heaven, and was made flesh by the Holy Spirit of the Virgin Mary, and became man. He was crucified also for us under Pontius Pilate. He suffered and was buried.' The resurrection and ascension is God's acceptance of that redeeming act and the evidence that God has intervened in history and that Christ's redeeming act has been efficacious—'On the third day·he rose again, in accord with the scriptures, and ascended into Heaven, and sits on the right hand of the Father.' The fate of men will depend on their conduct—'Christ will come again with glory to judge the living and dead.' Hence a man's destiny depends on whether or not he follows the way. There will be an ultimate victory for goodness on Earth, which is ground for striving to improve things ('of his Kingdom, there will be no end').

The Creed develops in embryo the doctrine of the Trinity, by affirming the divinity of God the Holy Spirit ('The Holy Spirit, the Lord and Giver of Life, who proceeds from the Father and the Son, who with the Father and the Son together is worshipped and glorified').[1] Thus it gives information about the divine nature unattainable by mere philosophical reflection unaided by revelation, and tells us the sort of God who is to be worshipped. In affirming that the Spirit 'spoke through the prophets' it affirms the basic reliability of the message of the Old Testament prophets in providing information about God and guidance on how to live.

It then affirms that the Christian way is to be led through belonging to the 'one Holy Catholic and Apostolic Church' and it specifies the means of the entry to that church—'one baptism for the remission of sins'. It affirms that diligent pursuit of the way will attain its goal— 'the resurrection of the dead, and the life of the world to come'.

The Nicene Creed thus provides a justification for supposing that pursuit of the Christian way will attain the purposes of religion.

The Belief Needed for Pursuit of a Religious Way

A man pursues a religious way in order to attain the goals or purposes of religion. We saw in Chapter 1 that you can only do an action to achieve some purpose if you believe that it is at least as probable that you will achieve that purpose by doing that action as by doing any rival action. This simple formula needs to be made complicated to deal with the case where an agent is endeavouring to fulfil more than one purpose. But we can ignore this complication here, for religions of any apparent depth unanimously teach that their goals are going to be attained only by men who pursue them to the exclusion of other goals (i.e. pursue other goals only in so far as their pursuit does not conflict with pursuit of religious goals). If you do not work very hard but do other things instead, you may still pass your earthly exams. But if you do not put your heavenly goals before other goals, you will not achieve the heavenly goals. This is because, on the Christian view, you will not have developed a character which fits you for Heaven.

---

[1] The doctrine of the Trinity is in effect stated here for it follows from Father, Son, and Spirit all being worshippable that all are God; although each of the three is not called a 'person'. The formal doctrine of the Incarnation, as formulated by the Council of Chalcedon in AD 451, is however only adumbrated in the Nicene Creed—since Christ is not explicitly stated to have two natures in one person.

So to pursue a way in order to achieve the purposes of religion, a man needs to believe that it is at least probable that pursuit of that way will attain those goals as that pursuit of any other way will. It would not merely be foolish or irrational, but logically impossible to pursue a religious way *in order to* obtain a certain goal, if you believed that pursuing the way would make you less likely to obtain the goal than you would otherwise be. I may not believe that pursuit of the Christian way is very likely to obtain my salvation, but I can still pursue it (and do so rationally) in order to obtain my salvation, if I believe that pursuit of no other way, e.g. the Buddhist way or the Muslim way, is more likely to obtain my salvation. Faced with a choice of six roads, I may not think it very likely that any named one leads to London; but I may still take one hopefully in order to get to London unless I think it more likely that a different road leads to London. In future, for the sake of simplicity of exposition, I shall assume that a man believes that one way is more likely to obtain his goal than is any other, and ignore the possibility that he believes that each of a number of ways is equally likely to obtain that goal. Hence I shall phrase the belief which a man needs in order to pursue a way as the belief that pursuit of his way is more likely to attain his goal than is pursuit of any other way.

The belief then which a man needs for his pursuit of the religious way is a means-end belief, a belief about a certain means (more probably than any other means) leading to the attainment of a certain end. But, as we saw in Chapter 1, means-end beliefs seldom stand on their own. They derive from more theoretical beliefs about what the world is like. Even the belief that following a certain road in my car will get me to London will derive from more theoretical beliefs—e.g. that I am now at Keele, that this road leads from Keele to London, that there are no holes and other obstacles in the road or bandits on the way, that the road will stay there until I get to London, that I have or can get enough petrol in my tank, etc., etc. Means-end beliefs seldom stand on their own; they normally derive from and get their justification from other beliefs which fit together into a system, some of whose elements are not mere means-ends beliefs. One could have means-ends beliefs which received little justification from more theoretical beliefs. I could believe that putting 20p in a certain slot will lead to my getting a bar of chocolate without having any belief about how this goal is achieved (i.e. how the machine works). The former belief could be based solely on past experiences of doing a similar thing. Even here, though, more theoretical beliefs seem to operate. My means-end belief must be reinforced by a general belief that machines do not normally disintegrate. But a belief that pursuing a certain route will obtain salvation is not going to be based on past experience that following such a way has yielded salvation before—there are no available statistics on the proportion of those following some religious way in the past who have attained their salvation (or either of the other purposes of religion). Since there are no such statistics, a man's means-end belief about the consequences of pursuing a religious way needs a basically theoretical justification, in terms of some creed from which it follows that pursuing the way will achieve certain purposes; and the creed itself needs to be justified in terms of basic beliefs. That is, intuitively, we would judge that if a man's means-end belief is to be rational$_2$ (see p. 46) it must be based on a creed which is based on experience. However, since all that is needed in respect of a means-end belief is belief that it is more probable that the way in question will attain the purposes of religion than that some other way will, all that is needed in respect of belief in a creed is belief that it is more probable that that creed is true than that any rival creed is true, a rival creed being one which justifies the pursuit of a different religious way.

It is because religions have somewhat similar goals that they are in competition and that this sort of justification is needed. However, in writing this, I am ignoring here the important complication that the goals are only *somewhat* similar. As I pointed out in Chapter 5, not all religions offer the same package. They do not all offer forgiveness from God. And they offer very different sorts of after-life. What exactly Buddhism's Nirvana is, is very unclear, but what is clear is that it is rather different from the Heaven which Christianity offers. I suggested (p. 135) that friendship with God is a very attractive aspect of the latter. If a man feels that one form of salvation is much more worth attaining than another, it follows from the results of Chapter 1 that he needs less in the way of belief that the way to pursue the former will attain its goal than he would otherwise do. If he believes that the Christian Heaven is more worth attaining than the Buddhist Nirvana, he can still pursue the Christian way to attain the former even if he believes that it is more likely that pursuit of the Buddhist way will attain its goals (including Nirvana) than that pursuit of the Christian way will attain its goals (including the Christian Heaven). However, although important, I do not think that men's judgements about the worth of the different goals offered differ so much as greatly to affect their conduct. Most men would be very happy if their conduct brought about salvation (and the other goals of religion) in any of the forms which different religions offer. What determines men's behaviour is not their beliefs about the different worths of the salvation offered, but their beliefs about the likelihoods of different creeds being true and so beliefs about the likelihoods of the different religious ways attaining their somewhat similar goals.

It follows that to pursue the Christian way one does not need to believe that it is more probable than not that there is a God; only to believe that this proposition together with the other credal propositions of Christianity is more probable than the total creed of any other religion, including a religion such as classical Buddhism which includes the proposition that there is no God (in the theist's sense). The other religious creeds with which the Christian Creed is contrasted will include non-Christian religions practised by millions, deviant forms of Christianity practised by few, and other religions theoretically alternative to Christianity but practised by no one. One who pursues the Christian way thus needs what I called in Chapter 4 a weak belief in the Christian Creed.

I have now provided further specification of how the alternatives with which a creed is being contrasted are to be picked out. Alternatives to an item p in a creed are contrary propositions q, r, which together with the rest of the creed, entail that men ought to perform different actions, in the process of pursuing the goals of religion, e.g. worship in different ways, treat other men in different ways, seek religious guidance from different sources, etc. The sort of weak belief that a creed is true which is required for the practice of religion is (see p. 121) the belief that if one acts on the assumption that it is true, one is more likely to achieve the goals of religion than if one acts on any contrary assumption. Christian, Jewish, and Muslim creeds dictate different ways of worship, different views of God on which to pray and meditate in order to grow in understanding of the nature of things, and different ways of serving others—e.g. they encourage different patterns of family life. (To a much more limited extent even different versions of Christianity dictate different ways to worship, live, and grow in religious understanding.) To pursue the Christian way you need a weak belief in the Christian Creed, but I cannot see that you need a strong belief, a belief that the various items of the Creed are more probable than not. A man does not need to believe that pursuit of some way will attain some goal, in order rationally to pursue that way to get that goal. A man who thinks the goal supremely worth attaining will pursue the way despite considerable odds against attaining it.

It follows that the community of those pursuing a way ought to ask from their members for no more than weak belief. I wrote in Chapter 4 that the Christian Church has never attempted to clarify publicly the kind of belief which is necessary for faith. This is because it has been totally unaware of the unclarity and ambiguity involved in the notion of believing a creed. My arguments suggest that it ought to be asking only for weak belief. If you insist that to be a Christian, a man must believe that each of the propositions of the Creed is more probable than its negation, it is as though you are telling a man who needs a fortune and wishes to buy a lottery ticket in the hope of getting it, that he is only allowed to buy the ticket if he believes that the odds are in favour of the ticket winning. That seems unreasonable. Of course the Church requires of its intending members something else than weak belief— strong purpose, a commitment to the pursuit of the goals of religion. A church is a society for those who seek its high goals.

I should add that, although weak religious belief should suffice for church membership, it is doubtful if a church could survive and spread without being led by men of stronger belief. You often need deeper conviction to sell a product than to use it. So there may be a pragmatic case for a church to demand rather stronger belief from its officers. But that is only a matter of evangelical tactics, and will depend on circumstances.

How much in content (as opposed to strength) ought a Church to ask of its members in the way of belief? How big ought to be a creed, belief in the truth of which is a condition of church membership? Different religious beliefs mean different ways of worship and service. Within a church, however large a creed it has, there will always be some beliefs about which its members differ. Even within the highly conservative Roman Catholic Church of the late nineteenth and early twentieth centuries there were divergent views on many large issues, for example about whether unbaptised babies go to Hell (see Appendix), and also interestingly about which past declarations of the Church were infallible and so necessarily to be believed by church members. These different beliefs clearly suggested different kinds of conduct. For example, if you believe that unbaptised babies go to Hell it is hard to justify not stealing as many as you can and quickly baptising them.

Clearly it is good that a man work out for himself which way will attain the goals of religion. But, equally clearly, in all human inquiries and pursuits, no man can achieve much by himself. He needs to build on the results of others, and to encourage and be encouraged by others. No man can discover for himself, starting from scratch, which way will attain the goals of religion. He needs a church, a society which can tell him how to live so as to attain these goals, and encourage and help him to do so. A man can work things out for himself if there are rival societies with clearly distinguished accounts of the religious way, between which he can choose to which to belong; and he can work things out for himself within the society which proclaims basically a true way if there is scope within the general account of the way given by that society for working it out in more detail. So men need a church which points them basically in the right direction, if they are to have an effective opportunity to attain the goals of religion. If men of too diverse views are admitted to the church, there will not be enough community of agreement on how the way is to be pursued to provide a message to the world, and guidance and encouragement to members. Yet if a church insists on too much in the way of belief, it will exclude from membership men in basic sympathy with its aims, who would by following the way in church membership come to have a very similar understanding of the world and pursue a very similar course of life to those within the church, and who, if excluded from the church, will not come to have this understanding or pursue this way. Also, it will prevent men from working so much out for themselves, which latter is, other things being equal, a good thing. It is a matter for the church to judge when the benefits of opening the church to men who do not have what the church considers completely true beliefs outweighs the harm—both to potential members and to existing members. Many religions are revealed religions. They purport through Bible or Pope or Prophet to have divine guidance on the essentials of the faith, and so on the limits to tolerable credal eccentricity.

In the course of specifying the weak beliefs needed for church membership, a church needs to make clear (as it has not always made clear in the past) the alternatives with which those beliefs are being contrasted. These will be picked out as those contrary beliefs by which, if a man is guided, he (or others who would be influenced by him if he were in the church) would be less likely to attain the goals of religion. Clearly, true belief is always more likely to lead to attaining any goal than is false belief; and the church must only insist on weak belief in those propositions which it believes to be more probably true than alternatives. But if a man is guided by some such alternatives, his conduct (on what he meditates, how he worships, etc.) will not be *much* affected. The church ought to specify as alternatives with which its beliefs are being contrasted, only those by which if a man is guided he is likely seriously to endanger the attainment of the goals of religion by himself or others.

To take an example which I used before—the Council of Chalcedon declared that Christ was one person with two natures, divine and human. Clearly thereafter a Christian was expected to believe this in contrast to the monophysite view that Christ had only one nature and the Nestorian view that Christ was two persons, each with a nature, divine and human. But it needs to be made clear whether a Christian needs also to believe the Chalcedonian formula to be more probable than its negation, or more probable than any equally detailed new formula which used new philosophical terminology (other than 'person' and 'nature') to express the divinity of Christ. Or, to take another example, the Nicene Creed claims that (1) Christ 'will come again with glory to judge the living and the dead' (i.e. those who are alive when he comes and those who are by then already dead). The Church might make clear that a man needs to believe (1) in contrast to (2) 'Christ will not come again to judge anyone' and (3) 'Christ will come again, but he will judge only those who are then alive'. These were, I suspect, the alternatives to which historically (1) was introduced as a contrast. The Church might make it clear that a man does not need to believe (1) in contrast to its negation, or even to (4) 'Christ will come again when all men are dead. He will judge all the dead.' The Church might hold that a man who was guided by (4) would to all intents and purposes pursue the same religious way as a man guided by (1). Both would meditate on a similar understanding of God, see him as the judge of all men and prepare to meet him as judge of themselves. The difference which believing that some men would be alive when Christ came as judge would make to our understanding of God and to the way we worshipped and led our lives, might be thought a small one.

Conclusion

I have argued that pursuit of a religious way, such as the Christian way, in order to attain the purposes of religion, involves a weak belief, e.g. that there is a God who has certain properties and has done certain things and provided certain means of salvation. The pursuit of the Christian way may therefore appropriately be described as acting on the assumption that there is a God who has certain properties and has done certain things and provided certain means of salvation. For the pursuer is doing those actions which he would do if he had a stronger belief. In pursuing the way to attain his salvation or that of others or to ensure that God is properly worshipped and obeyed, he is acting on the assumption that if he pursues the way God will ensure that these purposes are achieved (e.g. that God will provide salvation for him, or make it available to others, or accept his worship). He is thus acting on the assumption that God will provide for him what he wants or needs. There is some possibility that the religious man could be mistaken, and he could fail to attain his purposes. Hence (see Chapter 4) his action may appropriately be described as putting his trust in God or committing himself to God. He is committing himself to pursuit of the way which, at least in a weak sense, he believes that God has ordained, to gain the goals of salvation (for himself or others), or the rendering of proper worship and obedience which, he believes in at least a weak sense, God has promised to those who pursue the way.

A man may put his trust in something which, on balance, he does not believe to exist. A man in prison may be told that he will be rescued by 'The Big Chief' from the outer yard of the prison, if he can get there at night. On balance the prisoner does not believe this rumour; he does not think there is any such Big Chief. But the rumour has some plausibility; and the prisoner has no other hope of escaping. So he steals a file, files away the bars of his cell, and squeezes through the cell window to get into the outer yard of the prison. He is liable to be punished when all this is discovered, unless by then he has succeeded in escaping. The prisoner is not inappropriately described as putting his trust in the Big Chief.

So pursuit of the Christian way needs a certain belief and we may describe pursuing the way guided by that belief as evincing faith in God, since it involves acting on the assumption that he will do for us what we want or need, where there is some danger that he may not.

Appendix on the After-Life

There are a number of issues not so central to my main concern, which I did not discuss in the main part of the chapter, concerning the plausibility, given the goodness of God, of traditional Christian doctrines about the fate of men in the after-life in categories intermediate between the good and the bad, and about the ultimate fate of those who attain or lose Heaven. It would be appropriate to comment on these issues further here.

First, there is the issue of the fate of those who in the course of their lives have made of themselves persons who on balance follow the good way as they see it but with imperfect dedication, whose wills are on balance directed towards the good but who regret the absence of other things not so good. The traditional Catholic view is that such persons go through Purgatory to be made pure, but eventually reach Heaven. The traditional Protestant view is that there is no Purgatory; those with enough faith go straight to Heaven; those without it are permanently deprived of Heaven. Now persons of imperfect goodness would certainly find Heaven tough going before it became enjoyable—unless God in some way moulded their character for them, suppressed their desires for inferior goods. Unless this happened, the after-life for these people would be at first purgatorial. They would need purging for a shorter or longer period of time until finally they got to Heaven. Protestantism must hold that God immediately gets rid of the inferior desires of such men, although they have not with full dedication chosen that this shall happen and thus worked out for themselves the consequences of their basic choice for good.

The difficulty with the Catholic view is that if such persons are really in an irreversible process (cannot backslide so as eventually to lose the possibility of Heaven), then the process of purging would seem not to involve any choice by the agent (of whether or not to go through a particular part of the process). In that case, it is not clear why a good God could not do whatever purging is necessary briefly and painlessly. If, however, the process of purging is something which the human agent himself has to effect, then in view of the necessary stickiness of character to which I referred (p. 151), it is understandable why the process of changing his character is going to take a man's time and effort. A man's earlier character would not be his *character* if it was so easy for him to change. But in that case it would seem that a man might continue to choose wrongly, to give in to desires for lesser' goods and thus be in the situation of the backslider on Earth who risks losing the possibility of Heaven. What the Catholic must claim is that because on balance such men have made a basic choice for good (although they have not fully worked out the consequences of that choice); while they do need to keep on choosing to go through this or that part of the process, nevertheless, however much they backslide they never (unlike the backsliders on

Earth) lose the possibility of choosing the good. In consequence they may purge themselves in a short time; they may, if they backslide, purge themselves in a long time; or they may, if they always yield to desires for lesser goods, stay in Purgatory forever. But they will never lose the possibility of Heaven.

When the Catholic doctrine is expressed in this way, both Catholic and Protestant doctrines seem morally unobjectionable. The Christian may either hold that God has revealed (through Bible or Church) that one of these doctrines is the true one, or may maintain a healthy agnosticism.

A more serious difficulty for both traditional positions concerns the fate of those children or adults who die with a half-developed character, lacking fixity of dedication to the good but with a certain amount of good will. To send them to Heaven or even Purgatory would involve making them not merely what they have not yet chosen to make themselves, but what in part they have chosen not to make themselves. It would involve changing a man's character against his will. That seems immoral. Yet, to deprive such persons permanently of Heaven seems bad, for there is good in them which, given time, they might choose to develop in such a way as to make them fitted for Heaven.

It may be claimed that there are no persons in this category; that all men whom God allows to die, have in effect chosen good or evil. That may be correct, but it does not seem too plausible when one considers the many who die in adolescence, the paradigm age of partly developed character. The tradition has sometimes claimed that some such persons go to Limbo (see below), a place suitable for those of poor moral sensibilities, incapable of enjoying the joys of Heaven. It may well be that there are persons who lack moral capacities of any depth, and for them Limbo seems a suitable fate. Yet it does rather seem that many who die with wills unfixed for good or ill nevertheless have in part the capacity for the higher joys. Hence it seems to me that there is scope for the Christian tradition to maintain that not all fates are sealed at death. Some persons may have the opportunity in some further world to work out further their ultimate destiny.

The New Testament certainly warns that the fate of many is sealed at death for good or ill, and that a man should live his life conscious that his own fate is likely to be so sealed. But it can hardly be said to contain a rigid and explicit doctrine of the fates of all categories. A healthy agnosticism on some of these issues would seem suitable for the Christian tradition.

The Role of Creeds

The next issue concerns the fate of babies who die without having any opportunity to exercise a choice between good and ill. The traditional answer, Catholic and Protestant, is that the fate of babies, as of all others, is sealed at death. If they are baptised, they go to Heaven. If not, they do not. Some Christians have held that unbaptised babies go to Hell, a place of endless physical pain. Others, more liberal, have suggested that they go to some intermediate state, Limbo, a pleasant and enjoyable state but one where the joys do not have the depth of those of Heaven. (The doctrine that children dying unbaptised but guiltless of serious actual sin, go to the *limbus puerorum*, was common in the Middle Ages, and espoused by, among others, St. Thomas Aquinas. See the brief reference in *Summa Theologiae*, 1a, 2ae, 89. 6.) A few, yet more liberal, Christian theologians have suggested that unbaptised babies are given some subsequent opportunity to attain Heaven.

Now one who does not have a character could, I think, have a character imposed upon him. Freed from bodily inclinations and other sources of temptation, and given knowledge of good, he will, I argued in *The Existence of God* (pp. 98–101 and 156 ff.) inevitably pursue it. And perhaps there is good in giving a man a perfectly good character from the start, as well as allowing him to develop it over time. So the suggested fate of the baptised babies is plausible. On the other hand, there seems nothing wrong in God sending unbaptised babies to Limbo rather than Heaven. Babies do not have a character capable of enjoying Heaven, any more than do goldfish. And there seems no more obligation on God to give them such a character than always to create men rather than goldfish. There is nothing wrong in God creating lesser beings capable of lesser joys, or keeping such in being, rather than making only persons fitted for the highest joys. (See *The Existence of God*, pp. 114 f., and the article by Robert Merrihew Adams on which those pages are based, 'Must God Create the Best?', *Philosophical Review*, 1972, **81**, 317–32.) Whereas there would be something horribly wrong in the unbaptised babies going to Hell.

Next, is it plausible to suppose that a good God would keep permanently in Heaven those who on Earth choose the good way? The traditional view is that the inhabitant of Heaven cannot lose his good character and so stays forever in Heaven. He cannot, on this view, lose his good character because God gives to him such a vision of himself as a result of which he sees so clearly what is good that he has no temptation to pursue any other way. I have argued (*The Existence of God*, pp. 98–101 and 156–60) that a man who sees what is good will only do what is bad if he gives in to bodily or mental forces which are really no part of him. So a man who has attained to Heaven by choosing the good despite such forces could only choose the bad again, if God allows him to be exposed to such forces again. The traditional answer follows from the claim that God does not allow an inhabitant of Heaven to be so exposed. It is not an implausible claim that he does not do so. There is good in men having a choice of destiny over the considerable period of a human life, but there is also good in their choice of the good leading to the final removal of temptation.

The final issue concerns the fate of those who have finally rejected the good. Given that the traditional answer supported in this chapter is correct, that such persons have ceased to be persons capable of enjoying Heaven, what is their fate? The majority answer of Christian theologians down the centuries (though not one incorporated in the Catholic creeds, such as the Nicene Creed), is that they are subjected to endless physical pain in Hell. Now, no doubt the bad deserve much punishment. For God gave them life and opportunity of salvation but they ignored their creator, hurt his creatures, damaged his creation, and spent their lives seeking trivial pleasures for themselves. But for God to subject them to literally *endless* physical pain (*poena sensus*, in medieval terminology) does seem to me to be incompatible with the goodness of God. It seems to have the character of a barbarous vengeance; whatever the evil, a finite number of years of evil-doing does not deserve an infinite number of years of physical pain as punishment. The all-important punishment is to be deprived of eternal happiness (this is the *poena damni* in medieval terminology)—a fact which Augustine, a firm proponent of the doctrine of endless physical pain, himself pointed out.[1] This deprivation, I have suggested in this chapter, is plausibly an inevitable fate of those who have finally rejected the good. It seems to me that the central point of New Testament teaching is that an eternal fate is sealed—at any rate for many—at death; a good fate for the good and a bad fate for the bad. This appears to be the main point of such parables as the sheep and the goats.[2] It is always dangerous to take literally too many minor details of parables (such as the punishment being αἰώνιος, about which theologians dispute whether it is properly translated 'everlasting').[3] Given the main point, there seem to be various possible

---

[1] St. Augustine, *Enchiridion*, Ch. 102.

[2] Matt. 25: 31-46.

[3] There are some sayings of Christ's which carry a suggestion that any punishment

fates for those who have finally rejected the good. They might cease to exist after death. They might cease to exist after suffering some limited physical pain as part of the punishment for their wickedness. Or they might continue to exist forever, pursuing trivial pursuits (as amusingly depicted in Bernard Shaw's *Man and Superman*), perhaps not even realizing that the pursuits were trivial.

will be limited. For example, there is the warning to men to be reconciled quickly with their adversaries lest they be thrown into prison: 'You shall by no means come out from there until you have paid the last penny.' (Matt. 5: 26). As John Hick comments (*Death and Eternal Life*, London, 1976, p. 244), 'Since only a finite number of pennies can have a last one, we seem to be in the realm of graded debts and payments, rather than of absolute guilt and infinite penalty.' John 3: 19 suggests that sin is its own punishment.

7

The Comparison of Creeds

WE saw in Chapter 2 that a man who seeks true beliefs must seek beliefs with a high degree of probability, and that to do this he must seek rational$_5$ beliefs, that is, beliefs which result from adequate investigation (adequate assembling and checking of evidence, adequate criticism of inductive standards, and adequate investigation into what, given those standards, the evidence really shows). We saw in Chapter 3 that there is a duty to pursue some religious inquiry into whether or not there is a God; and that it is a good thing to pursue such inquiry a lot further than duty demands. Many of the reasons for which I argued in Chapter 3 that it was good to pursue inquiry into whether or not there is a God, were to the effect that a true belief that there was a God would be a first step towards a true belief about how the goals of religion would be attained; it would help towards an understanding of the world and how we ought to live in it, and towards the attainment of a deep and permanent well-being. We have now seen in Chapter 6 that what is needed for the attainment of these goals is a fuller belief, that is, a belief that a more detailed creed is true. Although all that is needed to direct our action along a religious way is the belief that one such creed is more probable than all others, yet since we shall only surely achieve our goals if we are guided by a creed that is true, we are much more likely to achieve our goals the greater the probability of the creed by which we are guided. Hence, given that the goals of religion are abundantly worth seeking (as I argued in Chapter 5), it is of great importance that we pursue inquiry in the hope of establishing one creed as very much more probable than others. That is, we ought to seek true representative evidence, check our inductive standards, etc. in order to have a rational$_5$ belief about the relative probabilities of creeds. For seeking such a belief is, as we have seen, all we can do towards getting a true belief about which (if any) religious creed is the true one. Knowledge of which religious creed is true is also abundantly worth having in itself—

quite apart from the use to which it can be put. For, as I argued in Chapter 3, knowledge of the deepest reality is a great good.

I argued in Chapter 3 that a duty to pursue investigation into whether or not there is a God arose from two sources: first, there was a general duty on all men to discover whether or not their existence depends on a God, since if there is a God, they will owe him worship and obedience; and secondly, there was a more specific duty on anyone in some kind of parental situation or who was an expert in the field, to pursue religious investigation in order to give to others the resulting supremely worthwhile knowledge. Now if the results of any inquiry into whether or not there is a God show that it is improbable that there is a God, there cannot be any general duty of the first kind to pursue further religious investigation. For if a man believes that it is improbable that there is a God, it follows that there is no duty of worship and obedience binding on him; and so no duty to discover how to worship and obey. Yet if a man concludes that it is probable that there is a God, it follows that he has a duty to worship and obey binding on him, and so he must investigate how best to fulfil it; and that involves investigating the claims of different creeds. However, I think that the expert or the person in a parental situation may still have a duty to compare creeds, even if on his evidence it is more probable than not that there is no God. For his duty is to show to others how best to attain goals of supreme worth. He must investigate whether non-theistic ways to salvation are likely to attain that salvation. And also those dependent on him need to know as surely as they can, even if it is probable that there is no God and non-theistic ways are unlikely to attain their goal, which is the way most likely to attain its goal. Even if (see p. 75) the agricultural biochemist believes that on balance it is improbable that more food can be got out of the land, if the people are very short of food, he still has a duty to investigate which method of fertilizing, irrigation, or crop rotation is more likely to produce an increase of yield (in the hope that his inquiries will show that one method is much more likely than any others to be successful). By analogy, if the religious investigator, who is an expert or in a parental situation, judges the goals of religion to be very worthwhile, it follows that he has a duty to pursue religious investigation even if he believes that it is not probable with respect to any one way that it will attain the goals of religion. So in these various circumstances it is a duty or at any rate a very worthwhile thing to investigate the relative probability of creeds, in order to produce a rational$_5$ belief about the relative probabilities of creeds, e.g. a belief that the Christian Creed is more probable than any rival creed which justifies a different religious way. The above conclusions about the duty to investigate the comparative probabilities of creeds hold, I urge, objectively for a man who has a certain belief about how probable it is that there is a God. If he does not support his beliefs about the comparative probabilities of creeds by proper investigation, they will not be rational$_5$. However, a man may not realize that these conclusions hold—e.g. although believing it probable that there is a God, he is conscious of no duty to investigate how God is to be worshipped. In that case, as in all cases where a man is unaware of a duty, he is not blameworthy for failure to investigate, and his beliefs about the comparative probabilities of creeds are rational$_3$, though not rational$_5$.

The process of showing the Christian Creed to be more probable than any rival creed which justifies a different religious way[1] can be analysed as needing three steps: first, a demonstration that it is probable to some degree on reasonably believed evidence that there is a God; secondly, a demonstration that it is more probable, if there is a God, that the other items of the Christian Creed are true than that the other items of some rival theistic creed are true; and thirdly, a demonstration that it is more probable that the Christian Creed as a whole is true than that any non-theistic religious creed is true.

The first task is the traditional task of natural theology and is far too big a subject to be discussed here. It was the subject of my earlier volume, *The Existence of God*. I concluded there that it is more probable than not that there is a God. But all that is necessary for weak belief in the Christian Creed is a much less probable belief—say, putting it loosely, that there is a significant probability that there is a God. For, given that, there is quite a chance that salvation may be had by pursuing one of the religious ways of theistic religions, since the attainment of salvation according to these religions consists in God providing that salvation (e.g. forgiveness and life after death).

---

[1] Having stated the task carefully at the beginning of the Chapter, I now express the task before the investigator in a looser way: 'showing the Christian Creed to be more probable than any rival creed . . .' in order to save the reader from over-complicated sentences. But to speak strictly, the task is not that. It is one thing to show that some belief is or is not probable on your present evidence. It is another thing to show that it is probable on as much evidence as you can readily obtain. The task of the investigator is to achieve a belief of the latter sort. (For the point of seeking more evidence, see Chapters 2 and 3, e.g. p. 72). However, in the case of a religious belief, disputes turn so often on what a given body of evidence shows. So showing what the evidence does show is always a major part of the investigator's task, and in practice his task often boils down to that stated in the text.

The next stage is to show that if there is a God it is more likely that the other items of the Christian Creed are true than that the other items of some rival creed are true. For given that there is a God, then if the other items of the Christian Creed are more probable than the other items of rival theistic creeds, the Christian Creed as a whole (item common with other theistic creeds plus different items) will be more probable than any other theistic creed as a whole (common item plus different items). We need to show that it is more probable that God became incarnate in Christ than that Muhammad was his chief prophet; that the way to worship regularly is by attendance at the Eucharist rather than by the five daily prayer-times, and so on. The choice between religious systems in these respects turns on a judgment about which is the true revelation of God. For the grounds for believing the other items of a theistic creed—that in this way God has intervened in history, that forgiveness is available in this way, that these are the fates for men in the after-life, that this is the way to live in this life—are normally that God has revealed these truths through the mouth of some human intermediary, whom we will call his prophet. I wish therefore now to discuss the kind of considerations which are relevant to assessing such claims to revelation. The discussion will be a brief discussion to indicate the kind of considerations which need to be investigated, rather than a thorough discussion of which is the true claim to revelation. I include the discussion to indicate the kind of investigation by which faith needs to be supported.

The Evidence of Revelation

A theistic religion claims that its prophet is a special messenger of God and that what he says about the nature of reality and how men ought to live is to be believed because it comes from God. It is also sometimes claimed that the prophet and his actions have eternal significance because of his special status. The Christian claim that Jesus Christ was both God and man who by his sacrificial life redeemed the world is obviously such a claim—indeed it is by far the strongest claim for divine intervention in human history made by any of the great religions.

Theistic religions are normally prepared to allow that God has spoken to men in a limited way through prophets other than their own unique prophet. Thus Islam is prepared to allow that God spoke to men through Jesus Christ. But the point is that, according to each religion, there is truth and falsity mixed in the deliverances of prophets other than its own, and that where there is dispute the sayings of its own prophet take precedence—for what he says is true without qualification (and, perhaps also, what he does is of unrepeatable significance).[1] If a religion claims that all prophets teach varying amounts of truth and falsity, and so purports to judge the worth of each prophet's teaching merely by considering what he says rather than the fact that he says it, that religion cannot be regarded in the traditional sense as a revealed religion, as teaching and supported by a revelation. For the grounds for believing any of what the religion asserts will not be that it has been revealed by God (for which in turn there is other evidence, including that other things which the prophet said are true); rather, the argument will always go the other way round—the grounds for believing that any of the things which a prophet teaches have been revealed by God are simply that they are true. A religion which claims a revelation in teaching claims that the prophet's message is to be believed, not because it can be known to be true independently of the prophet having said it, but because of the prophet's authority.[2]

So then, what is the evidence for claims that some prophet is in this way a special messenger of God? The traditional view down the centuries, advocated among others by Aquinas,[3] declared to be official Roman Catholic doctrine by the First Vatican Council[4] and classically expounded by Paley,[5] is that the evidence will be of various kinds but will include a central and crucial element of the miraculous.

In *Evidences of Christianity*, Paley argues that given that there is

[1] Occasionally, as in orthodox Judaism, it is claimed that there is more than one such prophet. I shall, however, in this chapter deal only with religions which claim that God revealed himself in a special way through just one such prophet. The application of the argument to more complicated cases should be apparent.

[2] Note that once a prophet is allowed to have the unique status, then through his word the unique status may be conferred on some other person, body or book. For example, if the prophet were to say 'whatever the church which I found teaches in such and such circumstances is true', it will follow from his saying this that whatever the church which he founds does teach in those circumstances is true. The different Christian denominations have of course tried to find this kind of commission in Christ's teaching.

[3] In *Summa Theologiae*, 2a, 2ae, 2. 9, ad. 3, and 2a, 2ae, 6. 1, Aquinas affirms that a man will rationally assent to some purported revealed truth if it has 'the authority of God's teaching confirmed by miracles' and 'what is greater, the inner inspiration of God inviting him to believe', i.e. in human terms, the plausibility of the doctrine proposed for belief.

[4] Vatican I, *Constitutio Dogmatica de Fide Catholica*, cap. 3 and *De Fide*, canons 3 and 4.

[5] W. Paley, *A View of The Evidences of Christianity* (first published 1794).

a God—who is, by definition, good—and that the human race lies in
ignorance of things important for them to know, it is *a priori* to some
extent to be expected that God would give a revelation to men. And
what things are these important things? If the arguments of this book
are correct, it is important for men to know the nature of the world
and man's place in it, how they ought to live, how deep long-term
happy well-being is to be achieved, how forgiveness is to be obtained
from God, how God is to be worshipped and obeyed. A revelation
such as the Christian revelation (as traditionally described) claims to
provide knowledge on all these matters. Paley however stresses—to
my mind totally disproportionately—the existence and nature of the
after-life at the expense of all other elements of revelation.[1]

Yet knowledge of all these things has great value, other than its
value in preparing men for the after-life. It is good that man should
understand the world, know how to live in it and how to obtain the
deepest well-being this Earth can provide; it is good too that man
should know how to worship and obey God and obtain forgiveness
from him—all this quite independently of the consequences in an
after-life for man of his doing these things. But it is also good that
man know how to obtain his eternal well-being.[2]

Men are capable of receiving such knowledge. But much of it could
not to all appearances be obtained by mere reflection on the natural
world. That God is three persons in one substance could hardly, if
true, be known to be true by such human reflection. I claimed, in *The
Existence of God*, that various phenomena, including chiefly very
general and publicly observable ones such as the orderliness of
nature, show the dependence of the world on a creator God. We
must, I argued, suppose him to be very powerful, wise, etc., if he is to
be able to bring about the existence and orderliness of the world; and
considerations of simplicity involve us inferring from 'very powerful
. . . etc.' to 'infinitely powerful . . . etc.' But it is hard to see how any
further details of his nature could be read off from the world. I have
no conclusive proof that this cannot be done. I simply appeal to the

---

[1] See Part III, Ch. 8. He writes of 'the great Christian doctrine of the resurrection of
the dead and of a future judgment', that 'other articles of the Christian faith, although
of infinite importance when placed beside any other topic of human inquiry, are only
the adjuncts and circumstances of this'.

[2] I emphasize again, however, the point made in the last chapter about the danger of
stressing and making it too well-known that the Christian way is a way to happiness
(rather than a way towards being in a supremely good situation doing supremely good
actions)—the danger that men might be encouraged to seek happiness rather than
goodness, and so lose the happiness.

apparent impossibility of seeing how it can be done; and to the fact that nobody today thinks that it can be done,[1] and that very few people in the past ever thought that it could be done. Likewise, mere reflection on the natural world could hardly show the details of how men ought to worship God, e.g. in the Eucharist on Sundays; or how forgiveness from God is to be obtained—through pleading the Passion of Christ. And so on.

Other such purported knowledge as is conveyed in revelations such as the Christian revelation, is purported knowledge of matters about which men produce arguments of a general philosophical character arising out of reflection on the natural world. That God is omnipotent, omniscient, etc., is, as we have seen, the subject of such argument. So too are the general principles of morality, such as that men ought to tell the truth, keep their promises, and show compassion. Now maybe all such arguments fail; it needs a detailed discussion of each case to show whether they do or not. However, I have argued in *The Existence of God* that arguments to show that there is a God omnipotent, omniscient, and perfectly free do work. And plausibly, reason can help to show claims about morality to be justified.[2]

However, if such knowledge of the omnipotence, omniscience, etc. of God and the general principles of morality can be obtained by natural means, it is evident that some men are too stupid to obtain the knowledge—the savage argues only to a much more lowly God—and some men will never reach that knowledge because of the climate of contrary opinion in which they grow up, the climate of an atheistic

[1] The claim that such doctrines as the Trinity could be authenticated without an appeal to revelation would not be made by modern radical Christians who wish to do without the notion of revelation in the above sense. They would say rather that these doctrines were not well-authenticated.

[2] For the reasons given above it seems to me that the Catholic tradition exemplified in Aquinas and the First Vatican Council was right to make its distinction between natural and revealed knowledge of God. (See p. 107.) Thus the First Vatican Council anathematized anyone who said 'that divine faith cannot be distinguished from the natural knowledge of God and morals, and that besides it is not required for divine faith that revealed truth be believed on the authority of God who reveals it.' (Vatican I, *De Fide*, canon 2.) However, I would add that among the evidence of God's existence is evidence of the miraculous in history (see *The Existence of God*, Ch. 12). And I would also claim that the First Vatican Council was wrong to hold that the existence of God can '*certainly* [*certo*] be known by the natural light of human reason from the things which are created' (*Constitutio Dogmatica de Fide Catholica*, cap. 2; my italics), if by 'certainly' is meant 'without there being the slightest ground for suspecting error'. I do not think that the arguments for the existence of God, although they make their conclusions probable, give it that degree of certainty. See *The Existence of God*.

authority which I sketched on pp. 60 f. It is sometimes through men yielding to bad desires, either to teach things which they do not really believe (in the interests of their state or party, church or career), or not to investigate further things which they are told on authority (through fear or laziness), that men come to hold beliefs and climates of opinion develop. Hence sin plays a role in moulding belief.

So the detailed truths of creeds will either not be known at all to men or (through men's stupidity, ignorance, and sin) be known only with difficulty. Yet these are the truths which are of crucial importance if men are to make themselves good men (true specimens of humanity), men worthy to obtain everlasting well-being. If there is a God (who is by definition good), he might to some degree be expected to intervene in history to reveal these truths which men could not discover for themselves and to give his authority to those to which reason pointed with insufficient force, for he has good reason to do this. There is also the reason to expect a revelation, not merely by teaching but by a human life, which the Christian tradition has always stressed but which Paley does not. Human sin and corruption need atonement. This is a primary reason why, on the traditional Christian doctrine outlined in the last chapter, a revelation in the form of a person who lived a sacrificial life was to be expected.[1]

So, given that there is good evidence that there is a God,[2] there is some reason *a priori* to expect that there will be a revelation. What historical evidence would show that it had taken place on a certain occasion? It is a basic principle of confirmation theory that evidence confirms a hypothesis (i.e. adds to its probability) if and only if that evidence is more to be expected if the hypothesis is true than it would otherwise be.[3] So given some prior probability that God would reveal himself in history, the evidence of history that he has done so will be such as is to be expected if the hypothesis is true, and not otherwise.

[1] Of course there may be some form of incoherence in supposing that God could become man; whether that is so would need a very substantial discussion. If there would be such an incoherence, God could not himself make atonement for the sins of men and this reason for expecting a revelation would not apply.

[2] The evidence may include some slight evidence of violations of the laws of nature and other faint footprints of divine intervention in history. Analogously, the evidence that Jones has visited a house may include (literal) footprints in the garden which could have been made by him (i.e. the prints were of the size of his shoes). But for other evidence we would not conclude that he has visited the house. Yet once we have reached that conclusion, we can then justifiably interpret the footprints as his, and so conclude which parts of the house he visited, e.g. the garden.

[3] On this see *The Existence of God*, Ch. 3, and especially pp. 67 f., for the formal statement of this principle.

The obvious kind of evidence, then, will be teaching such as God would be expected to give and actions such as God would be expected to do, of a kind and in circumstances in which they would not be expected to occur in the normal course of things.

What sort of teaching about the matters which man needs to know would God be expected to give through a prophet? Obviously teaching which is true and deep. Although the teaching itself must be true, it might however need to be embodied in the false historical and scientific presuppositions of the prophet's day if it is to be understood. For instance, suppose a prophet was teaching in a culture which believed that the world consisted of a flat and stationary earth surrounded by a heavenly dome in which Sun, Moon, planets, and stars moved. God wishes through the prophet to convey the message of the total dependence of the world on God. How is he to announce his message? There seem three possible ways. The prophet might say: 'It is God who holds the flat earth still and moves round it the heavenly lights.' Or he might say: 'Whatever the true scientific description of the world, it is God who brings about that state of affairs which that description describes.' Or he might begin by giving a true scientific account of the world and then say that God brings about that world. But if he is to announce his message in the third way, the religious truth can only be announced after a complete process of scientific education. And even if he is to announce it in the second way, the message will only be understood by a people who have done quite a lot of philosophical abstraction. They would have to have understood the possible falsity of most of their common-sense science, and have got used to the abstract concepts of states of affairs which might not be describable, and descriptions which might not apply to things. If the prophet's message is to be understood by a primitive culture, it is the first way of teaching which would have to be used. And unless one thinks that divine revelation can be given only to sophisticated peoples, that means that when a divine revelation is made to a primitive people, there is a distinction to be made between the prophet's message and the scientific and historical presuppositions in terms of which it is expressed.[1] This distinction would need to be made by a later and less

---

[1] This point has been made by many Christian theologians down the centuries. The past four centuries have seen it widely accepted in Christian theology but it was not unknown for theologians of earlier centuries to make it. For example, Novatian (*De Trinitate*, 6) claims that the Old Testament uses anthropomorphic language about God (talks of him as having hands, feet, etc.) 'not because God was like that but because in that way the people could understand . . . Therefore it is not God that is limited but the perception of the people is limited.' St. Hilary of Poitiers makes a similar point,

primitive society which knew a bit more about science and history, in order for it to see what was the religious message clothed in the false presuppositions. And of course if the later society was not sophisticated enough, it might fail to make the distinction, and so suppose the science and history to be part of the prophet's message. This could lead to its rejecting the message on the grounds that the science and history were false (the rational$_1$ reaction); or, worse (the irrational$_1$ reaction) adopting the old science and history (and rejecting the alleged advances here of more recent times) on the grounds that the prophet's message was true. It will, I hope, be unnecessary to give many historical examples of such reactions.

One all too sadly obvious modern one is the example of the different reactions to Darwin's theory of evolution. Christianity has regarded the Old Testament as in a sense and to a degree licensed by Christ. He took it largely for granted in his teaching, and the Church which he founded proclaimed it (with the exception of the laws about ritual and sacrifice) as God's message. The Old Testament in telling in Genesis 1 and 2 the Creation stories seems to presuppose that animal species came into being a few thousand years ago virtually simultaneously. The theory of evolution showed that they did not. So some rejected Christianity on the grounds that it taught what was scientifically false, and others rejected the theory of evolution on the grounds that it conflicted with true religion. But it seems odd to suppose that the religious message of what is evidently a piece of poetry was concerned with the exact time and method of animal arrival on the Earth, or that that was what those who composed it were attempting to tell the world. Their message concerned, not the details of the time and method of animal arrival, but the ultimate cause of that arrival.[1] To make the point that there is a distinction between a prophet's religious message and its scientific and historical presuppositions is not to deny that it may not always be easy to disentangle the message from the presuppositions, or to express it in more modern terms. One

---

speaking of the Bible 'enlightening our intelligence by using terms commonly understood' (*De Trinitate*, XII, 9). And Aquinas, trying to resolve a conflict between the book of Genesis and Aristotelian science, claimed that Genesis expressed the basic truth in an inaccurate way because 'Moses was speaking to an ignorant people' and needed to make assumptions which were strictly false in order for his basic point to be understood; see *Summa Theologiae*, 1a, 68. 3.

[1] See e.g. Alan Richardson, *Genesis 1–11* (London, 1953). Richardson calls the early Genesis stories 'parables'. The best way to see the points which these stories were intended to make is to contrast them with other 'creation' stories circulating in the Near East in the first millenium BC.

obvious step in going about this task is for the investigator to inquire into the circumstances of the prophet's utterance and see what he was denying, and contrast this with the assumptions about more mundane matters shared by the prophet and his opponents.

So then, with this qualification, the prophet must teach what is true. Must he teach only what is true? Can there be falsity mixed with his teaching? No: the whole body of what the prophet announces as his message must be true, for the reason given earlier: that it purports to be God's announcement to man of things beyond his power to discover for himself. However if a clear distinction could be made between the prophet's message and other things which he said but for which he did not claim any special authority, there is no reason to require that the latter be true.[1]

The prophet's teaching must be, not merely true, but deep. Men need moral teaching and instruction about the nature of reality which is not readily available to them.

What would be the evidence that the prophet's teaching is true? First, none of what he teaches must be evidently false. His teaching on morality, for example, must not involve his telling men that they ought to do what is evidently morally wrong—the prophet who recommends cheating and child torture can be dismissed straight away.[2] Likewise no factual teaching of the prophet must be proven false. If the prophet teaches that, whatever men do, the world will end in exactly thirty years time, and the world fails to end then; the prophet must be rejected.[3] Secondly, such parts of the prophet's

---

[1] Although there seems little ground for making that kind of distinction within the things which Jesus Christ is reported to have said in the Gospels, St. Paul interestingly made this sort of distinction among the things which he said. He distinguished between what he 'received from the Lord' (see e.g. 1 Cor. 11: 23) and what he wrote without the Lord's authority (see 1 Cor. 7: 12).

[2] Note however that if God is our creator, he has the right to command us to do things; and doing those things then becomes our duty, when it was not a duty before the command was issued. On this see *The Coherence of Theism*, pp. 203-9. Such commands might be made known to men through a prophet. Hence it is no objection to the prophet's teaching on morality that he tells us that it is our duty to do some action, when it would not be our duty to do that action but for a divine command.

[3] If the Gospel prophecies of the coming Last Judgement are interpreted as this kind of prediction, then of course Christ's claim to be an infallible prophet must be rejected. However it seems to me open to question whether the prophecies are to be taken as predictions at all, or rather simply as warnings of what will happen unless men repent (as Old Testament prophecies of doom were often intended to be understood. See the story of Jonah). If Christ's prophecies are to be taken as predictions, my own non-expert view is that careful examination of the text of the Gospels does not show that those predictions are in any way dated. There are certainly prophecies of victory which the Gospels expect to be fulfilled shortly. But the Gospels clearly envisage two kinds of victory—the

teaching as can be checked must be found to be true. Some of the prophet's moral teaching, for example, may coincide with our clear intuitions about morality.[1] Thirdly, it may be that some parts of the prophet's teaching which do not appear obviously true to start with are found, through experience and reflection, to be true. One way in which subsequent experience could confirm a prophet's teaching would be if the sort of teaching about God, his nature, and action in history which the prophet gives makes sense of the investigator's own private and public experience, in the sense of making probable a course of experience which would not otherwise be probable. The course of a man's life, the answering of his prayers, and particular 'religious experiences' within that life might be such as the God proclaimed by the prophet would be expected to bring about. All that would be further evidence of the truth of the prophet's teaching.

All of this is independent evidence is that some of what the prophet teaches is true. The fact that some of what the prophet teaches is seen to be true and deep is indeed some slight evidence that the other things which he said are true and deep. If a man says what is true on one deep matter, that is some evidence for supposing that he is a wise man, and so for supposing that what he says on other deep matters is true. But it is only slight evidence—many teachers who teach deep truths teach falsities also, and prophets who agree over one range of their teaching disagree over another range. That the moral teaching of Jesus Christ is true and deep is slender grounds for believing what he had to say about life after death.

Revelations include, and (as we have seen that Paley argued) can *a priori* be expected to include, things beyond human capacity independently to check. For example they typically assert the

Resurrection and the establishment of the Church; and the Last Judgement. And it does not seem evident to me that Christ forecast an immediate Last Judgement—indeed there are several parables which make quite clear that, although men should be ready for a Last Judgement, there was no knowing when it would occur. On the other hand, St. Paul certainly expected it to occur very soon. However there is a lot more to be said about this, and detailed arguments here are not appropriate in a philosophical work.

[1] Although Paley thinks that the conveying of moral instruction was not the main point of Jesus's teaching (which in his view was the affirming of reward in Heaven and punishment in Hell for good and bad conduct respectively), he does make the point that a revelation is confirmed by a prophet's moral teaching being true and deep. See his Part II, Chapter 2 'Of the Morality of the Gospel'. He argues that the moral teaching of Christianity is 'such as, without allowing some degree of reality to the character and pretension of the religion, it is difficult to account for'. He goes on to argue that Christianity commended virtues ignored by the ancient world and refused to commend ones which appealed to that world.

existence of a life after death; and they provide us with information about the sort of God who is to be worshipped in far more detail than a man could derive from examination of the created world, and they give us details of the way to worship him. Hence we need some evidence that what the prophet says is true when we cannot check independently whether it is or not. Analogy suggests the sort of evidence for which we ought to be looking. Suppose that in the days before wireless, telephones, and fast travel, a man claims to have visited a king of a distant country and to have brought back a message from him. What would show that the message comes from the king? First, the message may contain some prediction of an event of the future occurrence of which the messenger could have learnt only from the king; e.g. that the messenger's arrival would be followed by the arrival of some of the king's ships (the messenger having to all appearances travelled by land and so not having been able to meet such ships en route). Secondly, the messenger may bring some token which a man could only have obtained from the king, e.g. a precious stone of a kind only to be found in the king's country, and which is mined by the king alone and kept by him. The token might be the sort of token which people of the culture of those days traditionally gave to authenticate messages. By analogy, evidence that the prophet has his revelation from God and so is to be believed on deep matters where we have no independent means of checking, would be given, first, by his ability to predict some future event which he would have no means of predicting otherwise, i.e. by mere human powers. But any event in accordance with natural laws could be predicted by mere human powers. So this evidence needs to be evidence of an ability to predict events not in accordance with natural laws; and that, in a basically deterministic world, means violations of natural laws. The evidence would need also to suggest that the violations were brought about by God, and so were miracles. Secondly, evidence that the prophet had his revelation from God would be provided if the prophet's life was accompanied by events which, evidence suggested, were violations of natural laws produced by God in circumstances where such violations would naturally and by local convention be interpreted as vindicating the prophet's teaching. Both these further sources of evidence thus involve the occurrence of miracles.

Before taking the argument further, I need to spell out what I understand by a miracle and what would be evidence that an event was a miracle in my sense.[1] I understand by a miracle a violation of the laws of nature, that is, a non-repeatable exception to the operation of these laws, brought about by God. Laws of nature have the form of universal statements 'all As are B', and state how bodies behave of physical necessity. Thus Kepler's three laws of planetary motion state how the planets move. The first law states that all planets move in ellipses with the sun at one focus. If this purported law is to be a law of nature, planets must in general move as it states.

What however is to be said about an isolated exception to a purported law of nature? Suppose that one day Mars moves out of its elliptical path for a brief period and then returns to the path. There are two possibilities. This wandering of Mars may occur because of some current condition of the Universe (e.g. the proximity of Jupiter drawing Mars out of its elliptical path), such that if that condition were to be repeated the event would happen again. In this case the phenomenon is an entirely regular phenomenon. The trouble is that what might have appeared originally to be a basic law of nature proves now not to be one. It proves to be a consequence of a more fundamental law that the original purported law normally holds, but that under circumstances describable in general terms (e.g. 'when planets are close to each other') there are exceptions to it. Such repeatable exceptions to purported laws merely show that the purported laws are not basic laws of nature. The other possibility is that the exception to the law was not caused by some current condition, in such a way that if the condition were to recur the event would happen again. In this case we have a non-repeatable exception to a law of nature. But how are we to describe this event further? There are two possible moves. We may say that if there occurs an exception to a purported law of nature, the purported law can be no law. If the purported law says 'all As are B' and there is an A which is not B, then 'all As are B' is no law. The trouble with saying that is that the purported law may be a very good device for giving accurate predictions in our field of study; it may be by far the best general formula for describing what happens in the field which there is. (I understand by a general formula a formula which describes what happens in all circumstances of a certain kind, but does not mention by name particular individuals, times, or places.) To deny that the

[1] The following discussion of the nature and justification of claims that there has occurred a violation of a law of nature is an extremely brief extract from the short argument of Ch. 12 of *The Existence of God*. For fuller and more adequate discussion see my book, *The Concept of Miracle* (London, 1971).

purported law is a law, when there is no more accurate general formula, just because there is an isolated exception to its operation, is to ignore its enormous ability to predict what happens in the field.

For this reason it seems not unnatural to say that the purported law is no less a law for there being a non-repeatable exception to it; and then to describe the exception as a 'violation' of the law. At any rate this is a coherent way of talking, and I think that it is what those who use such expressions as 'violation' of a law of nature are getting at. In this case we must amend our understanding of what is a law of nature. To say that a generalization 'all *A*s are *B*' is a universal law of nature is to say that being *A* physically necessitates being *B*, and so that any *A* will be *B*—apart from violations.

But how do we know that some event such as the wandering of Mars from its elliptical path is a non-repeatable rather than a repeatable exception to a purported law of nature? We have grounds for believing that the exception is non-repeatable in so far as any attempt to amend the purported law of nature so that it predicted the wandering of Mars as well as all the other observed positions of Mars, would make it so complicated and *ad hoc* that we would have no grounds for trusting its future predictions. It is no good for example amending the law so that it reads: 'all planets move in ellipses with the Sun at one focus, except in years when there is a competition for the World Chess Championship between two players both of whose surnames begin with *K*.' Why not? Because this proposed law mentions properties which have no other place in physics (no other physical law invokes this sort of property) and it mentions them in an *ad hoc* way (that is, the proposed new law has the form 'so-and-so holds except under such-and-such circumstances', when the only reason for adding the exceptive clause is that otherwise the law would be incompatible with observations; the clause does not follow naturally from the theory.) What we need if we are to have a more adequate law is a general formula, of which it is an entirely natural consequence that the exception to the original law occurs when it does.

In these ways we could have grounds for believing that an exception to a purported law was non-repeatable and so a violation of a natural law. Claims of this sort are of course corrigible—we could be wrong; what seemed inexplicable by natural causes might be explicable after all. But then we could be wrong about most things, including claims of the opposite kind. When I drop a piece of chalk and it falls to the ground, every one supposes that here is an event perfectly explicable by natural laws. But we could be wrong. Maybe the laws of nature are much more complicated than we suppose, and Newton's and Einstein's laws are mere approximations to the true laws of mechanics. Maybe the true laws of mechanics predict that almost always when released from the hand, chalk will fall to the ground, but not today because of a slightly abnormal distribution of distant galaxies. However although the true laws of nature predict that the chalk will rise, in fact it falls. Here is a stark violation of natural laws, but one which no one detects because of their ignorance of natural laws. 'You could be wrong' is a knife which cuts both ways. What seem to be perfectly explicable events might prove, when we come to know the laws of nature much better, to be violations. But of course this is not very likely. The reasonable man goes by the available evidence here, and also in the converse case. He supposes that what is, on all the evidence, a violation of natural laws really is one. There is good reason to suppose that events such as the following if they occurred would be violations of laws of nature: levitation, that is, a man rising in the air against gravity without the operation of magnetism or any other known physical force; resurrection from the dead of a man whose heart has not been beating for twenty-four hours and who counts as dead by other currently used criteria; water turning into wine without the assistance of chemical apparatus or catalysts; a man growing a new arm from the stump of an old one.

Since the occurrence of a violation of natural laws cannot be explained in the normal way, either it has no explanation or it is to be explained in a different way. The obvious explanation exists if there is a God who is responsible for the whole order of nature, including its conformity to natural laws, and who therefore can on occasion suspend the normal operation of natural laws and bring about or allow some one else to bring about events, not via this normal route. We should suppose that events have explanations if suggested explanations are at all plausible. If there is quite a bit of evidence that there is a God responsible for the natural order,[1] then any violations are plausibly attributed to his agency and so plausibly recognized as miracles—at least so long as those violations are not ruled out by such evidence as we may have from other sources about God's character.[2] God's permitting a law of nature to be violated is clearly necessary for this to occur if he is the author of Nature; and in the

---

[1] As I claimed in *The Existence of God*.

[2] I argue in *The Coherence of Theism* that necessarily an omnipotent, omniscient, and perfectly free God must be perfectly good.

absence of evidence that any other agent had a hand in the miracle, it ought to be attributed to God's sole agency. But if there is evidence, say, that it happens after a command (as opposed to a request to God) for it to happen issued by another agent, then the miracle is to be attributed to a joint agency.

I have not considered here the kind of historical evidence needed to prove the occurrence of an event which if it occurred would be a violation, but clearly it will be of the same kind as the evidence for any other historical event. There is the evidence of one's own senses, the testimony of others (oral and written) and the evidence of traces (effects left by events, such as footprints, fingerprints, cigarette ash, etc.). I see no reason in principle why there should not be evidence of this kind to show the occurrence of a levitation or a resurrection from the dead.[1]

Now I claimed earlier that two further kinds of evidence for the genuineness of a prophet's revelation would be provided if there was evidence of the prophet's ability to predict miracles, and if there was evidence that his teaching was vindicated by miracles. Christian theology has traditionally claimed both these further sources of evidence for the truth of what Christ said.

The life of Christ was, according to the Gospels, full of 'miracles'. Some of the 'miracle' stories are perhaps not intended to be taken literally, some of them are ill-authenticated, and some of the 'miracles' were not violations of natural laws (e.g. perhaps certain cures of the mentally deranged come into this category). Yet some of the Gospel 'miracles', in particular the stories of healings of the blind and dumb and lame, seem to me to be intended to be taken literally by the Gospel writers, to be moderately well authenticated, and to be violations of natural laws, if they occurred. But the story of one 'miracle' above all, of course, has dominated Christian teaching from the earliest days until the present—the story of the Resurrection of Christ. It seems to this writer that the writers of gospels and epistles intended their readers to believe that although Christ was killed on the Cross, he subsequently came to life (in a transformed body which left its tomb). If the events of the first Easter occurred in anything like the form recorded in the Gospels, there is a clear case of a violation of a natural law. As a violation of natural law, it would (for reasons already stated) be plausibly explained by the action of God intervening in human history.

[1] Hume however thought otherwise. For discussion of his argument and for analysis of these kinds of evidence which we have for the occurrence of historical events and of their force, see my *The Concept of Miracle*, Ch. 4.

Christian theology has claimed as evidence of the genuineness of Christ's revelation, his prophetic power in the sense of his ability to predict future events to be brought about by God, including Christ's crucifixion and resurrection, the establishment of the Church and the fall of Jerusalem. At any rate the resurrection, if it occurred, would have been, I have claimed, a miracle; and so if Christ had the ability to predict it, that would show some knowledge of God's purposes. I do not pronounce on the disputed issue of whether Christ did predict his Resurrection,[1] or the other events, or whether there was anything miraculous in the latter.

Secondly, Christian theology has claimed that Christ's miracles, and above all the miracle of the Resurrection, marked God's vindication of Christ's teaching. The Resurrection meant that the sacrificial life of Jesus had not ended in disaster. If it occurred, it was the means of founding the Church and making the teaching of and about Jesus available to the world. Whatever is to be said about other purported miracles, the Resurrection (if it occurred) is for this reason reasonably interpreted as involving the divine judgement that it is good that the teaching of Jesus triumph. Since that teaching involves showing men the way to salvation, if it is good that it triumph, that must be because the way which it shows men does lead to salvation. For although God may have good reason for allowing evil to triumph, if it occurs through the free choice of men—because it is good that men should make a difference to the world through their free choice, or in accord with natural processes—as a warning to men as to the consequences of allowing such natural processes to continue;[2] he would seem to have no reason to intervene in nature to make it triumph. Apparently, miraculous triumphing is not to be expected but for divine action and approval and therefore plausibly signifies divine action and approval. Also, Jews of the first century AD would, I suggest, readily interpret miraculous intervention to secure the triumphing of Jesus's life and teaching as evidence of a divine 'signature' on that teaching and so of its truth (and perhaps also, if Christ's death was an atoning sacrifice, as the acceptance of that sacrifice). If God gives a message to men, the right interpretation of

[1] There is however just one consideration on the question of Christ having predicted his Resurrection which seems to me to have been unduly neglected by commentators. On the night before he was crucified, Christ instituted the eucharist, and the Church early understood that institution as the institution of a repeatable ceremony. You do not institute a ceremony of that kind to celebrate a failure; Christ must have held that his coming crucifixion would be in *some* sense a victory.

[2] See *The Existence of God*, Ch. 11.

the message is (in the absence of other considerations) the way in which it would naturally be interpreted by those who received it. For any giver of messages uses such devices as, given the conventions of his audience, will be interpreted in the right way.[1]

Similar considerations to those about a revelation via a prophet's teaching are relevant for assessing any claim that the prophet's life was in some sense God's life, viz. that the prophet was in some sense God incarnate (although claims to such revelation are not our main concern in this chapter). A primary issue here, as I noted earlier (p. 180, n. 1) is whether the concept of an incarnation is a coherent one at all—whether there is not some internal contradiction in the suggestion that the same individual was both God and man. If there is not, then to any claim that God has become incarnate on a particular occasion, there are relevant, first, *a priori* considerations about whether God is likely to become incarnate and under what circumstances. I noted earlier the *a priori* considerations put forward in favour of expecting God to bring about a Christian-type atonement. Then there will be evidence of two further kinds relevant to showing that God has on a particular occasion become incarnate. There will, first, be the quality of a certain prophet's human life—that it shows the kind of pattern which God would be expected to show if he accepted human limitations. It needs much argument to show what that pattern would be. But clearly, to make an atonement of the kind earlier referred to, a holy and sacrificial life is needed. Moral reflection and reflection on the prophet's life may help the investigator to see in it depths of holiness and sacrifice which are not in evidence at first sight. Yet there are many sacrificial lives lived by men on Earth. The evidence that a particular one was divine would be the testimony of the prophet himself (shown to teach true teaching by the criteria previously considered) or his accredited representative (e.g. a church—see p. 177, n. 2); that the prophet himself could work miracles at will (not merely pray successfully for them to happen); and that his life began and ended in a way which violated natural processes. For if through the prophet's life God entered and left the world in response to the current human condition, this would require

---

[1] The issue of the kind of intervention in history needed for a revelation is discussed in a discussion, 'Does Christianity need a Revelation?', between Basil Mitchell and Maurice Wiles, in *Theology*, 1980, **83**, 103–14. Mitchell argues along lines similar to mine, while Wiles claims that the sort of evidence needed to show the Christian revelation to have a miraculous character is not available, and that such a conception of revelation is not needed for Christian devotional practice to have point.

some interruption of the operation of natural processes which are
concerned with the created world and planned by God from the
beginning of the created world. For if the prophet's coming into the
world was a natural consequence of natural laws operative throughout human history (even if made so to operate by God's original
choice), his coming into the world (and so also his leaving it) would
not be the result of God's spontaneous response to the mess which
men had made of their lives and of the Earth.[1] So for more than one
reason, incarnation requires to be accompanied by miracle; and
evidence for such miracles in connection with a holy and sacrificial
life is evidence of incarnation.[2] Claims of an incarnation typically
need to be backed up by a claim to revelation in teaching (e.g. the
prophet or his accredited representative—a church—teaching that
the prophet was God incarnate); and there are major religions (e.g.
Judaism and Islam) which claim no incarnation and yet are to be
compared with Christianity in respect of a revelation in teaching.

Brief though my discussion of revelation has been, I believe that
it substantiates Paley's classical claim about revelation, especially
revelation in teaching. Paley writes: 'In what way can a revelation
be made, but by miracles? In none which we are able to conceive?'[3] I
have argued that Paley is right.

What a man needs to believe with respect to the claimed Christian
revelation, if he is to pursue the Christian way is, we have seen, not
that it is more probable than not that God revealed himself in Christ
but that, if there is a God, it is more probable that he revealed himself
in Christ than that he revealed himself through any other prophet
with a conflicting message. If the argument of this chapter is correct,
for another revelation to be more probable than the Christian
revelation, it would have to be backed by a more evident miracle, or
be backed by a miracle no less evident but containing more evidently

---

[1] Christian theologians down the centuries have disputed whether God would have
become incarnate in Christ if men had not sinned and needed atonement. St. Thomas
Aquinas, acknowledging the diversity of theological opinion, opts for the alternative
that he would not; there would have been no reason for an incarnation but for man's
sin: see *Summa Theologiae*, 3a, 1. 3. Reflection on the New Testament would, I believe,
support that view. However, on the alternative view, an incarnation could have been
planned from all eternity and so would not need a violation of natural laws for it
to occur.

[2] My account of the criteria for the occurrence of an incarnation are similar to those
given by Ninian Smart in *Reasons and Faiths* (London, 1958), Ch. 4; though he stresses
the need for the miraculous much less than I do—but see his brief remarks on the
Resurrection on p. 122.

[3] *A View of the Evidences of Christianity*, 'Preparatory Considerations'.

true and deep teaching, or perhaps, be backed by a miracle somewhat less evident but containing teaching far more evidently true and deep. I shall come shortly to the question of how much investigation of comparative religion is necessary before a man can have a rational₅ belief that this is so.

Paley's conclusion, after his investigation into this issue, was that no religion other than Christianity is backed by equally well-authenticated miracles. He claims that 'the only event in the history of the human species, which admits of comparison with the propagation of Christianity' is Islam. But he claims that 'Mahomet did not found his pretensions . . . upon proofs of supernatural agency, capable of being known and attested by others'.[1]

I believe that, whatever the deficiencies of Paley's detailed historical arguments (and he wrote long before the great advances in biblical criticism in the late nineteenth century), the approach of the *Evidences* to these matters is correct. The evidence of a revelation is the plausibility to the reflective investigator of a prophet's teaching (and—if an incarnation is claimed—the holiness of his life); and some kind of miraculous divine signature symbolically affirming and forwarding the prophet's teaching and work.

Comparison of Theistic and Non-theistic Religions

The final step in showing the Christian Creed to be more probable than any rival creed was, I suggested, to show that it is more probable that the Christian Creed as a whole is true than that any non-theistic creed is true. How is the Christian Creed to be compared with the creed of a non-theistic religion such as Buddhism? As they are so different each must be assessed separately for its probability as a whole, before we can see which is the more probable. Comparing total systems in this way can be a very difficult task. But we may be able to show one system inferior to another either if it fails to account for (or, in the extreme case, is rendered false by) data for which the other can account; or, if one contains certain important elements which are not in any way *a priori* probable and play no role in successful prediction of data.[2] The detailed teaching of a religion such as Buddhism may be able to be faulted on this kind of ground. Gautama the Buddha taught certain things, and different schools developed them in different ways. These things include teaching

[1] *A View of the Evidences of Christianity*, Part II, Section 3.
[2] For more detailed exposition of these points, see the *Existence of God*, Ch. 3.

about the way of life which is to be pursued, teaching that a man will be reincarnated after death in a higher or lower state according to the life which he has led on Earth, and that the man who pursues the good will eventually, after a long series of reincarnations, attain Nirvana, and that this is to be prized above all because thereby a man escapes the cycle of becoming.

Yet why is this to be believed? Gautama did not claim to have had a revelation from God in the theistic sense. He claimed to have discovered the truth; but in no way does Buddhism claim that the truth of what he said is in any way authenticated by anything miraculous connected with his life. Rather the appeal is to its intuitive plausibility, its *a priori* probability.[1] It must be left to an expositor of Buddhism to make his case for this, but whatever the plausibility of Buddhism's moral teaching, reincarnation as such does not seem to be probable *a priori*; we need evidence of it from a witness whose teaching is in some way authenticated. True, Hindus who also believe in reincarnation sometimes claim to have empirical evidence, in the purported testimony of children who claim to have lived previous lives and can tell true incidents from those lives which they could not otherwise have known. But even if this evidence were found strong, it would not have any tendency to show that the man who pursues the good eventually reaches Nirvana.[2]

It must be for the Buddhist to make his case for the prior probability of this latter claim. Yet the task of making that case seems to this author to have about it the sort of difficulty which would be had by a man trying to defend detailed Christian doctrines without an appeal to Revelation. Nature by itself does not reveal that sort of detail about its origin and destiny. We need testimony from someone who has reliable information and can show us his credentials. However, I may be mistaken about this through ignorance of the details of Buddhism; and this book does not attempt to pursue in detail the task of comparing religions, only to consider the general principles involved.

---

[1] 'The Buddha's insight is represented as being, not that of the dogmatist who asserts that such and such is the case and demands men's acceptance of his assertion in faith, but rather that of the analyst. And the analysis which is offered is both logical and psychological. Its appeal is in its self-authenticating quality.' Trevor Ling, *The Buddha* (Harmondsworth, Middlesex, 1976), p. 129. 'The Buddha stressed that no teaching should ever be accepted on the strength of tradition, of being handed down in holy scripture, of being in agreement with one's own views or because of trust in an authority. It should only be accepted when one has recognized it as wholesome.' H. W. Schumann, *Buddhism* (London, 1973), p. 24.

[2] In the sense in which I have understood Nirvana—see p. 129, n. 2. Argument is needed to show that Nirvana is a state worth having.

The Extent of Investigation Needed into Comparative Religion

If a belief about the relative probability of creeds is to be rational$_5$ it must be backed up by proper investigation. How much investigation is needed will depend on how important it is to have a true belief in this field. I urged at the beginning of this chapter that there is to a limited extent a duty to seek a true belief about which creed is the true one and that for many reasons it was greatly worthwhile to do so. However, with all beliefs there is little point in investigating if you are virtually certain of the answer; and 'the answer' in this case means which creed is the true creed. If a man is virtually certain in his own mind that Christianity in all its detail is true, there is little point in his even considering any rival religions, since if Christianity is true and they are rivals, they must be false. The amount of investigation needed will also depend on whether it is likely that investigation will achieve anything. I argued in Chapter 3 against some general arguments purporting to show that religious investigation into the existence of God will achieve nothing. Some of these aguments could be cast in a more general form, to attempt to show the uselessness of religious inquiry in general, but similar objections could be made against them. The amount of investigation needed will also again depend on the rival claims on our time.

How is a man who is convinced of the need to investigate the relative probabilities of creeds, to proceed? As I brought out in Chapter 2, the sort of investigation which a man ought to make must depend on the opportunities open to him and the evidence initially available to him, and that in turn will depend on what he is told by experts. He may be brought up in a community which has only heard of one religious creed, or at any rate does not have access to information about others. In that case he has no opportunity for further religious investigation. He must investigate the truth of that creed and, if there is some chance that pursuit of its religious way will attain its goals, pursue it if he seeks these goals.

If on the other hand, he has been brought up in a community which has heard of other creeds, then in order to have rational$_5$ beliefs, the investigator must make some inquiries about these other creeds. How much further inquiry is needed will depend on the results of his preliminary inquiries. Thus with respect to rival theistic religions he may find that all claims to revelation except one contain implausible moral or other factual teaching; and so, whether or not these others are backed up by good evidence of miracles is not relevant and need not be pursued. Or he may find that only one claim to revelation whose teaching has to any degree the right character, purports to be backed by evidence of miracles, or at any rate evidence of a serious and powerful kind. In such cases what his preliminary inquiries have done is render it very probable that any subsequent investigation of those other creeds will make no difference—that one claim alone to revelation is significantly more probable than any known one—and so there is no point in further investigation. As we have seen, Paley held that Christianity was in this unique situation.

The situation of many a man in the twentieth century is that there are a vast number of religious creeds which he could, if he chose, investigate. On which should his effort be concentrated? I suggest that, if he has access to information about them, a man should investigate the great world religions; and I suggest also that he should investigate at any rate cursorily the claims of religious creeds to which friends and acquaintances and other personal contacts seek to introduce him. The point of investigating the great religions arises from the fact that so many and so many serious and clever people familiar with modern knowledge owe them their allegiance, that there is some chance that there is some truth in them. The point of investigating religious creeds which are pressed upon one is twofold. First, it is quite easy to investigate these when some of the evidence is made so readily available to us. Secondly, I suggested in Chapter 3, there is perhaps some duty to believe what people tell us (when this is based on their experiences). And if there is not that, there is, I suggest, at least a duty to take seriously what friends or those with whom we come into personal contact tell us, certainly about matters of great importance. What a man thinks worth giving his life to serve deserves at least a passing inspection from us, if he assures us that it is of deep significance for us. The Mormon or Jehovah's Witness who knocks so unwelcome at our door is entitled to a small initial amount of serious attention. But I suggest that for most of us there is not nearly so much point in investigating the credal claims of religions which have not spread throughout the globe and into which we do not bump, as in investigating the other religions. The failure of the former to spread among those who do come into contact with them is some evidence that they are not worth more serious attention.

It is clear that in order to hold a rational₅ belief about the relative probabilities of creeds, there is need for more investigation in the Western world in the twentieth century than ever there has been at any other time and place in human history. This is so for two reasons.

First, it is far easier than ever it was to pursue such inquiries. The peasant in twelfth century England had no means of getting information about Buddhism; the farm-worker in twentieth-century England can borrow a book from the shelves of the public library. Hence any attempt today to pursue inquiry is far more likely to bear fruit, and so there needs to be more inquiry if a man's beliefs are to be rational$_5$. (See p. 82.) Secondly, we are now aware of the widespread support for creeds of the great religions which rival Christianity, which suggests that each of them has some evidence in its favour. This makes it less plausible to hold that Christianity is certainly true, and so rules out a possible argument against the need to investigate. (See p. 88.) In centuries to come such investigation into the relative probabilities of creeds may again become less necessary, for general investigation may have convinced so many people of the falsity of other creeds, that few people believe them. But for us in the West today a rational$_5$ belief about the relative merits of rival religions needs to be backed by a certain amount of investigation.

Epilogue: Faith is Voluntary

FOR the pursuit of a religious way a man needs to seek certain goals with certain weak beliefs. The choice whether to seek those goals is his. A man may choose to seek his own earthly well-being, or that of his family, or of his country, or of the world—or he may seek a deeper and longer-term well-being for himself and for others and the rendering of praise to God. The choice is his. Obviously any normal man will want earthly well-being for himself—food and drink, sex and sleep, laughter and children and spouse and parents, and so on. And one in whom natural instincts have not been repressed by bad upbringing or poor genotype will want these things for others close to him too. It may require a certain other than normal environment to produce a longing for the well-being of the world, as also to produce a longing for the goals of religion. But these goals are natural extensions of earthly goals. They involve wanting the well-being of those whom we have not met and those unfriendly to us as well as those whom we have met and those friendly to us; and wanting for them and for us a deep and long-term well-being as well as ordinary earthly well-being. There is a natural longing to understand the world; the desire to understand the 'nature of reality' is a natural extension of that longing. There is a natural longing to show respect to those who deserve it; the desire to render praise to whatever God there may be is a natural extension of that longing. There is a natural longing for friendship with persons of value; the longing for friendship with God is a natural extension of that longing—especially if, as some religions proclaim, God has called men to friendship with himself.

Some men may be aware only of limited goals, but others who have had contact with men of wide political and religious vision become aware of wider goals. A man will come to believe that some such goals are more worth pursuing than others. It is hard to see how a man who saw all its implications could believe other than that salvation was more worth having than mere earthly well-being. Along with judge-

ments about the comparative worth of various ends, a man will come
to have beliefs about how probable it is that he can attain those ends.
His belief in religious creeds may be weak or not so weak, and that
belief will give rise to a corresponding weak or strong means—end
belief about the efficacy of some religious way in the attainment of
salvation. What the man will seek will depend on the strength of his
purposes (by how much he prizes his salvation, that of others, and the
rendering of due worship and obedience to God, above earthly well-
being) and his beliefs about how likely it is that pursuit of the way will
achieve its purposes. He may think that salvation is to be prized
above earthly well-being, but he may judge that a religious way is so
unlikely to attain salvation (e.g. because he believes that it is unlikely
that there is a God) that he does not think it worth pursuing at the
expense of earthly well-being. Yet a man who prized salvation far
above everything else, would pursue it despite having a belief that it
was very unlikely that pursuit of any religious way would attain it.
However, a man who believed that it was certain that pursuit of a
religious way would not attain its goals (e.g. because he was convinced
that the concept of God or the concept of life after death were self-
contradictory) could not pursue that way to attain its goals.

A man's belief's about the worth of ends as well as his beliefs about
the efficacy of means (dependent on his belief in a creed) will result
from inquiry; and a man may come to have irrational beliefs either
because he has devoted less time than he felt that he ought to to these
matters, or because he has refused to be led in the direction in which
the evidence seems to point.[1] In both these ways error may be
culpable. A man's beliefs about the worth of ends do not however
automatically lead to his pursuing those ends with purposes of
strength proportional to his judgement of their worth. Bodily desires
may pull him back from pursuing what he sees to be the long-term
best goal. He must choose whether or not to yield to these desires.
Thus he may choose whether to pursue salvation or whether to
pursue temporary self-centred joys; whether to yield to sloth, or to
insist on following his rational judgement.

If a man's religious inquiries lead him to believe that it is more
probable that the Christian Creed is true than that any rival creed is
true, and he chooses to pursue the goals of religion he will be
exercising Christian faith. He needs that weak belief in order to
exercise Christian faith; and only if he has the belief can he make the

---

[1] For example, by forcing himself to use inductive standards which he initially
believed to be incorrect.

great choice as to whether to exercise that faith. It has been the opinion of the considerable majority of theologians down the centuries that Christian faith is voluntary.[1] If faith is simply belief, as Aquinas held, it can be voluntary only in the sense that we can choose, not our beliefs but whether to seek beliefs resulting from adequate inquiry into religious truth. However, the sort of faith that matters ('meritorious faith' in Thomist terms) is, I have urged, a matter of pursuing the goals of religion on certain assumptions believed to be more probable than rival assumptions, and in particular, on the assumption that God will do for one what one wants or needs. That faith, which is trust in God, is voluntary.

The following of a religious way may in the course of time convert weak belief into strong. Acting on an assumption which has any measure of success is likely to turn the assumption into belief. A man who found, through following the way, deeper and well-evidenced understanding of the world, a worthwhile way to live, and a deeper happiness; and felt convinced of divine presence and forgiveness, might indeed come to believe to be more probable than not the items of the creed which initially he believed only to be more probable than rivals.

By faith Abraham, when he was called, obeyed to go out unto a place which he was to receive for an inheritance; and he went out, not knowing whither he went. By faith he became a sojourner in the land of promise, as in a land not his own, dwelling in tents with Isaac and Jacob, the heirs with him of the same promise. For he looked for the city which has the foundations, whose builder and maker is God. By faith even Sarah herself received power to conceive seed when she was past age, since she counted him faithful who had promised. Wherefore also there sprang of one, and him as good as dead, so many as the stars of heaven in multitude, and as the sand, which is by the sea shore, innumerable.

These all died in faith, not having received the promises but

---

[1] One constantly emphasised on the Catholic side (e.g. by decrees of both the First and Second Vatican Councils. For the former, see *De Fide*, canon 5; for the latter see *Dignitatis Humanae*, 10); and also taught by Protestants apart from those much influenced by the classical Protestantism of Luther and Calvin. However, the decree of the First Vatican Council may be following Aquinas in assuming that faith (as opposed to formed faith) is just belief; and that, I have argued (pp. 25 f.) cannot be chosen.

having seen them and greeted them from afar, and having confessed that they were strangers and pilgrims on the earth. For they that say such things make it manifest that they are seeking after a country of their own. And if indeed they had been mindful of that country from which they went out, they would have had opportunity to return. But now they desire a better country, that is, a heavenly. Wherefore God is not ashamed of them, to be called their God; for he has prepared for them a city.[1]

[1] Epistle to the Hebrews 11: 8–16.

Index

actions, basic, 74 f.
Acts of the Apostles, 121, 125
ad hoc hypotheses, 62
Adams, R. M., 170
after-life, *see* Heaven, Hell, Limbo, *and* Purgatory
agnosticism, 123
Anselm, St., 55, 98
antinomianism, 113
a priori truths, 37
Aquinas, St. Thomas, 55, 102 f., 105-10, 111, 113, 124, 126, 131-3, 136, 151, 157, 170, 172, 179, 182, 192, 200
Aristotle, 76, 136
Articles, Thirty Nine, 110, 126
assumptions, acting on, 3, 31 f., 111 f., 118, 166 f.
atonement, 145 f., 159 f., 180, 190
Augustine, St., 106, 123, 133, 171
authority, role of, in determining belief, 42 f., 57 ff., 60 f., 67 ff.
Azande, the, 39

babies, fate of, in after-life, 170
baptism, 146, 160, 164, 170
Barnes, J., 55
Barth, K., 84, 111
Bayes's Theorem, 62
beatific vision, the, 77, 108, 131
beatitudo, 136
belief, and action, 8-13, 26-32, 86
  and evidence, 18-25
  and probability, 4-31. *See also* inductive standards
  basic, 21
  believing the consequences of one's, 11 f., 27
  conjunctivity of, 7 f.
  Dispositional theory of, 12, 16
  grounds for attributing, 13-18
  importance of true, 73-82, 99-103, 173 ff.
  initial, 34
  involuntary, 25 f., 102 f., 109
  means-end, 9, 12, 14 f., 161 f.
  mere, 106 f., 122
  necessary for church membership, 165 f.
  necessary for happiness, 98 f.
  necessary for Heaven, 93-6, 147-51
  necessary for pursuit of religious way, 160-5
  necessary for religious knowledge, 76 f., 80 f., 97 f., 173 f.
  necessary for worthwhile action, 96 f.
  non-rational, induction of, 88-102
  obligation to cultivate, *see* belief, importance of true
  passive, *see* belief, involuntary
  prior, 36 f., 43
  rational, *see* rational belief
  relative to alternatives, 3-8, 107, 119 ff., 163-6
  religious, definition of, 55, 73
  strong, 120, 200
  unconscious, 15, 18
  value of true, *see* belief, importance of true
  weak, 120, 163 f., 199 f.
Bible, not arguing for God, 86
Braithwaite, R. B., 12
Buddhism, 69, 73, 128 f., 135, 150 ff., 161 ff., 193 f., 197

Caesar's *Gallic War*, 42
Calvin, J., 113 f., 200
Chalcedon, Council of, 6 f., 160, 166
character formation, 114, 148-51, 168 ff.
charity, principle of, 13 f.
Chisholm, R. M., 20, 21
choice, normal situation of, 152-5
Christ, Jesus, 6 f., 57, 102 f., 104, 122, 144, 145 f., 159 f., 176, 179, 182, 183, 189-93

Christianity, *passim*
Church, the, 119, 124, 126, 144, 147, 149, 160, 164 ff., 177
circle, justification, in a, 21
Clement of Alexandria, 84, 135
Clifford, W. K., 79
cognitive freedom, 86
commitment, *see* trust
comparative religion, need for investigating, 173–6, 192–7
confession of faith, 106, 111
confirmation, 180. *See also* inductive standards
conjunction, definition of, 5
conscience, good and bad, 150 ff.
convergence of beliefs, 69 f.
Corinthians, First Epistle to the, 129, 183
cosmological argument, the, 55
cosmology, physical, 39
creed, definition of, 127. *See also* Nicene creed *and* belief
culpability, 29 f., 150 f., 170 ff.
Cyril of Jerusalem, St., 122

Danto, A. C., 75
Darwin, C., 58, 182
Descartes, R., 55
desire, 152–5
devils, faith of, 105, 108 f.
disjunction, definition of, 5
Dives and Lazarus, parable of, 156
Dummett, M. A. E., 16 f.

Einstein, A., 19, 42, 188
epistemic sense of 'looks', 20
eternity, 134 f., 170 ff.
Eucharist, as evidence of Christ's foreknowledge, 190
evidence, 18–21, 33–7
for religious beliefs, 55–61
evil, problem of, 60
evolution, theory of, *see* Darwin, C.
examples of lives of others, 59 f., 138, 158

faith, 3, 104–24, 198 ff.
formed, 109 f., 113, 200
implicit, 150
sufficient for salvation, 113, 114, 127, 151
Fascism, 128
Flew, A., 94

forgiveness, 80, 128 ff., 138, 140 f., 144 f., 175, 178 f.
free will, 60. *See also* choice, *and* character formation
friendship with God, 131–5, 162, 198

Galileo, 36, 58
gamblers' inductive standards, 38 ff.
Gautama the Buddha, 193 f.
generalization principle, 37 f., 40, 84
Genesis, Book of, 182
Gettier, E. L., 107
goals of religion, *see* purposes of religion
Goodman, N., 38
goodness, moral, definition of, 74
over-all, definition of, 73 f.
grace, 149

happiness, 133 f., 136, 148, 155, 178. *See also* Heaven
deep, definition of, 134
Heaven, 93–6, 125 f., 129, 131–7, 142, 147–56, 162, 168–72, 178, 198
Hebrews, Epistle to the, 107, 121, 141, 200
Hell, 93 ff., 164, 170, 171 f.
Hick, J., 84 f., 86, 124, 157, 172
Hilary of Poitiers, St., 181 f.
Hinduism, 129, 130, 194
historical beliefs, 56–9
Homilies, Book of, 110
Hugh of St. Victor, 107
Hume, D., 16, 25, 69, 83, 90 f., 99, 189

incarnation, 145 f., 159 f., 180, 191 ff.
incoherence of concept of God, 60
incorrigibility, 20
inductive standards, 13, 25 f., 35, 37–45, 47 f., 61 ff.
correct, 47 f.
primary and secondary, defined, 40
infallibility, 20
infinite regresses, 6, 21
Inge, W. R., 121 f., 123
inquiry, religious, arguments for believing pointless, 83–7
investigation, importance of, 51 ff., 66–70, 173 ff., 199 f.
Islam, 106, 150, 161, 163, 176, 191

James, Epistle of St., 109
James, W., 116

Jeffrey, R., 21
Jehovah's Witnesses, 196
John, Gospel according to St., 58, 68, 122, 172
Jonah, Book of, 183
Judaism, 129, 130, 163, 177, 191
Judgment, Last, 166, 183 f.

Kant, I., 37, 83
Kepler, J., 38 f.
Kierkegaard, S., 116
Kirk, K. E., 138
knowledge, limits to human, 83 ff., 106 ff.
valuable in itself, 76, 80, 130. *See also* understanding
Kraut, R., 136

laws of nature, 186 ff.
Lazarus, *see* Dives and Lazarus
Lehrer, K., 107
Levi, I., 4
Lewis, D., 13, 15
Limbo, 169, 170
Ling, T., 129, 194
love, 110, 118. *See also* character formation
Luke, Gospel according to St., 151, 156
Luther, M., 110, 112 f., 114 f., 200
Lutheran view of faith, 110-15, 117 f.

MacQuarrie, J., 84
Mahomet, *see* Muhammad
Mark, Gospel according to St., 56
Marxism, 128 f.
Matthew, Gospel according to St., 132, 147 f., 151, 155, 158, 172
Merneptah, 9
Mill, J. S., 134
miracles, 180, 185-93, 195 f.
Mitchell, B., 97 f., 191
Monophysitism, 6 f., 166
moral beliefs, 74 ff., 79 f., 179
Mormons, 196
Muhammad, 176, 193
Muslims, *see* Islam

natural theology, 55-71, 83-7, 175, 178 f.
negation, definition of, 4
Nestorianism, 6 f., 166
Newman, J. H., 30, 39, 87 f.
Newton, I., 48 f., 188

Nicene creed, 104, 105, 115, 119 f., 127, 143, 159 f., 166
Nirvana, 73, 129, 162, 194
Novatian, 181

obedience to God, duty of, 80, 138, 142, 158, 159, 167, 178, 199
O'Brien, T. C., 106
ontological argument, the, 55, 68
Origen, 59, 157
Osborn, E. F., 135

Paley, W., 69, 177 f., 180, 184, 192, 193, 196
Papias, 68
Pascal, B., 31 f., 81, 91, 93-6, 99, 116
Paul, St., 56, 58, 86, 113, 125, 129, 183
penitence, 144 f.
Peter, St., 121
Phillips, D. Z., 137, 140 f.
Plantinga, A., 37, 55
Pragmatist view of faith, 115-18, 123
prayer, petitionary, 59, 68, 140 f., 158
Price, H. H., 135
prima facie duties, 76 f., 100
probability, *see* belief and probability *and* confirmation
prophets, 176 f., 181-93
propositions, analytic, 36
basic, 20, 33-7
belief in, 124
initial, 33-6
prior, 36 f.
synthetic, 36
punishment for sin, 139, 171 f.
Purgatory, 168 f.
purposes, 8-18
of religion, 109 f., 113 f., 116 f., 118, 125-42, 198 ff.

Quietism, 138

Ramses II, 9 f.
rational belief, 33-103, 173-6
rational$_1$ belief, definition of, 45
rational$_2$ belief, definition of, 46 ff.
rational$_3$ belief, definition of, 49-53
rational$_4$ belief, definition of, 53
rational$_5$ belief, definition of, 53 f.
recognition, 121, 123
reincarnation, 194
religion, definition of, 128

religious belief, *see* belief, religious
religious experiences, 59, 68, 69
revelation, 92 f., 176–96
Richardson, A., 182
Romans, Epistle to the, 86, 113

salvation, 126–39, 141 f., 156 ff., 167, 175, 198 f. *See also* Heaven
Schumann, W., 194
scientific theories, evidence for, 38 f.
scoundrel, not a man of faith, 108 ff., 113
Shaw, B., 172
sheep and goats, parable of, 171
simplicity, principle of, 13–18, 38 f.
Simpson, R. W., 136
sin, 145 f., 180
    Original, 145, 153
Smart, N., 192
Smith, W. Cantwell, 103, 111, 121 f., 123, 124
soul, losing one's, 154 ff.
Stump, E., 158
Suetonius, 59
supererogation, works of, 126
Swinburne, R. G., *The Coherence of Theism*, 1, 36, 79, 132, 138, 142, 183, 188
    The Concept of Miracle, 186, 189
    The Existence of God, 1 f., 38, 48, 60, 62, 66, 83, 145, 149, 156, 170, 178 f., 186, 188, 190, 193
    An Introduction to Confirmation Theory, 5, 26

talents, parable of the, 151
teleological arguments, 56

Telfer, E., 136
Tertullian, 24 f.
testimony, principle of, 40 f., 57 f.
Thomist view of faith, 105–10, 118
time, rival claims on, 52 f., 87
Trent, Council of, 105, 110, 111, 137
Trinity, the, 146, 160, 178 f.
true teaching of prophet, 181–4
trust in God, 1, 110–15, 118, 121 f., 127, 167, 200

understanding the world, 130, 141, 143 f., 178, 198. *See also* belief, importance of true
universalism, 154 f., 157
Utilitarianism, 134

Vatican Council, First, 106, 177, 179, 200
    Second, 150 f., 200
vineyard, labourers in the, 147 f.
violations of natural laws, *see* miracles
vocation, 126

way, religious, belief needed for, 143–67, 199 f.
    definition of, 125 ff.
    purpose of, 129–42, 199 f.
well-being, deep and permanent, 77 f. *See also* Heaven *and* salvation
Wiles, M., 191
Williams, B. A. O., 135
Winch, P., 39
Wisdom, Book of, 86
Wittgenstein, L., 43
worship, duty of, 79 f., 126, 138, 140 ff., 158, 159, 167, 178, 198 f.